Dating _without_ Delusion

Living a Values-based Life
in a Dysfunctional World

Many thanks and acknowledgements

Here we are roaring towards 2024, with unprecedented unrest, social conflict, and personal anxiety/frustration. If you are Single the fallout may be more severe... and depressing. As a Singles Fellowship Leader, I aspire to help people who are not married to understand and achieve healthy relationship goals that culminate in lasting marriage; but the statics on divorce are overwhelming. So this is a daunting task, which requires all kinds of support from church leaders to printers and publishers. Along the way I have been strongly supported in three church venues. The first was at Mount Soledad Presbyterian in San Diego ('80s and '90s) where we enjoyed a Singles small group on Tuesday nights, and where the church hosted weekend conferences and seminars. Mark Slomka — then the pastor at Mt. Soledad and later at Faith Community in San Diego, strongly enabled a special kind of ongoing commitment to Single people. Apart from Mark's support, particularly in the early going, **Dating without Delusion** would be a faint memory.

Debra and I then moved to Washington State where we attended church in Post Falls Idaho at Real Life Ministries. In the that venue we did 6 week Singles Ministry sessions, 3 or 4 times per year. The church leaders enabled off-site weekend retreats specifically for Singles. Bill Krause — then the Senior Pastor — was a strong supporter and executive church leader for the Single s efforts. Mike Guindon, then the Marriage Pastor at Real Life Ministries, clearly saw the need for better relationship building to create solid ground for better marriages (see the back cover). Thank you both for the early foundations. Those events culminated in the first publication of **Dating without Delusion** in 2015.

At this juncture, Jay and his wife Debra attend The Rock on Point Loma in San Diego. For the past two years Jay has been leading a Singles Fellowship small group on Thursdays evening, and working on the republication of *Dating without Delusion*. The Pastors and group leaders at the Rock have been enabling these efforts. In all of these venues my wife Debra has provided patient support – many thanks to her.

Last but not least, Mel Lions (my typographer) has guided me through the minefield of the literary world which is set up to exploit ignorant authors like myself... he calls us guppies swimming with the sharks.

Second Edition | Copyright © 2023 Jay Parker
ISBN 979-8-9893296-1-8

Contents

Table of Contents

Table of Contents

Introduction/Prologue

Introduction

The One Word Problem → The One Word Solution

We all know the 'keep it simple' principle, so here is the 'keep it simple' summary for this book. The One Word to describe the *problem* this book addresses is *Divorce*. It's epidemic, its effects are long-lasting, and its influence often prevents us from individually moving forward toward healthier and more productive lives. At the national level, many of our society's problems are directly attributable to the effects of divorce. It's a sad thing to watch our government behave as if it can solve our many problems without addressing and understanding the root cause of our national sickness. Let's get it on the table right now: divorce is a cancer. You probably have been affected by divorce in one form or another; I certainly have. Both you and I need to understand and address those probably very damaging and very personal effects on our lives.

The One Word to describe the *solution* is *Values*. Everyone seems to think they have values, although they can't speak them. Without a good description of your Personal Values, how much impact do you think they have on your life? Spiritual Values, Relational Values, and Professional Values are the ones I'll suggest. At the end of the day, however, your values are yours: yours to own, yours to speak, and yours to live by. Great Personal Values are defining. Once you know them, they will have an enduring impact on your life. Divorce: a BIG problem. Having Personal Values is an enduring personal solution.

Who are You?

"Who are you?....who, who, who...I really want to know"

I saw The Who live in Boston when I was a teenager. It was a great concert; back in those days, they were smashing the big speakers by using their guitars like baseball bats. I never understood that whole 'destructo' thing, but it sure was exciting.

Today, I meet young people and ask (perhaps unfairly), "Who are you?" Now when I was a teenager, I didn't have the vaguest idea of who I was or who I was trying to be. When I was in my 20s, I was doing my best just to get through the next life hurdle. In these situations, well-meaning adults weren't doing a whole lot to help me. They thought going to college was a good idea but beyond that — and telling me to work hard to do it, they just didn't know how to help. So for many years I relied on my accomplishments: I graduated from; I played sports on my school teams; I was a member of the coin club, etc. Hey, at least these speak to commitment and work ethic! If you played field hockey, that was a good thing. If you won the league championship, you sacrificed and learned how to work together and to put the team's success — the greater good — at the top of your priorities. Very good stuff. But in the years over the horizon when you are 40, 50, and 60, field hockey won't have much say about who you are. Perhaps you met a lifelong friend on that team? A friendship of that nature has a lifelong impact. If you asked that friend who you were, what would they say? "She was a great teammate; we had a lot of fun together!" "He was always a reliable friend." Those are good things, parts of your living past. You need the past, plus something more, to move forward.

To be fair, I don't really expect great answers from young people. Just like me when I was young, they are doing their best just to get over the next speed bump. But when I ask the same question of people in their late 20s, 30s, 40s, 50s, and beyond, there is still a big element of confusion permeating their answers. The difference is that adults are *supposed* to know who they are... aren't they? I ask these questions informally and in relationship seminars. The result is usually the same: no answers. Or answers like, "I value integrity" or, "I want to love Jesus." Do you see the problem? In general I like people, and I like young people, but they don't have meaningful answers based upon introspective thinking. Beyond mushy generalities, the answers that do come back generally fall into three categories:[1]

1) They tell me what job they have, and what their role is at work. That is pretty mediocre info in terms of getting to know someone because at the end of the day, many people are in mismatched jobs for a paycheck trying to make ends meet. They know today's job is not going to define them. Work goals are answers which provide some life trajectory, but that's about it.

2) They tell me about their families of origin, where they grew up, or where they currently live. Unless you are from Queen Elizabeth's family or you're one of the Kennedys, these circumstances don't define you. And the tragedies that come from kids trying to be what their families want them to be are sometimes very painful. Many young people today are doing their best just to escape the turmoil of their childhood.

3) Embracing the 'Christian' label (which is a Bible directive: 1 Peter 4 v 16), carries the associated principle 'to give a defense...for the hope that is in you, with gentleness and reverence.'[2] The culture has attacked the label. Nevertheless claiming allegiance to Christ carries this sobering and weighty responsibility, doesn't it? The real you is not just a reflection of spiritual doctrine — it is the Spirit of God living uniquely in you.

Haven't you experienced this same kind of dialogue? There's nothing wrong with these conversations, except there often isn't any deeper personal insight to be had. Back to the key question: Who are You?

Imagine every relationship as a guitar string stretched between the tuning knob and the bridge (the fixed block at the other side of the neck and frets). A firm anchor at each end is the key to a good musical note. If one end or the other is not anchored firmly, you can't achieve just the right tension the string

---

[1] The faith-based answers from spiritually alive young people such as "I love Jesus" reflect a central spiritual decision full of deep and rich meaning. I'm suggesting this life decision requires careful reflection and more thoughtful articulation. Millions of people have accepted Christ, and God has an absolutely unique plan for each one of them. It's that ordained uniqueness that I hope will be reflected in Personal Values statements.

[2] ...sanctify Christ as Lord in your hearts, always being ready to make a defense to everyone who asks you to give an account for the hope that is in you, yet with gentleness and reverence (1 Peter 3 v 15 NASB)

needs to produce the perfect pitch. Relationships are like that. The best notes are produced when the string — the connection — is stretched between two established points. When you know yourself well, you are providing one side of the healthy relationship anchor. When the other person knows who they are, you both now have the possibility of creating a relationship that can be maintained in such a way that the perfect 'notes' can be played.

Good strings, like good relationships, always require tuning, but it is tuning from two well-anchored positions. Two people anchored in accurate self-awareness is the goal. If one person or the other has ambiguity — a.k.a., they're 'finding themselves' — you can't establish the right kind of healthy connection to allow just the right amount of relationship tension for the string to play with the lovely pitch you're looking for. Imagine if the guitar string is  not attached at one end. There is no possibility for the correct tension and the beautiful relationship notes. A completely unattached string lies curled up in the guitar case doing nothing: deteriorating. Un-anchored relationships are like that. There may be a lot of self-focused personality interaction without a purpose, but it will always be unsatisfying in a peculiar way.

I don't want to be judgmental; everyone has seasons of life where they are searching to find themselves. So give yourself and others room to do the 'finding,' if that's where you are in life. The lie, or the delusion, is that you will find yourself in the next man-woman relationship. A big part of this book is the premise that you — in yourself — in the core of your being, are an intricate finely woven tapestry waiting to be revealed. Do you want to hear beautiful melodic 'notes' coming out of your relationships? Look at the best relationships around you. People who share, understand, and accept similar values have enduring relationships. If the common values have a higher purpose — like serving others' needs in some unique venue — the personal bond between those people may be ever-growing and lifelong. Back to the key question: "Who are you?" I will say it over and over again:

Life is relationships; start making them better every day.[3]

Like the guitar string, you must provide a stable foundation on your side so other people in your life can know who you are, where you stand, and what to expect from you. You may say, "Jay, I thought this book was about dating? Let's stop the talk about guitar strings and get on to dating!" In this culture, sexual hookups, social media pressure, infatuation insanity (dating?) and serial monogamy are the inferno of relationships. Before you go further down the infatuation path with someone, please anchor yourself by understanding *your* unique Personal Values. This is a completely counter-cultural process. When you do your values work, you can slow down, breath, and relax in the clarity that your values provide. From this values foundation, we can delve into building relationships methodically — even romantic relationships! — dealing with the challenges as you go.

Why should I read this book? I'm married!

Good question. The simple one-word answer is *Relevance.* Despite our self-absorbed, me-is-everything culture, we all want to be relevant: to relate effectively with the people and world around us. As a married person, don't you want to have your relationships producing wonderful sounds like the well-tuned guitar? Of course you do, and that will be possible if you have fine-tuned and articulated your Personal Values clearly, and worked to really understand the Personal Values of your spouse. A wonderful congruity will be possible if your values consistently inform and undergird your life decisions.

Ask anyone you know — including your married friends — to tell you what their values are, and then watch the fumbling and stumbling as they try to make up something on the fly. Even people who do live values-based lives are usually pretty incompetent when it comes to clearly articulating them. Do you see how that slows the quality of the interactions you have with everyone around you? Working with great people and knowing outstanding people in the church context, I would guess I have more than the usual number of relationships with people who do live values-based lives. I know that *if* they thought about how they live, they would be able to make the transition to values statements that would be pretty solid. Here is a quick example.

[3] People of faith often answer with, "I want to know God above all else." And yes, your relationship with Him is paramount. It is a relationship 'to make better' every day. How are you making that relationship better every day?

Question: "Do you go to church? Really? Why?"
Possible answer: "Well, because I'm a Christian."

Woops... that answer just plugged into a society mindset that believes that 'Christians' are bigoted, narrow-minded, angry judgementalists. Why would I want to spend Sundays, or any day, with that? If Christians think for a moment, the reason you go to church is *not* because you label yourself (I hope). You go to church because God has told you to (I hope). How did he tell you to go to church? Well, you believe that God has spoken to us through the Bible (I hope), not that those 40+ authors were flailing around, trying to describe God. So has God said, "Go to Church"? Yes, He has... if you believe the Bible. Specifically, the directive, the commandment, comes out of the Bible (Exodus 20:8-11) and is reiterated by Jesus, the Apostle Paul, etc., etc. So it becomes incumbent upon us to know the Bible references and, perhaps just as importantly, to know why and how the Bible proves itself as coming from God, all the way from scripture fragments to full book Codices. It becomes incumbent on us to understand our worship lifestyle and how we are committed to live it.

The summary: we go to church because God, through Moses, gave us the 10 Commandments. And He said in the Number 4 Commandment, "Keep the Sabbath Holy." "Remember the Sabbath day to keep it holy. Six days you shall labor and do all your work, but the seventh day is a Sabbath unto the Lord your God."[4] So using this as the beginning of the discussion, we can dialogue how the commandment has informed and undergirded our Spiritual Personal Value, and our 'lifestyle of worship'. Does it? If so, then you can articulate how that value drives your choices; and specifically your choice to spend one day focused on the Lord. So a goal of this book is to help you find and focus on the Personal Core Values you want to live by. My premise is:

A value is not a value unless it drives your choices. (Jay)

If you don't believe that God has spoken, and is speaking. If you don't believe that Church is a directive, the reality is that *you* have some pretty defining beliefs. Own them; articulate them. If you are a person of faith, you have a similar personal responsibility to own and understand your values-based

---

[4] *New American Standard Bible* (NASB). Copyright 1962, 1963, 1971, 1972, 1973, 1975, 1977. The Lockman Foundation. LA Habra, CA. p. 105.

reasons behind your choice to go to church. Are you interested in being the best parent or grandparent you can be? Show your kids how to live a values-based life!

A quick real-life story. A couple of years back, it was time to teach ***Dating without Delusion*** again. One Wednesday evening at our church home group, we were talking about the class start-up process and who was going to attend etc. One of the husbands in our home group, which consists of seven married couples, is a very strategic/visionary businessman. He knows how to cut to the chase on deals and projects because he keeps a sharp focus on the 'end in mind.' He and his wife have become our good friends, but it surprised me when he said that he would like to come to the dating classes. Not only did he say he wanted to come...*he attended all six sessions.* Over 12 hours of class time, plus travel! Needless to say, I was impressed because even the Singles miss one or two sessions due to the situations which life throws at us. In particular, this man appreciated the discussions on Personal Core Values, and *he realized he could do a much better job of articulating* his own *values*. So at the end of the class, he takes me aside and in his no-frills, cut-to-the-chase-style he tells me, "Write the book!" In my laziness, I have let too many years go by without doing what should have been obvious to me. As you can guess, I took this direction seriously, even as direction from the Lord, and I hit the computer.

A second reason for you to spend time with me is *demographics*. In our new millennium, there are now as many Single adults as there are married adults. For every married adult — like yourself — there is a Single adult. How can that be, you ask? Generally, it's because marriages are continuing to fail, and young people are choosing not to marry or to marry later in life. Demographers have the challenge of tracking this trend, but it's pretty clear. Chances are you have some good, quality relationships with people who are Single. Whether they are divorced, widowed, or never married, these people are probably an important part of your life. Don't you want to inspire them to live values-based lives? If *you* and your spouse can live a values-clear life, that in itself will speak to the others in your network of relationships. How is your marriage 'speaking' to your Single friends, as well as the many young people you are influencing? If you have suffered a divorce, *your failure* is speaking pretty loudly, along with the millions of other people who fail at marriage very year — I share the pain of failure with you. Yes, your kids growing into adulthood are watching *you* and your spouse to see how marriage works.

How are your values 'speaking' to them? They are growing up watching you. Inexorably, your kids and your grandkids are marching toward the adult age (18). Don't you want to help them in a meaningful way? They do NOT want to hear the 'wisdom' of our Boomer generation; there is very little to learn from the ways in which we Boomers have fallen short. *Demonstrated* real-life marriage unity and commitment speaks the loudest. If you are parenting or grand-parenting, make sure to review and use the 'Parenting Target Zone' in the tools section (Part 3), which offers the parenting technique of relating to your kids and grandkids through your well thought-out values-based choices.

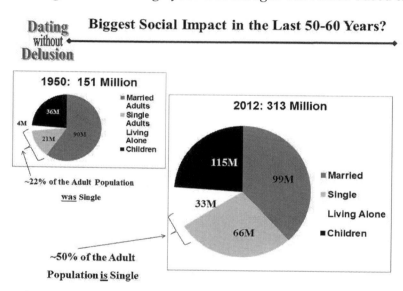

Now, please check out the demographics chart above. Census data illustrate how the number of people in marriage is shrinking. Pinpoint precision is not the issue here. The trend is the key. Your friends, your kids, and members of your immediate family are facing the world depicted in the chart. It used to be (in 1950) that 22 percent of the adult population was Single. In 2012, over 50 percent of the adult population was Single. People in healthy marriages often have relationships with people who are in healthy marriages. The network of 'operative' marriages is a dwindling but vital national resource. Increasingly, if you are in a good marriage, you have the responsibility to demonstrate that it *is* possible to succeed in marriage — you are a scarce real-life example.

Despite the divorce statistics that lurk behind the pie charts and the ominous trend lines, *our country has changed into something it has never been.* Increasingly, the huge Single population is encountering itself. They have seen many, many marriages fail. Very often they have one or more divorces in their own lives and background. They need to see healthy marriages in real life. They want to see marriages that work. Why? Because many Singles (definitely not all), in the depth of their desires, want to be in committed marriages that work. The problem is they have never seen a quality marriage function in real life. They have no model to learn from. Quoting Robert J. Samuelson from the Washington Post,

"Along with a budget deficit, *we have a family deficit*. It explains some stubborn poverty and our frustrations in combating it. We've learned what good families provide cannot be easily gotten elsewhere. For the nation, *this is the deficit that matters most*"[5] (italics mine).

Shared Personal Values are a necessary avenue to illustrate why and how marriages can be sustained. For those Singles who may never, or never again, be in a marriage, a values-based life is essential to the personal significance they need and want. Values-committed living holds the significance every human being longs for.

Can You Trust Me?

Here you are, on the threshold of a relationship book. It's not a book about theology, although we need theology to help unravel our relationship conundrum. It's not a book about psychology — but again, we need wise council from skilled psychologists if for nothing else but to get a grasp on who we are. Do you believe you are an absolutely unique individual? I do. I think you are a person that is a complex combination of childhood experiences and personal potentials. There are many factors trying to define my life, some good, some bad; the same thing is true for you. Our culture drives us to build intellectual walls because half of what goes on 'out there" is very dysfunctional, and we certainly don't know how to change it. Where the culture is concerned, the easiest attitude is to 'go with the flow.' Often our dialogue with one another becomes a superficial exchange of pleasantries until there is some outcry regarding the latest moral outrage — and there's a lot to be outraged about, as the culture becomes more dysfunctional and destructive. Politics by itself is

---

[5] Robert J. Samuelson, "Family deficit our most serious," 10/28/14 syndicated article. Samuelson was commenting on Isabel Sawhill's book, *Generation Unbound: Drifting into Sex and Parenthood without Marriage.*

now so polarized as to prevent any meaningful communication between people in opposing parties — they shouldn't be opposing in the first place. I think the calling to be in government is a tough one; if that is you, please bring your no-motherhood Personal Values to Washington. *And please recognize that the avenue to helping families is to first help people to create better marriages.* Perhaps really knowing ourselves, as opposed to what we think about the government's latest policy, is a better way to relate to the world around us. Perhaps getting the guitar strings anchored at our end is the way to move forward.

When you are finished with this book, you will know me pretty well because I'll use my values as a real-life example. But the goal is for *you* to know *yourself* more fully and more completely, and to have noble goals that promote your self-transparency. In that self-knowledge[6] is the secret to better relationships. That's how I'm going to encourage you to reach for constantly improving, high-quality relationships. Soon, you will see defining parts of my life that are Christian. You will see those elements because they are a fundamental part of me. To omit my life essentials would be dishonest, and that omission certainly wouldn't be transparent. Thankfully, my wife and I enjoy friendships with many people who are not Christians; they accept us in light of who we are, and on occasion we discuss our reasons for our belief. Our home group is a values-based, steadfast anchor of good relationships, honestly sharing life from a spiritual and faith-based point-of-view.

If you are a Christian, fine; I know you will receive this book's Bible references and the quotes from Jesus in a way that stimulates and validates your thinking. As we do our Bible work, remember that God himself is the author of the values that infuse your life. As you expose, understand, and articulate your values, you will see a very personal aspect of God the Creator. If you are not a Christian, then please accept the Bible references and quotes from Jesus *at least* on the same level as the other quoted authors, philosophers, and spectrum of men and women who lived lives that mattered.

I readily admit that often we Christians act oddly. It usually is our sometimes-feeble intent to get God into a situation we don't know how to handle. We Christians often try to offer salvation to people over a hamburger when those people aren't looking to be saved. We have little idea of the scars that

---

[6] For you Faith-based readers remember discovering ourselves is really a form of discovering the God who made us. Seeing the Creator through the creation. Colossians 1 vv 15-17.

childhood religious experiences have left in their lives. We try to offer a spiritual solution to a practical problem; though God is fully capable of practical solutions, this probably wasn't what you were asking for. Usually our spiritual motives are very sound. We know that God has dealt with us with both mercy and gentleness, and we want everyone to experience the same mercy and gentleness. Pretty good motives; often pretty poor execution. So if this happens to you, treat that Christian — and me — with a little patience. He will appreciate it — and so will I! I believe that spiritual person will be a good friend you can count on in the long run.

The best reason for you to give me your trust is the many people who have put out many hours of their time to participate in the seminar and to be very honestly transparent, sharing their lives, their past failures, and their future hopes. I'll offer many true-life stories to illustrate the relevance of the **Dating _without_ Delusion** principles to allow you to connect with the people who have gone before you. I will not offer names, which you don't need anyway. In those real-life stories, anonymity is essential. In the very few examples where I have to use a name, I will change it to preserve anonymity. For my part, I will share with you what I have learned from many people over many years, in the hope that our experiences and discoveries will enlighten you. Some stories are tragic and sad; some are funny and poignant. Learn from them all; enjoy them all.

As for the relationship process offered in **Dating _without_ Delusion,** please do a couple of simple things.

Accepting that 'life is relationships,' keep an open mind about enjoying your relationships in a more transparent way. You will sense a new level of personal clarity which can become the basis of your personal integrity.

1) Trust science, plus the empirical evidence and the Bible claim, proving you are a unique and special one-of-kind individual buried knee-deep in a culture that tries to stamp you with a 'you're just like everyone else' mold. Be ready to fight that culture in your mind. It's a tough challenge: _be ready to fight!_ Fight who? NOT other people, _instead_ fight the infusing culture which is designed to bring you down.

2) Take the **Dating _without_ Delusion** relationship process and the unique relationship challenges you are squarely facing, and adopt them and adapt them for yourself. Laugh at the stories, laugh at me, laugh at your-

self. Have fun!!

3) Lastly, I will do my best to leave *out* all the Christian buzz phrases that are vague and often confusing. I am a Christian because I accept the declared and documented facts about Jesus as truth, not because I get a set of perks and benefits. When I do use Bible references, you will see the practicality (and once again: truth) that is woven throughout its pages. You will see how compatible it is with good relationship living.

Can you trust me? I hope so.

Jay Parker, MSEL

Dating *without* Delusion
From 40,000 feet

A relationship book... in seminar format

Dating *without* Delusion has been around for more than 30 years; during those many classes and seminars, we used a heavy dose of PowerPoint. The slides and worksheets, bound into a seminar workbook, were provided to all of the attendees. As the years passed, more seminars, more feedback, and more integrated research combined to mature the content, which is the basis for the book you are reading today. Here's some coaching on how to use and read this book.

Many of you may be familiar with 'learning styles.' There are many discussions of how and why knowing yours is important. Learning Styles Online discusses seven learning styles:

- **Visual** (spatial): You prefer using pictures, images, and spatial understanding.
- **Aural** (auditory/musical): You prefer using sound and music.
- **Verbal** (linguistic): You prefer using words, both in speech and writing.
- **Physical** (kinesthetic): You prefer using your body, hands, and sense of touch.
- **Logical** (mathematical): You prefer using logic, reasoning, and systems.
- **Social** (interpersonal): You prefer to learn in groups or with other people.
- **Solitary** (intrapersonal): You prefer to work alone and use self-study.

This site offers a free assessment, which is a valuable exercise for anyone. I mention this because many people (significantly more than 60 percent?) have the visual/spatial learning style, as I do. I have always believed that a complex concept is better understood and retained if it can be depicted graphically. The graphic presentation is further enhanced when it is used in the seminar context because it has the added impact of being presented in the social (Interpersonal) context; in an interacting group. In **Dating without Delusion** classes, there is often highly animated dialogue between the people in the class: that's verbal and social/interpersonal. The end goal of the graphics is to make the book an 'easy read' for you — one that is also intensely practical and 'recallable.' Graphic depictions of essential principles probably get stored more effectively in your brain. A graphic may allow you to bring up and recall a relationship concept more easily. In the 'heat' of dating emotion, you'll need it. Let's look at a sample graphic.

Dating without Delusion

Don't Look for Violinists at Rap Concerts

(So What Did They Expect??)

📖 Know <u>Who</u> You Are…and…Pray!

📖 There's a Time & Season; Know The Season You're In

📖 When the Season is Right: Think of It As Looking for a Job

📖 You Must Look in the Right Places

📖 You Must Make Yourself Available

📖 You Need the Right Skill Set

AND…

… There's Only <u>One</u> Person You're Going to Change:

You Are <u>Not</u> Going to Change Anyone Else!

This one offers high-level suggestions for the dating mindset. There is a Gary Larson cartoon that depicts two female peacocks sitting at a bar table. On the other side of the room, a male peacock is putting his full plume on display. The caption reads, "Don't encourage him, Sylvia."[7] Why do we laugh? Because it's so true, that's why! Peacocks and players go to bars to hook up with someone, simple as that. I use this cartoon as an introduction to the 'Don't look for Violinists at Rap Concerts' excerpted in the slide above. The sub-title 'So what did they expect??' is meant to provoke seminar thinking. Here is the main point: The best a person can do is to know WHO they are: the first bullet point on the slide. Part One of this book is dedicated to help

---

[7] Sorry, I'd love to show you the Gary Larson cartoon, but they wouldn't even return my calls when I attempted to ask permission.

you do that. Now, let's discuss the graphic point-by-point.

Know who you are... and Pray! This is the first bullet on the graphic. If you want to be less spiritual, you can truncate this first bullet point to 'Know who you are!' You can easily envision the dialogue a slide like this creates in the class environment. My first suggestion to the lady peacocks is — 'So what did they expect?' — is this: if you know your Personal Values, you need to go to places to meet people who are likely to have a similar Personal Values foundation. Ergo, if you are a classical violinist, going to a rap concert might not be the best way to meet someone with a deep commitment to classical music. Get it? The problem pinpointed here is that people in general don't know what their values are and if they do have an inkling of a Personal Value, they don't use it to guide their actions and choices. Hence, the frustration of needing to meet somebody....anybody! Go to a bar! This phenomenon doesn't apply if your Personal Value is 'Party Every Day' because the bar/lounge/microbrew is a sneaky, pervasive value, driving your choice to get out there many nights a week.

The recent surge in dating websites reflects this problem. People are initiating relationships online in huge numbers. Why? Because working on rudimentary compatibility information is better than going to a bar. Even the Christian websites are increasing dramatically. Unfortunately, many women have complained to me, "He said he was a Christian, but he sure wasn't." Like everything else in our world, there are good and not-so-good websites. At least websites force people to define — at least in small part — who they are. "I like to hike" is at least as good as what a typical bar encounter might include, and a lot less risky.

Know the 'season' you're in. If you are recovering from a divorce or a recent breakup, if you have been recently widowed, you need time to recover and heal. When you have been rudely rejected or physically/sexually offended, this is not the time look for dates. When is the right season? When you have successfully reached the point in your life and emotions where a new relationship is an option, but not a necessity. There is a time and a season. Sometimes you should be ready for a new relationship; other times you need to recoup, recover, rest, and heal. That is not the time, not the season for a new romantic relationship. When you do reach the elusive but critical state — *ready for a relationship, but not needing one* — a very funny thing happens. You become more attractive! Here's what I've learned. When you don't need a relationship, you can avoid all of the 'clinginess' that desperate people broadcast. When you know who you are, you can confidently use your values to navigate the relationship rapids.

You must look in the right places. Violinists aren't going to find kindred spirits at rap concerts. Looking in the right places means being in the right places, doing the things that are really important to you. If you love reading, book clubs are an option. If you have a service heart for veterans, better check out the VA and the resources they offer — notice the intensity ramping up? If you love to work with challenged kids, all sorts of agencies and church organizations are waiting for you to get involved. And, of course, spiritual organizations have a broad combination of all of them. Get out there using your gifts to serve; the rewards of giving are many. A couple of seminars ago, a young couple came into class; they had chosen only to see one another (exclusively). Where had they met? In children's ministry, that's where. Cutting to the chase, they had similar 'service values:' serving other people (kids)in a similar fashion, in a common setting. All of that bodes well for their long-term relationship potential — and in fact, they are now married.

When the season is right, think of it as looking for a job. This is blunt, but important. When you look for a job, you prepare your resume. You practice the articulation of your abilities and skills. You make sure that you are fit (physically) and that you are dressed (attractively) for the interview. In dating, I say you must know who you are (your Personal Core Values) so that you can articulate your 'who' to the person you may want to date. Confident dress will be attractive, but not trendy or provocatively seductive. Guess I'm out of step with the culture...hang in there! You sense it, all the factors and happenings in your life — and perhaps God? — are telling you: this is the season. Objectives? To build quality relationships that move towards a 'Best Outcome.' Qualifications? Your relationship skills AND your Personal Values; your well communicated values. When the season is right, think of it as looking for a job. That means that you know your objectives, and your qualifications are ready for review.

You must make yourself available. I hear so many Singles say, "I don't date....x%&$#@!!!" What the heck does that mean? Are you going for a lifetime of no marriage and celibacy, perhaps to become a reclusive monk? Sorry for the sarcastic comment. I do have to bite my tongue when Single people articulate these poorly thought-out 'positions.' I can usually tell that they have been practicing this mantra over and over again. Many guys and gals, not having good relationship skills, revert to the "I don't date" slogan. It's an easy out, isn't it? These people know — or they should know — that they'll quickly change their tune if a quality values-based person shows up and treats them with respect. Later, I'll recall the example of the spiritually minded Beyoncé look-alike. The alternative? It's very simple to apply the 'right season' thinking shown above. Yes, there are some seasons when you will not be dating, to get some very important personal work/healing accomplished; if that's the case, please be ready to say so.

You must have the right skill set. Having Personal Values, being committed to your values, and communicating your values: these are the components of the right skill set. Remember Knowing, Speaking and Living Personal & Spiritual Values from the front cover? Do you have them? Beginning with your Personal Values is the essential starting point. I find that this challenge is a big one for everyone, and we'll spend some quality time to provoke your values thinking. I'll also cite some key nationally known references so you can be confident in the heavy emphasis that I put on Personal Values development. Part Two of this book deals with the relationship phases, and what kind of communication and commitment should happen during each phase.

Lastly, there is the big 'AND' on the slide.

There is only one person you are going to change... YOURSELF!
You are not going to change anyone else.

One of the big delusions we suffer from is expecting the other person to eventually change to suit our deepest needs and wants. Meaning that in the long run, they'll selflessly change to suit me. How many times has that worked out? If there is any change going on after marriage, it's more like, "OK, now we have a commitment, so now meet my needs!" Often we are attracted to the very same personalities that hurt us as children. At a recent class, an attractive woman came up and cited the problem of her recurring attraction to addictive personalities. Turns out she has the very distinctive spiritual gift: the gift of mercy. Just as she had done before, she was feeling attraction to men who needed care and rescue. Maybe she watched her mom try to rescue her dad? She has the challenge of recognizing and managing this situation, requiring a distinct change in her thinking and behavior. More later.

So now, point-by-point, you've worked through a **Dating without Delusion** slide with me. Summary: if you have a visual learning style, my hope is that the embedded slides (like this one) will help you gain and retain new knowledge and relationship wisdom. If you find yourself sitting in a bar environment and the bar patrons are behaving badly, maybe the Lord will remind you of the two lady peacocks complaining about the macho display of plumage. Then ask yourself, "Why am I here?" Many people believe that 'a picture is worth a thousand words.' Because I am so visual, I say a picture is worth 10,000 words; this is the rationale for the **Dating without Delusion** format. If you want to enjoy the full insight and impact of seeing and hearing people interact over key life principles, look for the next **Dating without Delusion** seminar. Most people say it's worth their time.

Triangles and Pyramids

The Egyptian pyramids are always a marvel; everyone who sees them is amazed. It's simply because of their size and longevity: they've withstood the

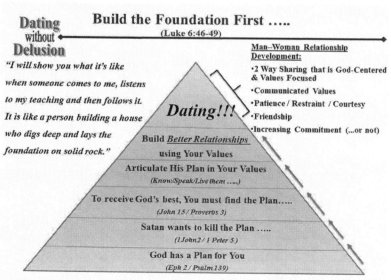

desert elements for thousands of years. One of the primary reasons for their durability is their shape: wide at the bottom, providing a stable base, and tapering to the pinnacle at the top. The idea is that stability can only be built upon a wide and immovable foundation. That is true for your life as well as for buildings and pyramids.

Using the pyramid shape, the graphic above depicts the **Dating *without* Delusion** foundational ideas and truths from the bottom/base to the top of the pyramid. Just like the actual pyramids, the bottom layers provide the base to move your thinking up to the next level. Looking at the picture you see in the bottom layer, 'God has a Plan for You.' The figure shows a couple of Bible references that are clear on this idea. For example, Ephesians 2:10 says, "We are His workmanship created in Christ Jesus for good works, *which He prepared beforehand*, that we should walk in them." (Italics mine)

If you've been told for your entire life that you can 'do whatever you want,' that you can become whoever you want to be, that you are the master of your own ship, the architect of your own destiny, this idea may be a revelation, or a very tough sticking point for you. The Bible is not ambiguous on this point, however. God has created and equipped you (and me) for a very specific role. If so, our life task changes from self-creation to *self-discovery*. The Bible is thick with these declarations. *The idea that you can create yourself is a delusion.* I think it is pretty easy to see how science and history back this idea. People like Albert Einstein, Thomas Edison, George Washington, and Martin Luther King are just a few of uncountable examples of people who followed God's leading to roles and discoveries that boggle the mind. Looking back across their lives those individuals would probably say that they were 'called' to their unique roles and purposes. Looking back and discerning a calling is not as impactful as looking forward through your very own values to see how you are 'called' to live your life.[8] Looking *back* is interesting. Looking *forward* with your Personal Values can be life changing.

Those are personal story highlights; what about low-lights? I argue that the two thieves on the crosses on either side of Jesus had divine destinies and purposes. Both thieves were caught breaking the law; they were proba-

---

[8] In the Christian world, people often expect and look for pastors to be 'called' to their very important and significant role, and this is undoubtedly critical. The Bible, however, does not limit callings to pastors. Quite the opposite: the Bible, addressing all the people in the early church, broadcasts the need to find personal callings. "I urge you to live a life worthy of the calling you have received" (Ephesians 4:1; NIV). "And we know that in all things God works for the good of those who love him, who have been called according to His purpose" (Romans 8:28). "And those He predestined, He also called; those he called he also justified; those He justified, He also glorified" (Romans 8:30; New International Version (NIV)).

bly career criminals — and the Romans were notoriously efficient at dealing with crime. The one thief who said, "Remember me, Jesus, when You come into your kingdom" received the promise, "Today you will be with Me in paradise." I believe that from this hopeless position, pinned to a cross, even this thief was used in a powerful way to fill a personal destiny. These highlight examples are encouragements to discover our purpose and live it out. The lowlight examples demonstrate that we can be used in dramatically significant ways, no matter what stage of life or circumstance we are in. In it all, 'God has a Plan' forms the wide concrete base of the pyramid. In the very front of Part Three there is a short but interesting discussion on the intricacies of God's design. At least for a moment, please accept the idea that you are intricately designed so we can move towards strongly defining your Personal Core Values.

The next layer up reads, 'Satan wants to kill the plan.' Acknowledging that an evil is permeating this world and accepting that it's Satan at work is not a huge leap. But beyond the bombings and mass shootings (which I contend are simple work for Satan) is the fact that highlight people, who discovered the path designed for them, are the ones who triumphed over evil and fulfilled their destiny. The evil perpetrated by a mass shooter is dramatic, but the eternal impact of keeping people from their manifest destiny is most important to our adversary. People equipped with key strengths and abilities can truly make a world-changing difference for good. Now, think about the tangled morass millions of people face as they go through a divorce. Instead of building up other people through their lives and marriages, they are rendered nearly useless by their relationship destruction. How does the opposition come? Through the culture. We need to uncover and discuss the 'Culture Battle' in some significant detail.

Next layer up reads, 'To receive God's best, you must find the plan.' It seems to me that it would be so much simpler if God would supernaturally imprint His plan for me on my brain. But He doesn't. Instead, He asks that we seek and accept His divine design for us. Our design comes in subtle reve-

Dating without Delusion — H.L. Mencken

"You can't do anything about the length of your life, but you can do something about its width and depth."

lations and circumstances, and through the focused self-discovery you'll do in this book. Sometimes this can be very frustrating (at least for me) because I am so impatient. Plus, there is always the danger of trying to launch some world-changing effort for which I'm not equipped. I think He does this because He wants to be in a moment-by-moment, circumstance-by-circumstance relationship with us. The essential question? How do I find God's very specific plan for my life?

To self-discover, we will discuss in detail how you are 'wired.' Your specific spiritual gifts inventory, your personality profile/disposition, your talents and strengths all are very detailed indicators of how you are equipped for the job. The idea is that _your_ specific role is for _you_ to fulfill in the place where you are positioned. You are equipped for _The Plan_ that is for you alone. Do you see it? Our deepest, innermost desire is to recognize our unique personal 'tools' and use them on the job they were designed for. My adopted brother — a long-time pastor in Maryland — talks about the 'markers' in your life. Those are the moments and circumstances when you had real impact, _serving others with irreplaceable encouragement._ Put the Gifts/Profiles/Strengths results with the markers and you will begin to discover The Plan — see the third layer up. The Plan, in turn, needs to be capsulated into your Personal Core Values. When you reach this Personal Values milestone — values that you will continually refine and re-articulate — then you are positioned.

Positioned for what? Positioned to build better relationships! When you can crisply articulate the driving Personal Values in your life, you begin to achieve what I will argue is an important goal: _Personal Transparency._ With personal transparency, other people can quickly grasp who you are and understand the choices you make. You will be equipped to understand and achieve the word we all like to bandy about: _Integrity._ Perhaps this won't make all of your relationships better, but it certainly will make them more honest and forthright (hmmm, I guess that _is_ better!).

At the peak of the pyramid is the unsearchable 'D' word: dating. With all of its pitfalls and innuendo, with all of its chameleon-like migration. The culture will try to ram its latest fad into your psyche, then it will change the 'rules' (there really aren't any), and then it will try to sneak its latest trend into your brain. The solution, I contend, is to define and refine your own definition of dating. After all, you're the one doing it, and you're the one who will have to deal with the aftermath of it. So we will redefine dating in such a way that you can use your Personal Values as a filter and guideline to move ahead. Most people in their heart of hearts view dating as a haphazard, unknowable challenge. Admittedly, it is very tough. In Part Two, I will offer you a very linear and comprehensible dating PROCESS. It's a process that builds upon the foundation of your Personal Values, and offers guidelines on communication and timing. The timing aspects of relationship development are very important for a host of reasons, and you'll learn that knowing where you are in the process is always invaluable. That's because sex and infatuation are VERY impatient — as my and your experience have proven.

In Part Two, we will discuss in detail the rationale for dating in the first place, the key decisions you have to make, how to make them and, very importantly, *what to communicate when* in the process. As with all processes, you may want to tailor this one for your specific circumstance, but any tailoring has to be done carefully. You will see that this *intentional* relationship-building can be *your* process. It is a process that you can own, adopt, and tailor for yourself.

The principle of establishing a firm foundation first is nicely captured by Jesus in the gospel of Luke chapter 6, which is inserted into the top left of the slide. Jesus is primarily talking about obedience in this particular instance, but He is also talking about establishing the foundation first, which is what the pyramid in the figure does. I love it when His words keep showing new facets and intricacies; they always are remembering and recalling the Old Testament.

So here we go back to the description at the base of the pyramid. God has a plan. He has created us "fearfully and wonderfully" (Psalm 139), with all our days "numbered, before there was even one." So where are you as a Single person? You can retreat to the false security of your Christian community, thinking that dating is not for you — Point 1, below. If you're a post-modern/millennial living in this culture, the other way you can easily kiss dating goodbye is to rely on random hook-ups — all leading to the downward spiral of emotional relationship frenzy and disintegration — Point 2. You can hold out and trust your feelings — Point 3 — waiting for just the right person to trigger all of your 'Phenomena of Recognition' feelings of infatuation (more later; please look forward to the discussion of 'Imago' with Harville Hendrix). Or, you can develop romantic relationships in the same way that you develop all of your relationships: based upon your Personal Values. This simply means that you will be developing your romantic relationships with the hope that each one has a best outcome. Your values can help you to determine

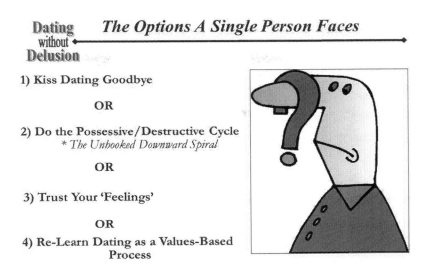

Dating without Delusion

The Options A Single Person Faces

1) Kiss Dating Goodbye

OR

2) Do the Possessive/Destructive Cycle
   * *The Unhooked Downward Spiral*

OR

3) Trust Your 'Feelings'

OR

4) Re-Learn Dating as a Values-Based Process

how to handle each of those emerging relationship situations. Remember, no two relationships are the same. For each one, there *is* a best outcome.

Recently, a very intelligent and attractive young woman sat in the seminar as we worked through the discussion on Personal Values. She is also a Single mom. Nodding her head in agreement with the values discussion, she spoke up and said she had made the decision to be the mom God wanted her to be. That, of course, didn't stop the barrage of interest from guys, both Christian and non-Christian. She related the story of a breakfast discussion (smart location!) she had with one of her potential suitors. He understood and seemed to accept her commitment to being a good mom, working on her faith-based values. Then the discussion turned to sex, her idea being that bringing men into her house was *not* what she was going to expose her children to. His response was something to the effect of, "'Well, I have to try before I buy." At least he was clear. And because this was a discussion that happened in the bright light of day (at a breakfast discussion, *not* on a date), it was easy for her to see this was not going to be any kind of experience she wanted to expose her kids to. I'm sure this wasn't the end of the story, but this intelligent, not-dating, and not-going-to-date-you discussion happened in a friendly environment, where this woman's spiritual and family values could be put on the table in a transparent way. You have many of your own stories to share. Let's start writing our stories with as good and even better outcomes.

One evening at the seminar...

"I don't date." The middle-aged man came to the front of the classroom after a ***Dating without Delusion*** evening class. His shoulders were aggressively arched forward, and he had a very serious look on his face. "I don't date," he said again. "I only spend time with people I trust." The complications and ramifications of this man's declaration were too many and too numerous to list, and I knew this was not the time; we had just spent two hours in seminar interaction. I've learned the hard way: these encounters are icebergs that are immensely complex. "Well, you never know when you might change your mind, and it's always a good idea to be prepared," I said. After those two hours, I knew there was no bandwidth left in either one of us to start delving into the personal history underlying this man's adamant announcement. Angry and adamant. After thinking about this encounter, the questions I could have asked him started to flood in:

- Are you never going to build a new relationship with a woman?
- Are you committed to being Single for the rest of your life?
- In those past failed relationships, did you share any of the responsibility?
- Are you simply going bury the pain and hurt of those previous experiences?
- Do you think that 'Fortress Mentality' is attractive to anyone?
- And how exactly do you determine 'who to trust'?

Then there is the possibility of meeting a woman with the spirituality of Mother Teresa and the looks of a Beyoncé, who says to you, "Gee, I would enjoy spending some time with you, could we go to church together?" (Excuse the hyperbole.) What would he say then? How would his "I don't date" principle hold up to that? Going to church with someone who is internally and externally attractive is a rare opportunity; are you going to approach that possible relationship with the strong and silent persona? Ultimately, the central question is if — just if — you met a woman (or man) who 'pushed all of your buttons,' why would she/he want to date you? This one central question is the one we all need to answer, and it is the 'why' of ***Dating without Delusion***.

Since I spent a long portion of my life as a Single adult, I experienced all the frustration of relationship building and disintegration. Through it all, I can honestly say that my goal, my motivation, my secret hope was to have a lifelong committed relationship, and my secret fear was that I wouldn't find one. Admitting I had this fear when I was Single was something I did NOT do, even though it was true. The fear was that I would continue on the failed relationship merry-go-round, experiencing more divorce and more emotional pain. With this conundrum came clear revelation:

> *"People who are really ready for a stable lifelong*
> *relationship don't need one."*[9]

As hard as it is to reach this state of mind and spirit, you need to do it because if you do meet someone who is 'right' for you, you want to grow that relationship carefully. Not on the wild mouse ride of infatuation, not based upon neediness and emotional desperation, but on some intelligent understanding of yourself. On the other hand, if you and God determine that you're going to continue as one of the millions of Single adults in America, you better be content with who you are. *You* are the one person you can't walk away from.

Let's look at one more real-life story from evenings at the seminar. In this case, a middle-aged woman came up after the class, and was pretty excited and energized. She told me how she was again interested in building a romantic relationship. For a number of years, she felt as though she needed to heal, and to heal on her own. Now, she was learning how to think and react differently to the idea of spending thoughtful and quality time with a man with values and integrity. She had developed an interest in a guy who she had known for quite a long time, so she had seen firsthand the depth and quality of his beliefs, his values, and character. With an absolute flash in her eyes she said, "I never knew what it could be like to develop an interest in someone I respect!!" Double exclamation point!! For all those years of dating with the culture mindset, she had relationships based upon an infatuation foundation — which is no foundation at all. I'm guessing she had sought relationships with men who were exciting, mysterious, and unpredictable: the 'bad boys.' Maybe because she had an unstable relationship with her fa-

---

[9] I borrowed this quote from Chip Ingraham in his *'Love, Sex, and Lasting Relationships'* video teaching series, which I recommend to you.

ther? We'll talk more about that later. Suffice it to say, she experienced some deep hurt in those emotionally energized dating days. This new kind of relationship was full of potentials that were way different. Honest conversation. Meaningful communication. For sure, a real other-gender friendship. *What a different world!*

Where we are going

Every day, counselors and psychologists all over the country do their level best to help struggling marriages; by and large, these noble efforts often fail. Recently, I heard my pastor say how hard it was for him, week after week, to meet with couple after couple on the brink of divorce. Marriage counseling also goes on in many different out-of-church venues, but the divorce rate seems to be a stubborn and ugly fixture in our society. For pastors or counseling professionals, there is no alternative but to keep on with their efforts to try to save marriages. My church, like so many others, offers all kinds of marital support: books, classes, conferences, studies, marriage mentoring and support groups — a veritable *arsenal* of material. Christians say God loves marriage, and I deeply believe this is true. Not to mention the flip side of a good marriage is an ugly divorce. The simple and straightforward way to attack this problem is to prepare people with relationship training *long before* they begin to build a serious/romantic relationship. This is exactly what you will be doing as you work through the pages of **Dating without Delusion.** It won't be a comfortable read, and sometimes it will just seem like a lot of work, but I think *you* are worth it — and so does God.

In Judith Wallerstein's *The Unexpected Legacy of Divorce*[10] (a book I highly recommend; please see 'Your Relationship Library' for a short synopsis) you can see in nasty detail how divorce infuses children with long-lasting depression, anger, and rebellion — or maybe just confusion. As those children move through adolescence into adulthood the effects are still there, often shaping their emotions deep into their adult lives. Divorce is a deadly evil that permeates our culture. I look out at our church environment and see firsthand the dedicated and prolonged effort that the pastoral/counseling staff puts into marriage and family. We even have an event called Marriage 911; you can guess what it's about.

---

[10] I will recommend a number of books for your 'Relationship Library.' This is one of the key books recommended, particularly for those people who have been affected by divorce in their childhood families or in their own marriages. For this example, Judith Wallerstein was a skilled family researcher at Cal Berkley.

Doesn't it strike you as odd that so _much_ effort is put into supporting marriage and so _little_ effort is put into _preparing_ for marriage? Often when a couple announces their engagement, the church responds by offering a pre-marriage class or curriculum. This relationship phase is what I call the 'Fog of Engagement', when infatuation runs high and dreams of the wedding day dance in the bride's head. In the 'Fog', relationship work usually takes a back seat to wedding preparation and the emotional excitement that swirls around it. So this is where I feel like a modern-day David with my puny efforts to encourage healthy dating, trying to kill the giant of Divorce, which is set up by an infatuation-based world. All of this is fought against a backdrop of lonely Singles, who are everywhere in our post-modern culture. So Mr. or Ms. Reader, here's the attack plan depicted below.

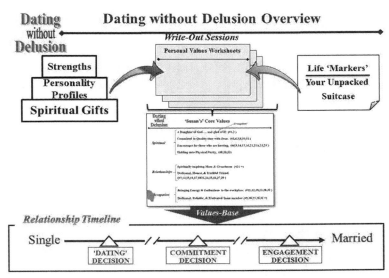

The idea is to equip you with essential and powerful understanding of yourself, by carefully examining your internal makeup and life experiences. This is a form of intrinsic learning[11] because it's fun to honestly learn about yourself. But you will also receive a very practical extrinsic benefit from doing this work: better relationships! The work I'll ask you to do is hard, but the outcome can be life-changing. From the basis of your refined self-un-

---

[11] Intrinsic motivation involves engaging in a behavior because it is personally rewarding; essentially, performing an activity for its own sake rather than the desire for some external reward. Extrinsic motivation occurs when we are motivated to perform a behavior or engage in an activity in order to earn a reward or avoid a punishment.

derstanding and self-awareness, the plan is to explain in granular detail how you can use that self-understanding in the relationship-building process. I'll ask you to use three specific, modern, and mature self-assessment tools to get a clear understanding of yourself. In the top left of the picture, the tools are shown as Spiritual Gifts, Personality Profiles, and Strengths Assessments. See them in the upper left corner of the picture? I'll also ask you to do some honest self-assessment to write down key life events (markers), and to do some honest self-examination so you can be clear on what you are 'bringing' from your childhood (see the upper right of the picture; often called your 'suitcase'). This is to see how you have been shaped and influenced by the key happenings in your life. By understanding how you are wired and how your life experiences have molded you, I'll ask you to dig into three Personal Values worksheets: Spiritual, Relational, and Occupational. These worksheet blanks are provided at the seminars and classes. In the actual seminar/classes, I help people to summarize — to synthesize — their worksheet efforts into a Personal Core Values summary. It's shown as 'Susan's Core Values' in the top-down flow of the graphic — don't spend time squinting at Susan's values; yours will be very different.

Over many years, I have seen many well-meaning values development books and systems which are largely ineffective. Mostly, they imply that you can pick your own values: a big mistake. I say you have to listen to your life, and God speaking to you through your life. Sometimes these values development systems attempt to cover the universe of morality and spirituality — another big mistake — and this results in page after page of impractical, un-retainable, over-the-top idealistic values lists. Hopefully I have learned from those, on your behalf. Your six or seven discovered, hard-earned, life-infused and well-articulated Personal Values, never any more, become the stone in your slingshot (using the David and Goliath analogy). What giant are you going to slay? You're going to slay the *delusion* that an infatuation-based relationship has any hope of surviving the rigors and challenges of a lifelong marriage. In the graphic, this is depicted as your *'values base'* and it is the central and essential element of **Part One** of this book. Unlike a novel or more traditional book, please don't think of this book as a 'page turner' or as entertainment; this will be work for you, and I hope you can embrace the personal challenge. I suggest that you read and digest Part One, and then start using your values in your day-to-day relationships. Reading Part Two will be interesting, but be ready to get back to the bookshelves when a romantic relationship actually emerges in your life.

Part Two of the book will take you through the *relationship timeline* — please see the bottom of the graphic. Part One is all about who you are. Part Two is about building relationships in an intentional, phased-based process. Clearly, *how* you behave should be based upon the clarity and common understanding of *who* you are. *How* you behave should be dependent on the maturity of knowing *where* you are in the sequential process of building that relationship. Relationship-building demands careful but meaningful communication in the early going and honest and transparent communication as you enter exclusive dating. In a recent ***Dating without Delusion*** class, a young guy summarized this thought when he said. "I'm glad to know there is a roadmap that I can follow." Step-by-step, using your values, you can move your critical relationship all the way to an enduring marriage relationship — or exit that same relationship when you find it does not have the values-based fundamentals a healthy marriage must have to survive. Admittedly, this is a tough challenge, and here's the advice. When a potentially great dating relationship comes onto the scene and you feel the infatuation and 'magnetic' attraction strike... please, sit down and do a slow read of Part Two. Part Two will help you remember where you are in the process of building a good relationship. It will remind you to go slow. Most importantly, it will remind you of what to communicate and when to communicate it.

Part Three is a collection of relationship tools I have developed and adapted over the years. A personal favorite is my adaptation of John Gottman's 'Four Horsemen.' It's relationship thinking to assist you when *contempt* sneaks into your mind and feelings in response to your partner's words or actions. Let's keep going. How about dealing with loneliness? What do you do when you're being hit-on by a married person? How about Single parenting? Would you consider a key technique to help you make the critical engagement decision? Like a manual, I have tucked some of these important tools into the back of the book so you can periodically go to the bookshelf and pull out a concept that will re-orient your thinking. My desire is for you to learn these techniques *now*, while you are thinking about dating, not to wait until your future marriage is in deep crisis.

Your Relationship Library is the last section, which offers a quick overview of the reference books I have leaned on. I quickly describe them with enough detail, I hope, to interest you in doing your own relationship research. These books are classics, and each one is timeless in its own way. For example, *The Unexpected Legacy of Divorce* is not a Christian book, but it is a one-of-kind landmark study of the effects of divorce on children. Judith Wallerstein from Cal Berkeley is the author, and the quality and thoroughness of her research provides important conclusions for our society — and you — to consider. Wallerstein also did a landmark study documented in *The Good Marriage*, defining four basic marriage types which are intensely instructive for couples on the path to the altar. Do you want to take a hard look at the Millennials? Laura Sessions Stepp does honest research into the effects of escalating sexual behavior within the upcoming generation. She carefully and honestly focuses on the young women of today's culture-setting generation through in-depth interview and analysis. *Getting the Love You Want* is the work of skilled psychologist Harville Hendrix. He wants to unravel the difficulties which stem from our childhood experiences and then persist within our marriages. In addressing the challenges of creating an open marriage he unpacks the source of our infatuations and attractions...and in so doing presents a powerful resource for *anyone* (like a Single person!) who wants to build better relationships. *The Gospel* is a distinctly spiritually based book that takes a fresh look at the New Testament. J.D. Greear is the author, and I believe he offers important thinking and perspectives for people of faith: 'Faith-thinkers'. Lastly I lean heavily on the Bible, as a reliable source of invaluable advice for effective living.

Each one has a profound impact because each one describes relationship phenomena found everywhere in our culture today. These key books have served me well. Perhaps they can be good relationship resources for you?

Your fight against the culture

Now remembering that I am a Christian, you may still be conjuring up all kinds of images, which may or may not be accurate; some may be very far from reality. You should also be aware that I am doing my best to make this book readable by both Christians and those who are not... feels like the razor's edge. The one thing that is *irreplaceable* is your willingness to think! The **Dating _without_ Delusion** approach is to stimulate thinking. Everyone has fallen into daily habit patterns that we follow *without thinking,* forgetting about the rationale for our choices and potentially problematic longer-term consequences. I believe this is an evil strategy aimed right at you — and me, too. To gear up for this fight, you first have to know the adversary. Sun Tzu, the ancient Chinese general, said, "If you know the enemy and know yourself, you need not fear the results of a hundred battles." So here we go, into the

Dating *without* Delusion **Sun Tzu**

"If ignorant both of your enemy and yourself, you are certain to be in peril."

battle against the culture. Has the culture just evolved? I don't think so. Bear with me as I take us on an intellectual ride, which is also a spiritual journey.

Suspending your disbelief

I think everyone likes to go to movies, at least once in a while. With that common ground, let's talk about *Mission Impossible*. A blockbuster hit over many sequels has the foundational conflict between our hero — usually Tom Cruise — and a seriously evil villain who wants to take down the world, or at least America. To enjoy the movie, we suspend our disbelief for an hour and a half to enjoy the stunt thrills that mostly are the 'Impossible' part of Mission Impossible. World disaster is avoided, and we leave the theater and go back to our real world.

But in the real world, the *personal* stakes are higher; most of us can't directly augment world stability, but we do have the say in own lives. In our battle, the villain is much more devious. Yes, I am talking about Satan. For a moment, please suspend your disbelief to envision the enemy you are up against. He is not the red tights and pitchfork cartoon character. He is slick, subtle, and devious, and he wants to bring you down — figuratively and literally.

Most people live, work, and play, giving Satan little thought. Most Christians fall into this same mode of living, and Satan loves it. He uses all kinds of subtle influences to bring us into personal disaster like addictions, pornography, divorces, bankruptcy, adulteries, and pride-invoked conflicts. (Remember: keep suspending your disbelief!) If you want to win this fight, you have to know your enemy and get ready for the poison darts he is going to throw at you. His primary weapon? It's the culture. Satan has great experience in bringing down many cultures, usually from inward corruption, e.g. Rome. If you don't think this culture is being brought down around our ears, Satan is *very* happy because you aren't in the fight. You're a willing participant in his society-destroying scheme. But if you pay attention, you will see many people being swept down the sewer pipe by the pervasive ethos of our culture. The examples are too many to list, but when you turn on the news tonight, you'll see the latest cultural cancer in one form or another.

At this writing, we are in the aftermath of the Marysville and Florida State shootings. Last year, it was the Penn State/Sandusky trial. We are trying to rebound from Dark Knight shootings, the Sikh temple shootings, and shootings at the Navy Yard. It's happening every week! The most evil: the Newtown school shootings. What about the Boston Marathon bombing? It seems that mall shootings are weekly events. Junior high school sex parties are happening in what used to be conservative neighborhoods, and the greed of financial institutions has continued in spite of worldwide deficits and national economic failures. Please forgive my negativism; chalk it up to objectivity.[12]

---

[12] The other night on CBS news we saw a policeman shoot a man in the back, school educators convicted of helping students cheat on tests, and DEA officers indicted for using government $ to hire prostitutes. Back-to-Back stories!

Knowing your enemy is the key. If you are objective about his influences and his relentless damage, you will be more open to fighting back — and also knowing the true God. So let's take a look at the culture. Check out Jude Law in the slide below. The emphasis is on image, not on personal character. Here's what the small print says, "My only obligation is to keep myself and oth-

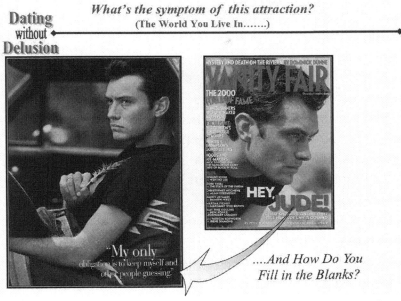

What's the symptom of this attraction?
(The World You Live In.......)

Dating without Delusion

"My only obligation is to keep myself and other people guessing."

....*And How Do You Fill in the Blanks?*

er people guessing," which was a subtle but pervasive attitude at the turn of the century. Now, it is ingrained in the culture. It revolves around image and appearance: style over substance, fun lifestyle at all costs. I happen to like Jude Law as an actor, but his image statement here is one that defies any meaningful understanding of him as a person. It is the absolute opposite of what I call personal transparency. My goal, and hopefully the goal of the ***Dating without Delusion*** experience, is for us to develop genuine *personal transparency.* In short, I want you to get to know me in a simple and straightforward way, and I want to know you without a lot of innuendo and evasive dialogue. But embedded in this culture is a set of lies that are being broadcast relentlessly at you and at your kids — remember, many of the Single readers are also Single parents. Physical appearance is everything; you must have the xyz thing — particularly the latest technology xyx — and lifestyle is paramount.

Read this from George Barna:[13]

---

[13] "Prime Time with God" online daily devotional from George Barna; Oct. 15, 2013. Ephesians Four Ministries.

There are many motivations for work. Some might say it is simply to put food on the table. George Barna, the American researcher on religious habits, found disturbing results from his study on the motivations of many Christians in American society. "We are not a society that simply enjoys its time off. <u>We are driven by our leisure appetites.</u> It is increasingly common to hear of people turning down job offers because the hours or other responsibilities would interfere with their hobbies, fitness regimens, and other free time activities. Even our spending habits show that playing has become a major priority. The average household spends more money on entertainment than it does clothing, health care, furniture or gasoline." (Underlines mine)

His study also found that many people define success in surprisingly non-Christian terms: He found that 66 percent of Americans define success in life as the acquisition of sufficient money, education, material possessions or career prestige; only seven percent related success to their faith condition and its influence upon their life. *"The Christian Church has stagnated, largely due to its comfort with routines and rituals that are neither challenging nor relevant for millions of people,"* said Barna.

Watch Out for the Cultural Lies
(Both You <u>and</u> Your Kids)

Dating without Delusion ←————————————————————→

1. **You can become whatever you want** ....
2. **You need to do what everyone else does** .....
3. **You can do what everyone else does (without consequences)**
4. **You are how you look** ....
5. **You must act & speak like others** ....
6. **Performance and Results are everything** ......
7. **Self Gratification is the goal** ...... **SEX** is assumed
8. **Maligning (......if you don't join them: 1 Peter 4:4)**
9. **?**

Open your eyes and you will see people all around you driving towards those 'play' goals with every ounce of energy they can muster. The alternative? We can work hard to develop personal transparency: first, work hard to articulate your Personal Values, then work hard at being committed to them — meaning, we will work hard to live by them. But it will be in the face of cultural lies that have worked into the fabric of our culture and thinking. In the slide above, consider how you might have been 'influenced.'

Reaching the culture's definition of 'success' is just one of the culture's pervasive influences. You've heard some of these since you were a kid — and your kids are being shaped by the same kind of faulty thinking. One of the most pervasive lies is: *'You can be whatever you want.'* (See the first bullet in the slide above.) It is recited as almost a national religion. The idea, of course, is that our nation will always reward the hard work and dreams of our young people. While that may be true, we will discuss in depth why each one of us is made with talents, skills, and strengths that are absolutely unique. However, they don't allow us to 'be whatever you want.' I remember very vividly one evening, my youngest stepson (about six years old at the time) said at the dinner table, "I'm going to play football for the Dallas Cowboys!" Dilemma! As a parent, you never want to douse healthy enthusiasm; on the other hand, I guessed he did not have the mental and physical capacity or the physical dedication it would take to achieve this goal. I suggested he start a rigorous workout routine to start getting ready for his athletic career in pro football. The workout suffering would be a path for his self-discovery. As you can guess, the workout regimen never materialized. He is now an accomplished and talented chef, and well suited for it. Thankfully, I do believe his internal composition is in sync with his persona, talents, and strengths.

Many other lies are driven at us through social media and relentless societal peer pressure. As we work to understand who we are, the cultural lies will become more evident. The last bullet capsulizes this pressure. 'They malign you' comes out of the Bible, where Peter was writing to the early church, one of many Bible examples. Peter is calling us to live for the will of God, and I repeatedly argue that it is a will for you that is personally findable. Then Peter says that when you decline the carousing offered by the culture, "They are surprised that you do not run with them to the same excess of dissipation, and they *malign* you."[14] You know what maligning is: it's badgering, ridiculing, criticizing because you don't do what they do. It's peer pressure, big peer pressure. And if you are unsure of why you don't want to go to the x,y,z club and do Jell-O shooters and the latest Gucci drug, you are going to be demeaned and your emotions assaulted by the ridicule.

Now remember when you were a kid and the gang was off on some 'adven-

---

[14] *New American Standard Bible.* Copyright 1962, 1963, 1971, 1972, 1973, 1975, 1977. The Lockman Foundation. LA Habra, CA. p. 1653. (Italics added)

ture' that started to turn dark corners. When I was a kid, we climbed neighborhood garage roofs, ripped off the composite shingles, and used them like
Frisbee projectiles to attack the other guys on the next garage roof over. The
damage was substantial. But just imagine if one of those high-velocity spinning shingles hit someone in the head or eye. *Really* dangerous. You have your
own stupid story. Remember how you knew what was right — that was God
— but you hated the thought of the ridicule that you would face if you didn't
go along. This is what kids face every day. Now they face it through the Face-
book/Twitter/Instagram social media, which is ubiquitous...meaning that it
goes with them *everywhere* and it's there *all the time*. Studies clearly show kids
are addicted to social media, even though they simultaneously are bullied in
the digital environment. They could be sitting in a great concert, which should
be fun, and simultaneously they are getting thrashed through social media. Or
they might be in a good class or on a fun outing to the mountain, and in comes
that demeaning little electronic voice that is being read by 75 other students.
As a kid, I know I did not have the personal fortitude to deal with this kind of
ridicule. I would have shriveled up, or gotten angry and lashed out.

Kids are trying to discover who they are. If they make a personal discovery, even in small part, they have a chance to successfully deflect the maligning. But apart from a new meaningful personal direction, they have little
chance against the digital peer pressure. Consider what Lee Siegel says in
Newsweek:

> *Even for the most gregarious children, the Web's constant reminder of the
> majority opinion makes them fearful of trying to do or say anything that doesn't
> please the crowd. Yet appealing to the Web's masses also offers them the temptation
> to say things they would never have ordinarily uttered in public — things that can
> come back to haunt them later in life.*[15]

The same is true for you and me. If we know who we are, we have a chance
of deflecting the heat. Then comes a period of loneliness because you no
longer are a part of that group you relied on for social connection. Time to
find a new group (ASAP) of people connected by a higher purpose that you
can share — not easy. This kind of vicious circle is all around us...and the
slick adversary and his demon-boys are impressed with the depth of their
manipulation and control.

---

[15] Siegel, Lee. *The Kids Aren't Alright*. Newsweek; 16 October 2012. pp. 18,19.

The central strategy of your enemy

As you know, I contend there is a divine design that is stamped into your DNA. Within that higher purpose is a sharply focused plan — think back to the pyramid view from 40,000'. Revitalized thinking can enable your gifting to serve other people in an effective and transforming fashion. Satan knows this, and he hates you. By effectively dragging you into the cultural morass, he can keep you in his grasp and use you to drag other people into the same kind of self-serving, superficial life. Now, imagine bad relationships taken into cohabitating, or badly matched marriages. People in these circumstances are consumed with arguments, divorces, lawsuits, child custody battles, and a range of dysfunctional circumstances. All of these are time consuming, emotionally consuming, and resource consuming, preventing you from doing anything for anyone else because you are trying your best to manage that latest disaster. "He's a real jerk." "She's a b-----" are the ways we try to deflect our responsibility for the mess we've made (so, why did you pick her; why did you pick him?).

Now, look at it from your enemy's viewpoint; he has driven two lives into the depths of ineffectiveness. Two people are consumed with managing the mess instead of realizing their personal destinies. The slick enemy scores a big victory. For him, dead people, shot on the street, may be light entertainment. Divorced or multiple-divorced relationships are much more damaging because they re-create themselves. Not only do they annihilate effective living for people and parents, they very effectively infuse the children and the culture with deep uncertainty and dysfunction. The summation of divorce across our country creates the concept that divorce is normal, that it is acceptable, that it is no big deal. This is a LIE!

C.S. Lewis is my favorite author, primarily because he thinks on a much higher level than I do, dragging my thinking to a higher plane. He doesn't ride intellectual fads. If he were still with us, he would probably agree that he is a 'fad-buster' (Lewis passed away in 1963). One of the many books he published is *The Screwtape Letters*. You may remember the premise. Uncle Screwtape is a senior demon that writes a series of letters to his demon-nephew Wormwood, coaching him on the most effective life-destroying strategies for the 'subjects' — that would be us. In this excerpt, remember that the 'Enemy' of the demons is God. Let's listen in:

"*Of course I know that the Enemy also wants to detach men from themselves, but in a different way. Remember always that He really likes the little vermin, and sets an absurd value on the distinctness of every one of them. When He talks of their losing their selves He only means abandoning the clamor of their self-will; once they have done that, He really gives them back all their personality and boasts (I am afraid sincerely) that when they are wholly His they will be more themselves than ever. Hence while He is delighted to see them sacrificing even their innocent wills to His, He hates to see them drifting away from their own nature for any other reason. And we should always encourage them to do so. The deepest likings and impulses of any man are the raw material, the starting point with which the Enemy has furnished him. To get him away from those is therefore a point gained; even in things indifferent it is always desirable to substitute the standards of the world or convention, or fashion for a human's own likings and dislikings.*" *(Underlines mine)*

'An absurd value on the distinctness of every one of them' is the demon's recognition that God has designed a completely unique persona, with talent, strength, and values set into each of us. Please recall the base of our pyramid in the 40,000' introduction: 'God has a Plan.' God has a plan *for you.* And now, consider the demonic strategy. 'It is always desirable to substitute the standards of the world or convention, or fashion for a human's own liking and disliking.' The paraphrase is, '...let's use the culture to divert the subject's attention away from his one-of-a-kind purpose.'

Do you see it? Culture is the demonic tool of choice. If the culture is the demonic weapon, what is the strategy? The evil strategy at its essence is to rip out the base layer of the pyramid: the plan. If our enemy can take out the foundation, then we will no longer be of any threat to him. Selfishness leads to the modern wave of divorce, disabling people from others-centered living. Let's listen to a modern voice, Gary Thomas in *Sacred Search*:

"*You have no idea how much kingdom time is wasted on ill matched people trying to make their marriages a little less insufferable. I want you to gain a positive picture — a vision — for how much kingdom work could be accomplished by two well matched people working in harmony to seek the kingdom of God, grow in righteousness and fulfill their unique calling in Christ.*"[16]

---

[16] Thomas, Gary. Published by David. C, Cook. Colorado Springs, CO, 2013. P. 250.

Satan tries to eliminate the idea that we have a central and defining purpose — then we are reduced to wallowing around in our own self-invented soup. No focus, no defining purpose, continually shifting and unstable. Does this make sense? To your enemy it does.

Divorce: Permeating our culture

Back in the '90s, I was flying across the country — in those days, my company had me flying on American — and there was a nice little airline magazine called American Way. Here's what I read:

SURVIVING THE '90s with JIM SHAHIN _Inoculation, Please_

Divorce is like a flu that everybody seems to be catching. Is there a doctor in the house? Everyone around me, it seems, is getting divorced. The couple whose life seemed charmed — she brilliant and vivacious and successful, he handsome and driven and praised in his field. The onetime high-school sweethearts whose relationship was nothing if not tumultuous over the course of their two decades and two children. The couple with two children whose relationship spanned the breadth of two coasts. The couple, never well-suited, who married out of desperation and ultimately imploded. Everyone. Dropped as if from sniper fire. A couple we had only recently hit it off with — bam. A couple who'd gotten married around the same time we had several years ago — bam. A couple I'd known since high school — bam. It got almost comical: the week before leaving with another couple on a trip to France, good friends of theirs in Paris announced they were splitting up — a bam heard 'round the world. My wife, Jessica, and I started feeling like a jinx on love. We had both witnessed the demise of marriages before, of course. But not so many so close to us in such a short period of time. It's been like an outbreak of the flu. And you fear that, like the flu, exposure makes you vulnerable. Unfortunately, there is no inoculation. Divorce stories are all different and they are all the same: something went awry. The particulars? Well, only the people involved really know and even they don't — really. They have some ideas, but those ideas are like some hazily detected blip on a radar screen. Finally, the thing is

explained away. And the explanation, usually elaborate with evidence, anecdote, and character reference, is inevitably maddening and simple: <u>One of them was unhappy, too unhappy to try anymore</u>. That's when the world for both of them is forever rearranged. "You're with somebody for years and years and then they're gone, not there anymore," one friend said. "You're hurled into this emotional void." As they struggle to emerge from that void, they seem a bit punch-drunk, staggering into the harsh daylight of their new worlds, trying to feel good about what they've left behind (especially if they initiated the breakup), trying only to figure out what happened (especially if they didn't). Some go on dating sprees. Some jump immediately into another serious relationship... counseling... hangs around friends more... etc.... etc. (underline mine)

That was back in the '90s, you say; why do you quote that, Jay? I want you see that the 90's culture has set the course and ethos of the world we live in today. The people Jim describes are the mostly-divorced parents of the Gen X/Millennial generations growing up in our society today. One study I dug up ranked stress on a point scale; here's how it looks:

Stress Levels
- Death of Spouse: 100
- *Divorce:* 73
- Marital separation: 65
- Death of close family member: 63
- Jail term: 63
- Personal injury or illness: 53
- Marriage: 50
- Fired at work: 47

In this ranking, only 'death of a spouse' ranks more stressful than divorce. As you look at that lady above, mourning the divorce problem, sure, divorce *used to be* a scandal, or as the inscription above her reads, 'The Great Society Sensation.' Today in our culture, divorce is the *normal* state of affairs. Everyone knows people who have been divorced multiple times and we think nothing of it: we're not even a bit surprised. The study ranking refers to stress imposed upon parents. Are you joking? What about the kids? The worst problem is modeling relationship failure for our kids to repeat.

Look at the next graphic. That kid is walking away, angry and confused. Mostly, his world is turned upside down and he doesn't know what is going to happen to him. Part of him thinks that *he* is the problem. I am divorced, my wife divorced (twice), and I know there is impact on our sons. What can we do? The first and best thing is know who you are, then move forward with real-life commitments, possibly to marry based upon your values-based identity (refer to Part One the second 'C,' Commitment). Meaning, let's go for

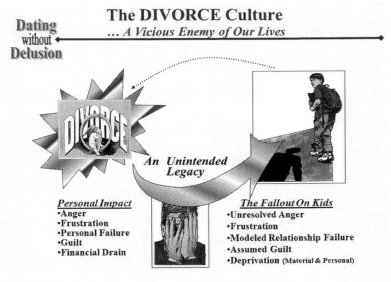

The DIVORCE Culture
... A Vicious Enemy of Our Lives

Dating without Delusion

An Unintended Legacy

Personal Impact
•Anger
•Frustration
•Personal Failure
•Guilt
•Financial Drain

The Fallout On Kids
•Unresolved Anger
•Frustration
•Modeled Relationship Failure
•Assumed Guilt
•Deprivation (Material & Personal)

no-more divorce in our personal lives! Let's make this a clear and compelling goal. If you happen to be in a second or third marriage, the best you now can do is to be faithful and committed to your current spouse. Or if you're Single, to your next spouse. Or maybe you should first be faithful to yourself? The best families I know have enduring first marriages modeling a lifelong commitment one spouse to another for the kids to learn from. This spoken and demonstrated commitment creates an aura of stability for the kids. I have said in the seminars over and over: *The best thing you can do for your kids is to love your spouse.* Most of the people I'm talking to are already divorced, making this impossible apart from reconciliation, which is rare. The best they can do is work hard to allow their kids reasonable access to the other parent. They have to start living their parenting values on their own, even if that other parent is living a dysfunctional life. Very rare are great marriages with the 'commitment' kind of love that sets up their kids so that they can, in turn, live out their own commitments in quality next-generation marriages. So many of us have gotten into tough divorces; now we must move on from where we are. We need to deal with our mistakes (ask forgiveness), reconcile, or move on to a commitment that we can keep — that's where Debra and I are at the 33-year mark in our marriage.

The 'Gray Divorce' phenomena

No divorce in the first place is the **Dating without Delusion** objective. In our society, even seemingly good marriages are breaking apart for people over 50; it's called Gray Divorce. People raise their kids, send them out into the world, and then discover that the person they married doesn't share the same values they do. The one defining shared value — the kids — just moved out to go to work or college. In March 2012, the Wall Street Journal ran a full two-page piece on gray divorce. It cited the numbers of divorces for people over 50: more than 600,000 per year in 2009 in the U.S. Projected ahead, over-50 divorces will reach 800,000 per year by 2030. In 2009, more than one in four divorces was by people ages 50+.[17] Quoting the Journal: *"The trend defies any explanation, but it springs at least in part from Boomers' status as the first generation to enter into marriage with goals largely focused on self-fulfillment."*

In my opinion, the trend is a direct outcome of people who do not know themselves or their values. Their relationship lacked a values-based foundation. Remember the base of the pyramid? These people may have some compatibility, and raising their kids is a noble undertaking. In the short-term (18–20 years), parenting was a common value they shared, and it likely held them together. But when parenting was done, their relationship lacked 'values compatibility' (my term).

I contend that we *all* desire self-fulfillment. From a spiritual standpoint, I contend that we all desire to become who we are meant to be; that's rock solid self-fulfillment. The lady in the Wall Street Journal piece — Dawn — is the divorced lady quoted in the article. She is very straight and to the point: they stayed together all those years because of the kids, but now nothing was left. She says,

"He was so uncompassionate and I had turned to my religion, and he would never go to church with me. I realized that I was alone in the marriage and would be better off with someone *whose values and interests* were more

---

[17] Thomas, Susan Gregory. *The Wall Street Journal,* March 3-4, 2012 Review, pp. C-1,2.

like mine." (italics mine.)

Do you see that sharing a compatibility activity, like going on bike rides, was not going to save their marriage? Do you see that the one common personal value that Dawn and her former husband shared was the kids? Now out of the house, the kids no longer provided the _raison d'être_ (reason for being). It's the Personal Values thing again. My guess: Dawn and her husband married in the first place for a bunch of infatuation-based, passionate, and superficial reasons — and those reasons could not stand the test of time.

Remember, this section of the book is a dissection of today's culture. Gray divorce directly impacts today's culture. Why? Because Dawn and her husband, who is now out of the house and gone, have provided an example for their kids to emulate. Instead of being living examples of marriage dedication and commitment, they have provided a model of brokenness. Did they buy into the happiness model of the Millennials? Or did they unwittingly contribute to the ethos of today's culture? I think it's both.

Mark Slomka (please sees the Introduction and cover flap) and I were recently talking about the gay marriage issue. Now because you know I'm a Christian and Mark is a pastor, you're thinking, "Oh boy, here we go." Not so fast, please. From a political standpoint, I advocate FREEDOM based upon pervasive and relentless personal responsibility. People who believe we can alter God's design for marriage by allowing gay people to marry don't comprehend the depth and intricacy of His design for the man-to-woman bond. Marriage will stand, despite the little 'acknowledgment' efforts of our government.

As far as gay people are concerned, I don't even begin to comprehend the complexities of how they are what they are. I do know God loves these people as much as He loves me. And if nothing else has come through so far, it is that you and I must own _who_ we are through crisp articulation of Personal Values: a challenge for everyone, gay and heterosexual alike. But, you say, marriage as the Bible defines it is being undermined by gay initiatives. Perhaps. My discussion with Mark focused on the much bigger problem, which is the damage our multiple-marriage, multiple divorce culture has foisted upon our society. (I am a guilty one.) And it's a naturally expanding, ever exacerbating (worsening) problem. As you see in the slide above — and as many psychologists would quickly point out — divorce begets more divorce. The fallout on kids is a legacy divorced parents _don't_ understand. Divorce injects the worst kind of stress on everyone in the family. And our adversary (Screwtape) laughs in the shadows.

Values-Roles-Goals root cause analysis

For whatever reason, the up-and-coming generation — the 20s through early '30s generation — seems to always set the tone for the broader culture. Don't you agree? Those very younger people, adolescents and early teens, get lots of margin.[18] They're sometimes ignored because they have little experience and, in many instances, they're not taken very seriously. My generation, on the other hand, the Boomers, are fading into irrelevance as we get older and less 'engaged.' However, we set the tone for the culture back in the late '60s and '70s. And didn't we love it! But today's culture (now evolved to Generation Z) is set by the Millennials (Born ~1980 to 2000), or Gen Yers, or Gen ME. Sometimes they are called the Gen Me, Me, ME generation (GenME[3]). Perhaps you've heard of some other tag? Regardless of the name, *they are today's culture-setters,* and they're expressing a lot of frustration and dissatisfaction. Let's take a look at it.

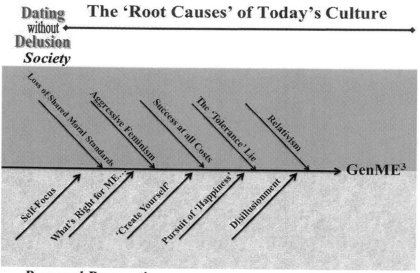

Personal Perspective

As you see in the graphic above, the overarching society has changed, with a very pervasive effect on the young people growing up in it. The chart

---

[18] We now are experiencing Generation Z: Born from 1997-2012. Many of these young people are experiencing significant depression.

is called a 'wishbone.' All of the 'bones' angled into the GenME3 world are contributing factors to the generational personality of the GenME3ers. Society's influence intersects with 'modern' Personal perspectives of todays's culture to create a cultural soup that surrounds us all. The first effect was created when my generation — the Boomers — lost our connection to any shared morality. The examples and standards Boomers established as parents were very diffused, defaulting to money and 'success,' whatever that meant. Work hard! Be Honest! Go to school! A young person growing up in that world had little choice but to self-create self-focused attitudes and behaviors. The emphasis was to start making decisions based upon 'what's right for me.' The Boomer generation set an indelible standard of wealth and material possessions that may never again be equaled. Material success was a tough standard for Millennials to achieve, and the scramble to achieve it seems to have become embedded in every young person's critical choices. The idea is that you can invent yourself in any way, just as long as it quickly achieves those very visible material goals ($$$).

Laura Sessions Stepp focuses in on the Millennials. In *Unhooked*, she carefully reported on the behavior of young college women (GenME[3]ers). *Unhooked* documents their disdain for committed relationships and their drive for personal success. When it comes to relationships, listen to one of the young women in *Unhooked*:

> "My generation... actually our Society... is into taking shortcuts...Get rich faster. Skip this step. Win instant approval. Hookups are like the shortcut to intimacy, while dating is the long way around, the scenic route. We want to get there, wherever 'there' is as quickly as possible, and I think we've lost the ability to enjoy the journey.

> "Sometimes we forget how much the 'end' depends on the means you took to get there. Sometimes patience is a virtue. I think some people (in her generation) are starting to realize the intimacy learned from a hookup is no match for the intimacy learned from a relationship. However they aren't sure what the difference is. They don't recognize that the process of dating/getting to know someone/caring for someone is very important in creating the depth of feeling you will have for them." (underline mine)

This young — at the time — GenME[3]er was realizing the 'depth of effect' that society had impressed upon her. The hookup-quick road to relationship success *seemed* like an avenue to happiness, but she and her friends found out differently. From her perspective, here are three observations. See if you agree.

First: There is no indication that this gal has any concern about the morality of her behavior or any intellectual connection to underlying moral values. Please remember, I am not being judgmental. I am not recommending that she accept my moral principles. However, shouldn't she have some of her own? Her primary thoughts zero-in on doing relationships better, or differently, to live more effectively. Make no mistake, however: she has a pervasive material values base. Success-focus is also the reason behind the 'tolerance' attitudes. Do whatever's right for you... as long as it doesn't affect me. Suggestions that there are higher standards that need to be adopted personally aren't received very well.

Second: Her level of disillusionment is palpable — meaning you can almost touch it. See the disillusionment wishbone depicted in the root cause graphic above? She describes a deep internal disillusionment that says, "Where do I go from here?"

Third: Though she doesn't say it, this woman wants to understand what the possible relationship *solutions* are. The good news is that she seems open to suggestions, which we older adults aren't providing. In *Unhooked,* Laura Stepp is working hard just to understand what's going on in the culture. Laura is disciplined *not* to broadcast recommendations, preferring instead to paint an unbiased picture of what's going on in the minds and lives of the young women she works with. And this is my experience, also. The Millennials are open to hear possible solutions, but they will absolutely reserve the right to self-create — to pick their own solutions. Pretty tough when you have limited life experience, and relationship failure is all around you. Hopefully this is where **Dating _without_ Delusion** will kick in. 'Self-creation' is one of the delusions I hope you are discarding, in favor of 'self-discovery.'

Now, let's look at one last and most-important effect the new culture has foisted upon our society. Please accept for a moment that back in the good ol' days, values and values-based choices were the foundation for behavior — at least at some level. This is why Grandma pines away, reminiscing about how stable and predictable the world was back then. Stability and predictability are *not* what this new culture promotes. Just the opposite: this world drives you to invent yourself, to do your own thing, to be unlike anyone else. But if you hear what the woman says in the excerpt above, you hear something more like, "I found myself acting like everyone else around me and I hated it."

The Values-Roles-Goals decision stream

In ***Dating without Delusion***, I am arguing that you *are* unlike anyone else. In the good ol' days, there was a different pressure to conform and really, that old culture was far from perfect. In fact, many young people back in the 50's and 60's felt as if older people in society were rigid, judgmental, and close-minded. During that time, the moral fabric was disintegrating, and older people who grew up with understood standards had no idea how to reverse the trend. They watched Elvis to Bon Jovi and had no idea what was happening, but they knew change was coming like a tsunami. They shook their heads in disbelief. When *they* grew up, their adopted/Personal Values *did* impact their personal choices.

So here is the overall effect. As you see on the left, values *used* to drive choices. In the 'perfect' world, your values could and would affect your choice of your role; you could set aligned goals and objectives and they would very

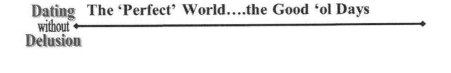

tangibly affect your day-to-day personal choices. The problem back then was that other people were choosing and imposing those largely morality-based values on the younger generation, and the younger generation — including me — didn't like it. So even way back in the 60's, 70's, and 80's, we were deciding to start making choices 'for me.' The problem 'for me' back then, and the problem for the Millennials today, is that I had no solid values base to work from. Isn't it true? If you have no well thought-out principles to work from, you have to default to 'what feels right.' Look at what happens when values are nonexistent, in the next graphic below. In the absence of meaningful values, young people decide to establish goals for themselves, which in itself is a very admirable exercise. We all have to aim for something, right?

So aiming for goals that are GenME culture-friendly leads people to set *extrinsic* goals. What is extrinsic? Simply, it is recognition and affirmation coming to you from the outside, such as awards, accolades, and money. Intrinsic motivation, on the other hand, comes from deep inside, where you feel a permeating sense of satisfaction from doing what you really enjoy. It's finding how you are designed — to be a part of something bigger than yourself. Remember, this is not a psychology book; you may want to spend some more time digging into this extrinsic/intrinsic concept: a very revealing exercise for anyone. Here, I see today's culture emphasizing and prioritizing *extrinsic goals* above all else. Extrinsic examples include:

- Be successful, be well known, or even famous
- Be recognized as *the* authority: gain power and prestige
- Retire by the time I am 50 (or 40...)
- Have enough money to _____, or just be wealthy
- Have a great family (surrounding *me*)
- The kicker: Be happy!

Imagine a person who uses wealth and prestige as the criteria for pursuing a career. Based upon this *extrinsic* goal, they choose their *role* for the wrong reasons. They target money and riches. After achieving that status — wealth, fame, power, etc. — they can't wait to "bail out of it and do what I want." Do we all have and use extrinsic motivations? Of course we do. We need to pay the bills. But as you see in the graphic on the next page, a funny thing happens when Personal Values disappear. Do you see how Personal Values have been replaced in the left-to-right decision stream? Personal *Goals* have moved to the front of the thinking process. Again those Personal Goals are often strongly extrinsic: success, money, fame, power, recognition, independence... and most of all 'happiness'. In *Unhooked,* Laura Stepp pinpoints a culture that elevates a woman's sense of self-determination; this emerges from pervasive baby boomer culture parenting with a 'success at all costs' mentality. Do you see how the past culture set the stage for the loss of Personal Values? Do you see how success-based goals have become the primary influence in our culture? Are you bucking this cultural trend? Have you found some noble way to serve others, and to serve them expecting nothing in return (except perhaps some gratification and joy)? I hope so, and of course I know people who are able to live this selfless way get rewarded mightily. They are the exception, however.

Now, think about relationship building for a moment. Do you see extrinsic goal setting as a reliable foundation for strong relationships? I don't. Goals

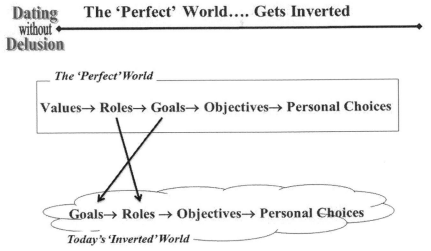

Dating without Delusion   The 'Perfect' World.... Gets Inverted

The 'Perfect' World

Values→ Roles→ Goals→ Objectives→ Personal Choices

Goals→ Roles → Objectives→ Personal Choices

Today's 'Inverted' World

do not replace values. As goals shift and change, is goal-setting going to undergird a strong marriage for the span of a lifetime? Probably not. Personal Values, on the other hand, are enduring. If you build your relationships on values forged in the furnace of self-discovery, I argue that you will enjoy relationships that can stand the test of time. But...you *will* be bucking the culture.

Devil's Ping-Pong

If you have become embroiled in a messy divorce, Satan has effectively sidelined you. If Satan can divert you into the infatuation game you are 'out of commission'. This is because relationships built on infatuation do not have any staying power. From his view, Satan is eminently successful when an infatuation-based relationship leads to a marriage because the chances of that marriage surviving are tiny. The divorce wreckage is the validation of the strategy that Screwtape and his demon-boys have worked on us.

The secondary strategy is when we find our way to give back, — perhaps because we find faith in God? Based upon our new faith, we become increasingly dangerous adversaries to the demon world. In the actualization of our planned/destined selves, we become increasingly resistant to the culture, open to God, and meaningfully relevant to our circle of life relationships. Theologically and intellectually grounded Christians know that they are destined for eternal life, and Satan knows it too. To minimize the damage, Satan uses the culture and all of the trappings of 'religion' to put us into a nasty little game that I call Devil's Ping-Pong. If he can't embroil you in a divorce, he pulls out Devil's Ping-Pong. This is Satan's tactic of bouncing us between the extremes of religious arrogance and religious self-condemnation and depression. Let's dissect both 'prongs' of this attack.

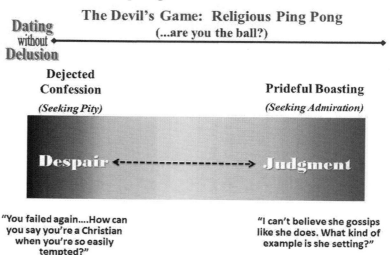

Suppose you skirted the divorce mud pit. Or suppose you are a confident and reasonably content Single person. Add a measure of faith to that profile and you have become a potentially dangerous person (to Satan). Someone who can really damage the demonic strategy. Someone who can have a positive, encouraging effect on those around him. The demon-boys know you and the potential hurt you can put on them. What is the devil tactic to counter that? It's particularly effective against us faith people, but it's effective against anybody

In church, we hear about all of the good things we should do. Most of us want to be positive contributors to our society...to the common good. This works really well against me and my baby boomer counterparts. When I see what the good things are, I pick one or two and get up to get out there to do them. When the pastor urges me to read and pray, I try to sit down and do it.

Name your own stuff. When we work to be better, we may succeed for a short while, and then comes the nagging little demon voice. "Aren't you doing well, Jay? Why don't all the other people you know, like Debra, pray like you do? Why don't they spend more time in the Bible like you do?" The slide above shows a little example of judgmentalism: "I can't believe she gossips like she does!" Notice this tactic always builds you up, while it assumes a subtle attitude of superiority. Now that I am reading the Bible more, I want you to know it and like me for it: that's my desire for your approval, your admiration. Sure enough, my personality profile, from DiSC, tells me I'll have this very problem. As a 'Persuader,' I am reminded that under pressure, "I'll become organized to look good." I have the sneaky little desire for prestige and status. Here's the deal: because I know myself, I know I'm an easy mark to get 'ponged' to the right side of the picture above. Even in writing this book, I'm seeking your approval. Heck even my Love Language is 'Words of Affirmation'. I want you to like me. I want the book to be a bestseller. Realizing all of this, I start looking to get off the Ping-Pong table. I know that 'Pride goes before destruction,' that I need to 'think more highly of others than myself.' I know to tell Satan to get off my back. I'm in the fight.[19]

What about the 'ping' side? Remember all those exhortations to do well, to do better, to be more spiritual, to do more good work? Sure enough, you can do that stuff for a while but sooner or later you'll fall short. Then what? Then the self-incrimination starts. The little demon-boys start whispering, "You're such a pathetic Christian. You shouldn't even go back to church, or hang around those people who are doing so much better than you." I resist the soft porn that's all around me, and then I cave in to some TV show or a Victoria's secret commercial and the little condemnation voices start up. You've felt it: the depressing realization that you have failed. If the failure is prolonged, you really feel like a failure and you do feel depressed, to the point where you need pity. You've been 'pinged.' Consider 'dual captivity' from JD Greear's _The Gospel_.[20]

> "_Most people live in a 'dual captivity': they are captive to the sinful lusts of their heart; but they are also captive to the rules of their religion. Sin makes them desire the wrong things; their religion keeps them from doing what they now desire._

---

[19] The Millennials tell me the church is seen (by their generation) as collection of angry and judgmental people who are increasingly irrelevant.

[20] Greear, J.D. _The Gospel_. B&H Publishing. Nashville, TN, 2012. p. 99.

Seeing the glory of God revealed in the gospel gives us freedom from both sin and religion. The gospel sets us free from the threat of condemnation and <u>changes our hearts so that we want to know and serve God</u>." (Underline mine)

Sounds like a description of Ping-Pong, doesn't it? J.D. Greear encourages us, as Faith people know, to remember we have a secret weapon. I like the prayer from *The Gospel*.

There is nothing I can do to make You love me more,
and there is nothing I can do to make You love me less.

In other words, God's love and acceptance is NOT dependent on your performance, or impeded by your failure. Or helped by your success. This realization is the first part of your strategy to get off the Ping-Pong table. If you are not a Faith person, this kind of surrender attitude may be difficult for you. The ongoing challenge is to block the ping and the pong. And do what?

My job, from a spiritual and a practical perspective, is for Jay to become Jay. Your job is for you to be you. We'll use some real life examples from my life. For discussion we'll also look back at the life of King David. We'll discuss a twenty-first century violinmaker's great-grandson who was wired for his calling. I have no idea of his spiritual persuasion. One thing is for sure: he didn't invent those violin-making skill potentials. In his fullest expression of how he is built, he will be able to leverage his gifts, skills, talents, and strengths to give back. To serve. Perhaps he sponsors the Young Men's Violin Coalition; maybe he creates a worship orchestra that can do the Hallelujah Chorus at Christmas. Of course I'm making all this stuff up. I'm guessing; it's the violinmaker's job to figure it out for himself. All of which brings us back to the Ping-Pong table. How do you stop 'being the ball?'

Check out the slide on the next page. That triangle in the middle of the picture represents a person who knows their Personal Values; they know how to speak and how to articulate their Personal Values; they make life decisions using their Personal Values as a critical guide. The violinmaker's great-grandson embraces who he is and uses his giftings to give back to the Young Men's Violin Coalition. He instructs, he coaches, he organizes performances. Most of all, he encourages kids to enjoy commitment, to learn teamwork, to see that being a part of something like an orchestra — something where the whole is much greater than the sum of the parts — is an absolutely transforming thing. He senses which kids are wired to be lifetime violinists and which kids need to move on to something else. He can do these things because he is thankful for the gifts (blessings?) he has received. He is finding that giving back is really one of the best rewards in life. He knows that his gifting — his wiring — is really good, and that he has received his ability ultimately from God. These realizations keep him from being puffed up (no PING).

When the violinmaker's great-grandson (who is called to create violins.... more later) goes to church and there is a lot of talk about volunteering and

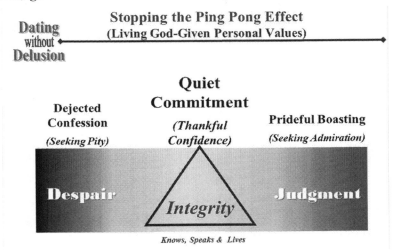

serving, he knows that he _is_ serving, probably the way that God wants him to serve. He can easily say no to the many calls for volunteers to go to Africa on mission trips because he is a violinmaker, not a missionary. No guilt complex here (No PONG). On the other hand, when the initiative comes to create a Young African Men's Violin Coalition, he may have to ask himself if he is being re-directed. What's the point here? The point is that the great-grand-son can live his life with a quiet confidence. With a thankfulness. When the Young Men's Violin Coalition receives awards — when it receives accolades and public attention, he can quietly and confidently know that he is doing what he is supposed to do (watch out for the PONG!).

Keep your focus on the upper call, on the good and important values-based things, and you won't have the time or the energy to waste on the evil dis-tractions. When we are occupied in doing what is right, we have less time to waste on the junk (a.k.a. the sin). No doubt our lower natures will try to raise their ugly heads, but we will have many reasons to turn our backs on them. When various temptations push me around, I remember what I _know_ God wants me to do. I know God has called me to serve Singles. My call to be a 'Trusted Husband' is critical. If I fail it, I will be disqualified from my calling to work on behalf of Single men and women. Do you see it: no P̶O̶N̶G̶!

That tight triangle in the middle of the picture — the one that blocks the Devil's Ping-Pong game — represents YOU, living a life undergirded by God-given Personal Values. My experience is clear. Most people don't know their Personal Values. My message to you is also clear, I hope. If you don't know your Personal Values, get ready for some Ping-Pong with you-know-who...and you will be the ball.

GenME³/Millennial Ping-Pong

Now look back for a moment at our culture discussion. Remember the effect for the GenME³ — the Millennials — when they substitute goals for values? Recall the whole idea of extrinsic motivation becoming the driving force for these culture-setting 27- to 42-year-olds, driving for success and notoriety, for lifestyle and pervasive happiness. Now, look what happens when the Millennial gets on the Ping-Pong table. On the right side of the graphic, you see the Millennial who is positive, optimistic, and focused on success. Many of these young people are strongly driven towards the happiness goals they out-

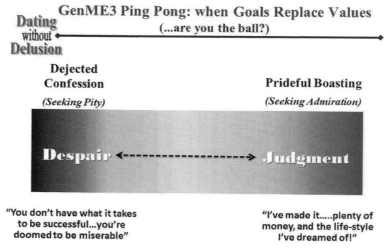

line for themselves. It's a tough posture to criticize because the kind and level of success they articulate is impressive. The 'I want to retire by the time I am 45' and other milestone goals really are eye-poppers, particularly for Boomer guys like me who have struggled through decades of education, work, disappointments, and setbacks... and an occasional achievement milestone. But for the young people who do achieve these impressive lifestyle goals, there waits the little pride problem: that air of self-importance and confidence that is very pervasive and maybe very annoying.

But let's talk about the Millennial goal-setters who don't make the money, or get the recognition, the ones who look ahead and see a grinding career without glamorous prospects. For these people — and there's lots of them — happiness is a much tougher objective. For them, the 'despair' side of the Ping-Pong table might become a more regular experience (see above). When the person with high goals can't see how to achieve them, despair and depression begin to set in. The culture puts an extreme value on those extrinsic goals. What's left if I can't achieve them? I think despair and depression are some of the underlying mental health causes for the blizzard of shootings, suicides, and addictions. Makes sad sense, don't you agree?

As I am finishing this manuscript, the Marysville shooting goes down (October 25, 2014), and everyone is shocked (again) and asks (again), "How could this happen?" Very prophetically, the day before (October 24, 2014), a National Institute of Justice-sponsored study looking at 12–18 year olds reported on teen relationships and intimate violence. The report says:

"Nearly 20 percent of both boys and girls reported themselves as victims of physical and sexual abuse in dating relationships — but the researchers reported what they called a startling finding when they asked about psychological abuse, broadly defined as actions ranging from name calling to excessive tracking of a victim. More than 60 percent of each gender reported being victims and perpetrators of such behavior... Using a definition under which adolescent relationship abuse can occur in person or through electronic means, in public or private, or between current or past dating partners the survey estimates 25 million adolescents are victim and nearly 23 million are perpetrators."[21]

The young shooter had just been rebuffed by his former girlfriend. His dreams of dating happiness were shattered, and I'm sure there was plenty of emotional abuse streaming around on the Internet to provoke him. His happy relationship goals were gone, and he was angry enough to exact violent revenge. Do I know all this? Once again, from a distance, I can only speculate. But if you look at the number of abuse victims and perpetrators reported in the study cited above, you can expect more of this kind of violence. When

---

[21] Crary, David, Associated Press. Most dating teens report being victims and perpetrators of psychological abuse.

you look at it from this perspective, you can easily understand the cause is not so random. The culture is exacting a heavy toll on the Millennials (and now Generation Z). Remember, I believe the culture, which they so strongly influence, is exacting a heavy toll *on us all.*

As the slide of this section depicts below, the Culture is a real and formidable 'block' between you and a healthy[22] dating experience. So realistically how can you prevent yourself from getting embroiled in all the dysfunctions of the culture? The simple answer is the development of Personal Values and developing a healthy view of dating as a controlled process. Before we move into Personal Values development and the actual dating process, we need to have a short but foundational discussion of 'Persona Inversion' — Next.

Persona inversion?

This tool provides a visual for people to understand how a values-based life differs from a culture-soaked mindset and existence. I strongly suggest this for Faith people but it can work for anybody. Let's look at the graphic on the next page. For this discussion consider the 'Persona' to be the sum total of your body, mind, and spirit. It's the collective way you interact with people, your appearance, your speaking and inflection and the principles you espouse. So consider the circles to be a graphic representation of your entire 'Persona.' On the left, you see a depiction of a person's values, their emotion, and their intellect. In our culture, real and well-understood Personal Values are very rare. This is why we face such a challenge getting them written down in the seminar. That small circle in the center of the red circle represents a values blind spot. Unknown values have little impact on personal decisions or behavior. The next ring is a representation of our intellect: the real and genuine engagement of our minds in making life choices. Intellect, of course, may be significantly larger for those people disposed to critical thinking. How much 'Critical thinking' can you do apart from Personal Values? Do academics do a lot of this kind of thinking? Perhaps the 'Intellect' circle should be much larger for people who engage in lots of critical thinking? Then there is the emotionally based dominant part of the persona: emotions. For those of us who are older, we can think back to our younger days when our emotions were the real driving force behind our choices and behavior.

---

[22] As the slide of this section depicts, the Culture is a real and formidable 'block' between you

For today's younger generations, the commitment to lifestyle and playtime is so pervasive, often you don't comprehend how much power it holds over you. Of course, we all face the challenge of living in a culture that does this to us. So what's the point?

The point is _our mindset can be reset._ By knowing our God-given intrinsic values, we can consciously use those values to inform and empower our choices.

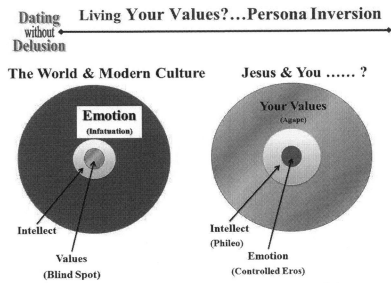

On the right side of the picture, you see the dominant part of the persona circle is the _Values_ part. The next layer is the _Intellect_ layer; in the center of the circle, you see the _Emotions_ layer as a controlled, smaller element of the persona. Getting to the picture on the right is no trivial task, however. As we have struggled with the articulation of our driving, choice-producing values, so will we struggle with this inversion. For myself, even with a crisp and succinct values set, I feel as if I fall very short of the values-centric person that God wants me to be.

It's the struggle between knowing and doing. Our activity-based, get moving, stop messing around culture gets us moving all right... but are we moving in the right direction? Here I fall back on key words from the Bible and J.D. Greear in _The Gospel_:

> _Imagine how overwhelming it was when Jesus lays the Great Commission on the disciples. "Basically you must take the gospel to every person in every country in the world because I am the only way they can be saved, and you are the only way they can hear about me" (Acts 6:1–8). Big mission. Lots of work involved._

Better get started working right away. Surprisingly, however, the first thing Jesus told them to do is go and wait. Do nothing. Nothing, that is, but wait for the coming of the Holy Spirit... Apart from Me, you can do nothing. (John 15:5,6). The point reiterated from cover to cover in the Bible is, 'God doesn't need you for anything.' You and I are utterly powerless to bring about salvation and hearing. This healing message is at the core of the gospel. The gospel aims to shatter pride and independence from every angle. The gospel's first work is to make us sit in <u>*stunned awe*</u> *at what has been done for us." (Underline mine)*

So now, as you sit and see the huge void between the two circles, if you realize — as I do — that I spend too much time behaving like a person driven by his emotions, what are we going to do? The void exists between being and doing. Even the 'defining your Core Values' (as I have been barking at you for the majority of this book) is an activity that is premature.

Picture the circle on the right, as a graphic depiction of your whole being. To fill up that right-hand circle, you have to sit, be quiet and wait, just like the disciples. In your silence, you have to wait: to wait dependently on God to do the filling. Picture the right-hand circle as a balloon; picture God's breath as the filling power. Be filled up by knowing how He has equipped you. As many years as I have been a Christian, I have yet to successfully do this on a regular basis. But when I do it, it is powerful. It's quiet... quiet dependence... quiet in relationship with the Lord. This is the power that is the foundation for the confidence that comes from your God-created values.

The Three Essential Parts of Love

"All You Need is Love" - The Beatles

"If I have the gift of prophecy and know all mysteries and all knowledge, and if I have all faith so as to remove mountains but do not have love, I am nothing." The Apostle Paul (1 Corinthians 13:2)

It is the most misused, misunderstood word in our vocabulary. We *love* football, golf, Thanksgiving dinner; we love our moms, TV shows, movies, YouTube; we love our dogs and other pets. Even Webster has trouble covering the gamut of meanings (see the slide on next page). But we need a better understanding of love in relationships, don't you think? In a dating book, we necessarily have to get to a better comprehension of 'love.' In many ways, it's kind of a starting point for the rest of our discussions. Somewhere, I dug up an interview with a bunch of 4-8 year-olds. Listen to what they have to say about 'Love' when asked, "What does Love mean?" The answers they gave were broader and deeper than anyone could have imagined. You'll see that the 4-8 year-olds know real 'love' when they see it. Look below and see what you think:

- "Love is that first feeling you feel before all the bad stuff gets in the way."

- "When my grandmother got arthritis, she couldn't bend over and paint her toenails anymore. So my grandfather does it for her all the time, even when his hands got arthritis too. That's love."

- "When someone loves you, the way they say your name is different."

- "You know that your name is safe in their mouth."

- "Love is when a girl puts on perfume and a boy puts on shaving cologne and they go out and smell each other."

- "Love is when you go out to eat and give somebody most of your French fries without making them give you any of theirs."

- "Love is when someone hurts you and you get so mad but you don't yell at them because you know it would hurt their feelings."

- "Love is what makes you smile when you're tired."

- "Love is when my mommy makes coffee for my daddy and she takes a sip before giving it to him, to make sure the taste is OK."

- "Love is when you kiss all the time. Then when you get tired of kissing, you still want to be together and you talk more. My mommy and daddy are like that. They look gross when they kiss."

- "Love is what's in the room with you at Christmas if you stop opening presents and listen."

- "If you want to learn to love better, you should start with a friend who you hate."

- "Love is hugging. Love is kissing. Love is saying no."

- "When you tell someone something bad about yourself and you're scared they won't love you anymore. But then you find out not only do they still love you, they love you even more."

- "There are two kinds of love: Our love. God's love. But God makes both kinds of them."

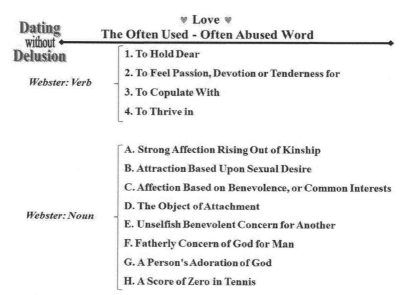

♥ Love ♥
The Often Used - Often Abused Word

Dating without Delusion

Webster: Verb
1. To Hold Dear
2. To Feel Passion, Devotion or Tenderness for
3. To Copulate With
4. To Thrive in

Webster: Noun
A. Strong Affection Rising Out of Kinship
B. Attraction Based Upon Sexual Desire
C. Affection Based on Benevolence, or Common Interests
D. The Object of Attachment
E. Unselfish Benevolent Concern for Another
F. Fatherly Concern of God for Man
G. A Person's Adoration of God
H. A Score of Zero in Tennis

These kid definitions could be the subject for a whole book or a daily devotional (next project!). And most of the kids' definitions have some great 'verse backup' in scripture. For the moment, I'll stick with the first response: "Love is that first feeling you feel before all the bad stuff gets in the way." This kid knows that there is a big difference between fluffy, blown-up emotions and the realities of life. She knows that all of the gushy infatuation can only last for a while before the reality and complexity of the man-woman relationship has to be dealt with.

I have learned much from Chip Ingram, a pastor who has developed some great videos for Singles relationship instruction. He has a great series for Singles called *Love, Sex, and Lasting Relationships*. In this video, which you can view online, Chip talks about the Hollywood relationship model: find 'em, fall in love with 'em, fail in the relationship...then repeat the cycle (over and over again). The challenge he is pinpointing is that many people depend heavily upon their emotional surges to find and start relationships (a.k.a. he's hot... she's hot). Even the relationships that have pretty well understood values similarity, and a whole host of compatibility things, aren't going to rescue you from the 'bad stuff' that the little girl has seen up close and personal. J.D. Greear, author of *The Gospel*, talking about his marriage and looking back on dating, says:

"I remember my wife and I crooning to each other a few months before we got married, 'We never fight — we must be perfect for each other!' And we didn't fight. At that point. Throughout the entire year of our dating relationship and engagement, I cannot remember a Single altercation. Well, we made up for lost time during the first six months of our marriage."[23]

And off they went to counseling.

The 'Dynamic Migration'

Yes, you <u>are</u> going to have strong disagreements, which you need to be prepared for. This brings us to the slide below. The Greek definition of love, refined through the centuries, includes a fourth love, Storge, which refers to the family love parents feel for children, kids feel for grandparents, and so on. The slide shows below the other three loves. The problem our culture promotes is every relationship starts, and usually ends, with Eros: the emotional/physical aspect of love. What I am going to tell you, is very counter-cultural.

I say you *should* begin with Agape, the ability for selfless giving, and Phileo, the friendship element of love. But let's be realistic; those emotional feelings are powerful, and they are being fueled every day by our infatuation culture —

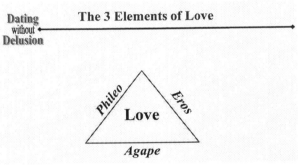

as you read earlier in The Culture Battle. Like everyone around you, your emotions will try to drive your behavior. Recognizing these other more stable 'loves', I hope to convince you *to slow down!*

So let's 'Begin with the end in mind' (Stephen Covey's *7 Habits of Highly Effective People*). What is the 'end,' the goal, the objective of an effective and successful dating mindset? Of course the goal is a lifelong commitment in marriage. If that is your goal — if that was my goal — we better understand

---

[23] *The Gospel*, pg. 113.

how love is supposed to work over the long-term commitment of a marriage. Realistically, can you depend upon the emotional upheavals of Eros to sustain your relationship over 25, 35, 65 years? Better not. Obviously even the most romantically intense marriages must have a more solid and reliable footing.

Here's what I have discovered by watching successful marriages operate, and personally from experiencing a long-term (33 years and counting) marriage myself. On your *best* days, Eros may permeate your marriage but experienced, mature people know that there will be plenty of days when your mate thinks you are pretty edgy, boring, and maybe even stupidly offensive. That's when the other loves must be present and relied upon to sustain you through the difficult times. Do you and your potential mate have a basis for true friendship? I like to say that you and he/she 'care about the same things.' It *isn't* activities, although activities may certainly help. It *is* having similar points of view on some things and enjoying the same life experiences in the relationship. Most of all it is sharing, having a little two-way intellectual back and forth. It's respecting and supporting the other person's values, beliefs, and some of their opinions: that's Phileo. Then there is Agape. Very simply, it is giving *when you don't feel like it.* When your relationship is getting stressed, sometimes you need to exercise gracious patience. There is a human element of it and there is a distinct spiritual aspect, also. The Bible uses Agape extensively. So what is it? A great spiritual teacher I learned under many decades ago described it this way (also see the bottom of the next slide):

> Agape Love: *"Giving all that you are, or all that you could be,*
> *for the sake of the one you love... expecting nothing in return"*

The 'expecting nothing in return' is the hard part.[24] As a faith guy, I think this is impossible to do without spiritual help. When I exercise 'Love', I always seem to want something in return. I want you to like me. I love it when you thank me. I ever so subtly expect you to 'reciprocate' when I have served you. We humans are trained by the culture to operate on this give-and-take basis: you scratch my back, I'll scratch yours; the ol' quid pro quo. Agape, on the other hand, operates in a selfless manner, looking to meet the need of the

---

[24] For Faith thinkers, Jesus provides us with a perfectly executed Agape example. He gave His life, His all, His everything for our salvation, expecting nothing in return. Greear encourages us to look at our own sin first, and it will soften our hearts and criticism of our 'significant other.'

one you love. Is this love achievable? Not often. For me in my marriage, I try to keep this love in mind, and then ask God for the help I need to deliver it.

In dating, you are floating along in the throes of infatuation and Eros, and all of its mushy emotion is overwhelming your senses. Remember, that feeling will fade, sooner or later. Eros will make many return visits, *but it won't be reliable.* I hope you see the power and necessity of having a spiritual base... a spiritual perspective that undergirds your relationship. Sooner or later, ugly circumstances will necessitate selfless-giving. And you know, as do most people, sooner or later, you *will* face tough circumstances. We want to face those circumstances with someone who we 'Love' and trust. In early dating, it is unrealistic and pre-mature for the person you are dating to express this kind of love to you. However, as you get to know this person, you should hope to see them exercise this selfless, giving love to important people in their lives. You watch as a woman goes into kids' ministry and really, genuinely cares for those kids. A man's mother is ill, and he extends kindness and love to her as he takes her to the doctor, or visits her in the hospital, or goes over to her house to make sure she's OK. As you see Agape being exercised in someone's life, you are learning: learning the person you are watching has selfless-giving capacity, which someday might be *very* important to you.

So here's the key: when your emotions (Eros) wane, can you, will you, depend on one of the other 'loves' to sustain your commitment to your spouse? Look at the Dynamic 'Migration' in the next graphic. When emotions fail,

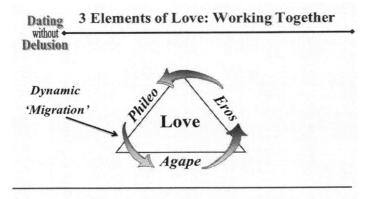

Agape Love: "Giving All That You Are, or All That You Could Be, for the Sake of the One You Love...Expecting Nothing In Return"

can your relationship continue to build itself through migration and dependence on the other 'loves'? The practicality of marriage living requires all three. You may argue that Agape is all you need to sustain married life. If you say that, I will say you married the wrong person. A full understanding of love, combined with a purposeful and *intentional* dating process, will bring you 'full spectrum' relationships. Sometimes the best outcome for a dating relationship is a true and lasting friendship. Or, at some point you may find yourself committed to the one person who will be your marriage partner for life. The dating process we will discuss in Part Two is specifically designed to help you determine if the relationship you are currently pursuing has the potential to have this kind of 'full spectrum' love relationship... or not.

1 Corinthians 13... comes after 1 Corinthians 12?

Think back on the many marriage ceremonies you have attended. For me, it seems like a hundred. Think of the marriages you have been a part of: best man, bridesmaid, or some other key participation. Just for the fun of it, Debra was trying to keep track of the many marriages we've been to; it's a lot. And that number is spiking upward because many of our kids, nephews, nieces, and their contemporaries are reaching that mid-20's, early 30's age range: For Gen Xers and Millennials. I guess, getting married is the thing to do — that's also a book in itself. At one point, Debra and I were splitting up (geographically) to attend distantly separated ceremonies. She would travel to one marriage and I would go to another.

So if your experience is anything like mine, you know that the groom and particularly the bride want to make that day have a magical significance. They want their marriage to transcend earthly bounds and go to a higher plane. They want their marriage to be something that the guests and family will *never* forget. So like Debra and me, you can probably look back on some wing-doozies. Cruises... on the lake... at the castle....you've seen some pretty amazing — and expensive — stuff. If your experience is at all like ours, you sit in the audience watching the ceremony and at a key moment, someone will stand up to do a Bible reading. And there it is, the description of love from 1 Corinthians 13. OK, let's go with it.

The immediately obvious thing, and the title of this book section, is that 1 Corinthians 13 comes after 1 Corinthians 12. Well 'duh,' you say. What my pastor, elders, and theologian friends repeatedly tell me is to always read the Bible in context. Christians like me often pull verses out of context to gain validity...or whatever. But here is Paul the Apostle writing to the Corinthian church, which was a sociological and spiritual mess, trying to correct their errors and to encourage better behavior. So in 1 Corinthians 12, Paul was encouraging each and every person in the first century Corinthian church to use their God-given gifts to serve one another.

Here in 1 Corinthians 12 is Paul's 'body analogy:' like a physical body with many different and varied parts, we are a spiritual body with many different

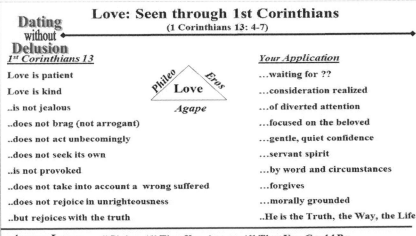

Love: Seen through 1st Corinthians
(1 Corinthians 13: 4-7)

Dating without Delusion

1ˢᵗ Corinthians 13	*Your Application*
Love is patient	...waiting for ??
Love is kind	...consideration realized
..is not jealous	...of diverted attention
..does not brag (not arrogant)	...focused on the beloved
..does not act unbecomingly	...gentle, quiet confidence
..does not seek its own	...servant spirit
..is not provoked	...by word and circumstances
..does not take into account a wrong suffered	...forgives
..does not rejoice in unrighteousness	...morally grounded
..but rejoices with the truth	..He is the Truth, the Way, the Life

Love — Phileo, Eros, Agape

Agape Love: *"Giving All That You Are, or All That You Could Be,*
for the Sake of the One You Love ...Expecting Nothing In Return"

and intricately designed functions. Just like the parts of a physical body, the people in a church must work to do what their gifts have equipped them to do. Go back and read chapter 12. "If the whole body were an eye, where would hearing be?" (verse 17) "And the eye cannot say to the hand 'I have no need of you' or the head to the feet 'I have no need of you'" (verse 25). "But God has so composed the body...that there should be no division in the body, but that the members should have the same care for one another" (verse 24, 25).

Paul then goes on to talk about the gifts that God has placed in the church, comparing the gifts and their functioning to the functioning of the different parts of the body: eyes, feet, hands, etc. Yes, we all are different. This is a foundational concept for ***Dating without Delusion***. Yes, we are all called to serve one another, each of us with our unique contributions. Do you see that Paul is addressing the whole of the Corinthian church? Now comes the transition, in verse 31: "And I show you a still more excellent way." In my Bible — and most others — the artificial chapter break right after this verse was added afterwards by translators/publishers. In chapter 13, Paul continues to describe how the unique gifts of each person should be used to serve one another. How? Well, in Love, of course. Does this mean that the Love Chapter doesn't apply to marriage? No. I believe that it applies to *every* relationship, *including marriage*. It's a higher call for all of the people who profess faith in God, and for those who want to live to a higher calling. It's a call to listen to the Love attributes spelled out in this now very famous chapter. So if we're going to keep calling out these Love verses — which you'll probably hear at the next marriage ceremony — let's get serious about what they are saying to us. On the graphic above, you see the attributes of love on the left-hand side of the slide. On the right-hand side, I've done my best to suggest what the implication of each Love attribute might be. And since this is a dating book, I'll suggest that these Love descriptions have an added importance for dating and marriage relationships.

One of the interesting seminar discussions looking at these love attributes is to call out which of the three loves (Agape, Phileo, or Eros) is central. For example, Paul starts with:

Love is patient. So if you look to the right side of the slide, I ask, "...waiting for what?" You've all seen impatience. Impatient to get married, impatient to get the next thing, impatient for sex, impatient to _____ (fill in the blank). If impatience marks your dating relationship — or any relationship for that matter — you are in the danger zone. My culturally relevant summary might be, "If you want it bad, you'll get it bad." Do you recall Chip Ingram's warning about Hollywood-style relationships? A lot of hype with no foundation. Of the three Loves, which one helps this impatience problem? Perhaps a little Phileo: we care about the same things enough to wait, to share them at the right time, in stride, after I/we have seen all the implications. Certainly Agape helps because when Agape gets working in me, I start to put my own needs into the second seat and look at what my dating partner's — or perhaps my future spouse's — needs first. What about Eros? Eros is the impatient one, isn't it? I *have* to have it — or maybe even have to have you — NOW. That kind of impatience doesn't fit the 'others-centeredness' of Paul's love description. Is Eros bad? No, it's GREAT... at the right time, in the right commitment-centered context. Do you see how this de-structuring of the Love Chapter creates some great seminar dialogue? Let's keep going.

Love is kind. You know what kindness is. Its motivation is to somehow meet the true need of the other person. It's gracious, timely, and based upon great personal insight — insight into the *other* person, not you. Kindness can often be sacrificial: I had to go out of my way and put myself out to make the kindness personal. Of course Agape is the love behind kindness: selfless giving. If I do a 'kindness' that has unspoken expectations behind it — with many other strings attached — it's really not kindness at all. It's a disguised set-up for reciprocation.

Love is not jealous is a culture-buster. Our culture teaches jealousy in every sitcom and dating show that's broadcast. It's possessiveness. In infatuation-based relationships, the clinging, can't-do-anything-without-thinking-about-her makes him jealous *all* the time. Just think about the insecurity of jealousy. He can't do anything without her freaking out. Why? Because she can't trust him. He can't trust her. Real full-spectrum love is marked by trust and confidence. Debra fully supports the work I do with Singles. There I am, out past 9 p.m. for Tuesday night teaching, going to a Singles home group while Debra is visiting in San Diego. Debra trusts; Debra can turn away from any jealousy because she loves and trusts. That's a trust I have to guard carefully, and work to preserve.

Love does not brag (not arrogant). Arrogance is the attitude that outwardly expresses pride. It is self-consumed. Braggarts are so wrapped up in themselves that they cannot even begin to understand other people's sensitivities and needs. Alternatively, real love is focused on the beloved. He is truly happy when she is happy. She loves to see him at his best, enjoying the things he loves. I contend that pride is the self-soaked attitude that brings us down harder than any other. I contend it is the #1 sin on God's list — primarily because it leads to so many other problems. Read the Garden of Eden story and see how Satan used pride to usher Adam and Eve out of the Garden.

Love does not act unbecomingly. It's gentle, quiet confidence. If we know the intricate, Personal Values-based details of our partner/spouse, we can relax in the confidence that he will make wise choices based upon his spoken values. That she will live and speak (without gossip) of the common commitment and the interpersonal understanding we both share.

Love does not seek its own. Its own what? It's the opposite of always trying to get my own way. It's NOT thinking about what I want to do first. This is a challenge I face. It's the opposite of a servant spirit. 'Seeking its own' is thinking about what suits me, and taking the other person's needs and wants into consideration only after the fact. Love — and particularly Agape love — doesn't do that.

Love is not provoked. This means provoked by word and circumstances. And this provocation is *guaranteed* to happen in your life and in the life of your eventual spouse. You will, at some point, want to react with anger, frustration, disappointment, discouragement. So the question really is, will that provocation trigger a reaction that you can't control? Anger that bursts out. Dramatic out-of-control reactions, like driving way too fast. As I'll tell you later, I am personally pre-wired for angry reactions. It's a challenge for me not to be provoked. Even in the best pre-marriage and marriage relationships, circumstances will put your relationship at risk, but true love reacts with a wonderful calm... a peace that is beyond understanding.

Love does not take into account a wrong suffered. If I were Paul, I would have put this attribute much higher on 'the list' simply because I am painfully aware of the times I use whining and complaining as a drag-out retribution technique. You get it: your significant other has been rude and hurtful, and she realizes it and asks for forgiveness. But I just want to exact a little retribution — that's a fancy word for payback. Hurtful payback. Often I wind up hurting Debra or others because I just can't let go of the wrongs I've suffered. So I fail this test all too often. I am trying to learn to forgive as opposed to dragging out bad, revengeful attitudes, but it's not easy. Those attitudes need to be shortstopped with simple and genuine forgiveness. Forgiveness is an easy word to say, but it's a hard application. Simply by forgiving the wrong-behavior... isn't that easier said than done! When you have been wronged and/or offended, you feel contempt for the other person, which is difficult to deal with. Even if you are a person of faith and you ask for the Lord's help, it's still hard.

At this point, let's link the truth of first century scripture with the analysis and objectivity of modern twenty-first century psychology. Go to the tools section and do a quick read on the 'Four Horsemen' from John Gottman. Gottman contends the Four Horsemen — *Contempt, Criticism, Defensiveness,* and *Stonewalling* — are at the root of many failed relationships and divorces.

The beginning of this downward relationship spiral is contempt, and the contempt is often triggered by a wrong suffered. As Paul says in 1 Corinthians, *true love doesn't even take the wrong into account.* You can easily see that the reality of these verses is a really big challenge. I want you, as a Single person, to face it now. Talk about love is cheap and rolls off the tongue so easily. Beware: there is an Everest-sized mountain to actually living love out. These are the essential tests of true love. This is how true loved gets put into action.

Again for people who are dating, remember this stern warning: infatuation dies at the 12 to 15-month mark. Then, two people have to continue life with one another face-to-face — with all the complex life problems, many of which we 'camouflage' during the dating frenzy. We are going to have to live with wrongs suffered. The worst-case scenario can include the three Scarlet A's: Abuse, Abandonment, and Adultery. But even 'normal' or 'regular' interactions between a man and a woman have the sneaky potential to create subtle contempt for the other person. Hard things to forgive; hard things not to take into account. Date well, and you will be prepared for these tough situations and have a relationship built on real love, not emotion.

Love does not rejoice in unrighteousness. In a nutshell, this attribute is talking about being morally grounded. It's your firm adherence to a set of moral standards. The key question for you is, *what* moral standards compose your guidelines? For Christians, the 10 Commandments provide the clear standard. It was provided to Moses at Mt. Sinai, and validated by Jesus on a number of occasions. In the seminar, you can see why it's frustrating for me when people who profess Christianity don't know the 10 Commandments. (Much more discussion is coming on integrity later in the Personal Values discussion.) In today's on-the-fly society, making up your own moral standard seems to be the trend; you can easily see the problem with this relativism. In my own/ your own mental ambiguity, we can adjust our 'standards' to fit the situation at hand. What moral standard keeps you from 'unrighteousness?'

Love rejoices with the truth. Do you have any truth in your life? The culture is training us to believe that there are no absolutes. Again, it's called Relativism: Truth versus Situations. Not only do I urge you to seek and find truth, I urge you to seek, find, know, speak, and live your Personal Values. Make your values become a part of the truth in your life. If your values can become woven into your daily life, you can live with transparency and integrity (which we will talk about later). My Personal Values can become the standard I attempt to live by: *Personal Truths.*

As for this many-faceted description of Love, I am intimidated beyond any kind of self-reliance. *"Love is not provoked; love does not seek its own."* It's easy to say that I have love, but every one of these love attributes seems out of my reach. I know I can't even begin to approach the life marked by the kind of love presented here. When I feel this intimidation, it serves as a spark, as a reminder of my need for Faith. For me, He is the Truth, the Way, and the Life.

Here's what I guess. I guess that many people pull out this 1 Corinthians 13 scripture and place it as a centerpiece in their marriage ceremony. Then life kicks in, and 1 Corinthians 13 — often with all of the rest of the Bible — goes back on the shelf. OK, what are we going to do about it? If you're Single; if you're married; either way, this kind of love — the real stuff — is essential. I suggest you copy the slide on page 70 and post it on your refrigerator[25]... or perhaps on your bathroom mirror. Without these in-our-face reminders, the word 'Love' will slide back into cultural vernacular, back to meaningless mush. Let's keep it at the forefront of our thinking. Remember how we began this discussion: "If I have all faith so as to remove mountains but do not have love, I am nothing."

Love is responsive...or reactive?

My answer is, both. Eros and all of its energy and impatience is the 'reactive' one. Eros reacts to hormone stimulation with excitement, anticipation, and usually delusion. It behaves much like a twitch. Phileo — friendship love — is much more sharing-based. Many complementary ideas and thoughtful discussions are the trademarks of Phileo. These kinds of interactions bring to mind a coming together or perhaps an intellectual give-and-take. Sharing brings to mind the mutual sharpening of two intellects and minds.

Then there is Agape, with the very extreme definition: 'Giving, expecting nothing in return.' How can that work? From the spiritual standpoint, looking at the love Jesus has for each one of us, I do see selfless giving. All through the gospels (Mathew, Mark, Luke and John), He is healing, guiding, giving,

---

[25] By the end of this book, you will have enough graphics to wallpaper a small room. As a visual learner, I know I need to see the reminders repeatedly. Do you have another technique? If so, use it and leverage it to the max to be reminded about the essentials... like true love.

teaching, and feeding the 5,000 in an overwhelmingly 'others-focused' manner. Seeing someone give selflessly in your life is both amazing and intimidating. It is amazing simply because self-LESS-ness is the absolute opposite of the self-CENTERED-ness of our culture. Mostly I look at selfless giving in amazement because I see myself as most often *not* being able to do that. But in my marriage, when I see Debra have moments of selfless giving, it is both wonderful and inspiring. Seeing selfless giving often creates my desire to give selflessly. *This best love is responsive.* Spending spiritual time with God, perhaps through the Bible; seeing Jesus heal and bless, creates a responsive thankfulness in me. When someone selflessly considers me, somewhere deep in my inner being I am inspired to that same kind of living and giving. Agape, for me is the responsive love.

In dating, as time goes by and you share an expanding universe of experiences with the person you are dating, sooner or later you will have the opportunity to see your dating partner in those circumstances where his giving steps up to meet someone's real need. Where her selflessness has true empathy and mercy. Or not. If you don't have the opportunity to see that other person in the authentic giving mode, he or she might not have the inner fortitude it takes for a lifetime marriage commitment. If you do see that person doing some genuine giving, you should be strongly encouraged.

Can love 'fill up' a relationship?

In the early going of a mutual, attraction-based relationship, it certainly *feels* like it could. Infatuation and Eros make you *feel* as if there is no one else in the world. Then the infatuation starts to fade. Hopefully the dynamic migration of the other loves starts to kick in as you share the other loves. So can love fill up a relationship? Remember, Eros and infatuation are going to shrink. They will inevitably wane. Agape is powerful, and Phileo can be wonderful as your relationship grows. My issues and dysfunctions certainly are difficult for my wife to deal with. Hers are difficult for me to deal with. Our love for one another — all three kinds — can be sustaining — but at the end of this discussion, I need the spiritual element from God, to provide the filling power that I don't have inside me. Depending on the Lord is a wonderful, always present resource which provides the filling. The practical effect takes the pressure off of my marriage and off of Debra. People who are loaded with infatuation don't believe this, however. They *feel* as if their newfound love is all consuming and overflowing. Then when the relationship matures, it is difficult to discover that your (marriage?) relationship doesn't have the filling power. Does this revelation lead to a divorce? Hopefully people realize that a 'filled-up' life comes from many sources.

Avoiding a poisonous expectation

One final point in this Love discussion. You are a complex and wonderful combination of personality, strengths, and capabilities. Even if you find the 'perfect' mate, can you rely on just that one person to meet all of your relationship needs? Better not. Eros-based emotional relationships certainly can't. Even in relationships that have full spectrum 'Love,' we are complex men and women who need to have *other relationship venues,* primarily healthy family and extended family relationships and values-based friendships. This is an important realization when you are dating. *If the other person is totally absorbed in only you, the bright red warning lights should start to flash.* The problem? *It is a delusion to expect all of your relationship needs to be met by one other person* — even God doesn't want to be that one person; see Genesis. We need to allow our most important relationship person to have the freedom and encouragement to nurture other healthy relationships. Your significant other should have a same-gender accountability partner. In dating, you should always encourage healthy relationships for your potential future spouse. I hope you don't think that I'm talking about potentially problematic other-gender friendships...and yes, you know which relationships hold infatuation pitfalls. I *am* talking about my wife's ongoing commitment to her family. I am talking about her friends from home group (spiritually based), her friends from swim club (Phileo, compatibility based), and her lifetime friends from her former flight attendant career. I would be a fool not to encourage her to enjoy those

Dating ??

freedoms. When you get to Part Two, you'll see the little cartoon on the Part Two divider page (shown here above). If you try to talk about dating without having a very stable base, this is how most people feel: Yaaaaarghhhhhh!

In one of the seminars, a young guy was sketching on his Styrofoam cup, and he very accurately captured the frustration surrounding the whole topic of dating. This is exactly the reason that we will spend half of this book discussing Personal Values, your commitment to them, and how you communicate them, all as a balance for the chemistry and infatuation elements that drive attraction. I call Infatuation 'the 'evil little twin' of Compatibility. Talking about relationship phases or date/no date decisions would be random and disconnected, apart from a wise and wide foundation. Remember the pyramid, 40,000' perspective? Like the pyramids, Part Two of this book is built upon the lower foundational layers starting with 'God has a plan for you...'

In Part One of this book, I asked you to believe in the intricate sovereignty of God — the intricacies of how He made you. He's made you with uniqueness and a specific purpose in mind. If you don't yet accept that you have a divine purpose; a calling, please accept the science of DNA, personality strengths, and profiles to provide an overwhelming case for your individuality. The challenge is to mud-wrestle with yourself — and maybe the Lord — to get those values articulated. Most people who attend the **_Dating without Delusion_** classes accept the premise that Personal Values are essential, but they often can't get over the hurdle of actually defining and articulating

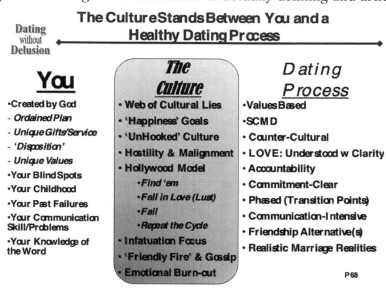

The Culture Stands Between You and a Healthy Dating Process

them. I attribute this to the straightforward difficulty of it, and I acknowledge the work of the slick adversary (guess you know his name, Rolling Stones). Getting your Personal Values understood always offers you a clear path of communication, and it always drives your choices, sometimes in a clear way, sometimes in an uncomfortable way. Part One work gives you the bottom four layers of the pyramid (go back to the 40,000' Introduction for a review if necessary). If you have those bottom four layers, you can use your values with your friends and family. The wise thing to do is to practice using values in all of your relationships. As you exercise life-choices using your Personal Values, you will be working your values refinement. Continually, we can be working on better values articulation and better values understanding. Listen to people you respect to give you honest response and feedback. Honest feedback is wonderful. It allows *you* to keep working on *you*. So before you start Part One of the book, I'm asking you to Commit: to live on the *right* side of the 'World We Live In'. Perhaps it means you have cut off a spiraling out of control relationship. Do it now. The sooner the better.

If you knuckle under to the culture, you very comfortably can live (at least for the short term) in 'un-relationships.' In the morality of a Christian environment, that's probably not going to work. If you're not a Christian but you've made it this far with me, will you go a little further? In your heart, you know that the left hand Post-Millennial Un-Relationship world is fueled by Infatuation — the 'evil little twin' — and the marriage relationships coming out of that world are on a collision course with divorce. Who would ever want to suffer through that? Look at the GAP, the chasm, the void between these two different types of relationships. Choose wisely. Choose the right side where values-centered relationships live, and let's get on to the dating half of this book.

What about the online dating sites?

You know them: *Match.com, It's Our Time, eHarmony, Christian Mingle,* and on and on. As far as I can tell, the websites are being used more and more by people intent on meeting someone to date. I have heard that over 30 percent of new relationships are initiated on-line. Many of the people I meet and interact with in the seminars are using websites to begin person-to-person dialogue. This is a trend that no doubt will accelerate. In short, I have taken the time to look at a few of these sites. My conclusion? At their best, they will establish some 'compatibilities' such as preferred/shared activities. Sometimes they very inappropriately ask for income levels and other 'out-of bounds' information. But as I see it, they do little to reveal a person's deeply held values. My oldest stepson filled out one of the profiles and wow, did he ever 'game it'! I couldn't even begin to recognize the person he described on the web. So are the websites bad? Time for a real-life story — this one I got third-hand.

It's a real-life story about two people who initiated a good dialogue on-line. They used one of the eHarmony, Match.com, OurTime.com resources to start an enjoyable interchange. They decide that they really 'like' each other, and agree that they should get together for a drink at a local restaurant. They have posted pictures that are as flattering as possible, and they have completed pretty detailed profiles. Of course, the profiles are all about Compatibility, NOT ABOUT VALUES! BIG problem! So as they go to the restaurant to share this drink, I would guess they are both hoping for the 'bells and whistles' of infatuation to fire off in their heads when they meet for the first time. A little Compatibility, mix in the 'evil little twin,' of Infatuation and they'll have the formula to launch this relationship, right? Remember, this formula is a highway to disappointment!

She enters the restaurant and he stands up to introduce himself, and guess what? He 'fudged' on his height! He is a 'couple' of inches shorter (more like five!) than what he put in his online profile. She has one drink and walks out the door. Let's do a remote post-mortem.

He didn't 'fudge'... he lied about his height. Although she could assault his dishonesty, no doubt it was more about his insecurity. If they actually shared real values, this would not be enough of a reason to ditch the whole relationship. I'll guess that her father was tall and she had some imago needs that 'turned her off' when this man didn't fit her profile. What if he lied about his height and said he was 3″ _taller_ than his true height? Get it? He reports on-line that he is 5′8″, and he's actually 5′11″. I bet she would have gotten past his dishonesty pretty fast. Pretty decent sharing over the phone and the Internet, which took significant time, didn't build any kind of resilient relationship; it only built infatuation expectations which were unanchored in any kind of values realty. Like the unattached guitar strings, this relationship was fragile, directionless, and easily abandoned. Now you see why I am not very enamored with online dating. I accept it as a modern day reality which is gaining momentum. In the end analysis, I see relationships being built that have all kinds of soft vulnerability.

In the seminar when I ask, "Was that right?" you can imagine the energy of the dialogue that ensues. Of course he lied on the website, and it's easy to judge his dishonesty. But what about her? Did she post an older picture, or perhaps one that had been touched up? Was that lying? Perhaps her dad was a taller man and she subconsciously overreacted? With some thought, she might have excused his insecurity for the sake of the good interpersonal relationship they had already established on the phone. As it turned out, she prioritized her emotional reaction and made a decision based on her feelings. If they had shared values, cutting off this relationship might have been a big mistake. I'll guess that the superficialities of the websites and some decent conversation on the phone weren't enough for her to value this relationship over his insecurity. Who really knows? So are the websites bad? Giving them the benefit of the doubt, they allow people to meet one another. As the story shows, keep your expectations for website interaction very low. Maybe someday we'll build a relationship website based upon Personal Core Values. One project at a time. In the interim, they don't give you the intellectual foundation to confidently start a dating relationship. You must use your own Personal Values to do it yourself.

Part One:

Your Values → The Essential Foundation

The highway to your Personal Core Values

Here's my recurring experience: I ask many people in all kinds of circumstances: in the seminar, sharing time with friends and acquaintances, etc. to simply tell me about their Personal Values. I'd like to say that 1 person out of 100 clearly articulated a Personal Value or two. That's not my experience. Most people get a puzzled look and make up something on the fly. Do your own investigation. Ask "What Personal Values do you live by?" and you'll get to share my experience. "Integrity," "Family," "Love," and "I love Jesus" are the often-repeated answers. "Trust" is another favorite. On the other hand real Personal Values are very unique and personally definitive.

To begin this discussion, let's use a football analogy. There are 11 players on the field at any one time, but there are many more positions and roles to be filled on a football team. Offensive positions, defensive positions, punting, kickoffs, kick returning, the list goes on and on. Any good coach can look at a potential player and immediately have an idea of how that specific person can fit into the team. Here's a big guy, close to 300 lbs. who has a developed physique. The coach is narrowing down the candidate positions — the potential roles — this guy can fulfill. How fast can this man run? How quick and coordinated are his feet? It looks as if he has superior upper body strength. The coach looks at this player and sees a potentially good offensive lineman. The key *role* is being defined.

Now, the challenge is to determine how to best use this player's unique attributes to ensure he will be successful in actual games. Perhaps his exceptional upper body strength can assist his blocking? Perhaps his quick feet allow him to block very fast pass rushers? These strengths will allow this player to excel in his assigned role. This player can fit into the role as an offensive lineman who uses his strength and foot coordination to play left tackle on the team's offense. Do you see what has happened? The player has discovered his position, his *role*, and has begun to learn how to use his very unique skills, his *talents*, to fill that role. These descriptors, or *amplifiers*, describe in very crisp phrases how he is going to fill, to play, the position for which he has been selected. The player improves and excels because he knows his specific role and has a vision of how he will fulfill it. He knows he must work to improve on his natural abilities by working to become stronger, by working to become even faster. Values go one big step deeper. Perhaps our offensive lineman discovers he can set an example through demonstrated dedication and sacrifice. He lives to help his teammates improve and persevere — he is unanimously selected as the team captain. He leads the team to persevere and excel. The season becomes a memorable one, shaping the lives of many players and coaches. This man's leadership and his sacrificial dedicated approach to success will be long remembered after his football career is over. Leadership, focused work ethic, and the ability to create a collaborative environment are what he brings. His leadership and lead-by-example approach are the essence of his life — the things which will bring him forward.

As a football coach, just like most football coaches, I became very adept at looking at a player run and in a matter of seconds, I'd have a good idea of which position he would best fill. It might take a whole season to really understand a player — to see the deep qualities which define him as a person. These qualities and callings are what values are about.

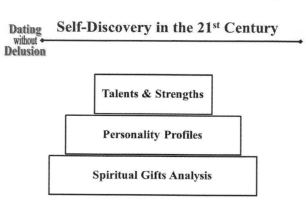

Have you ever taken a job mainly to pay the bills, and then discovered it drove you crazy because you weren't a good 'fit?' In the real world, roles are often not well defined; expectations are not clearly understood or communicated. From your very personal perspective, you don't know how to communicate why you would/should fill a particular role. The rest of the world is not so self-evident, is it? This is what Personal Values are all about. They're about knowing yourself and being able to describe yourself in a short and unambiguous way. Without these two elements —

knowing yourself, and articulating who you are — life decisions can very quickly become situational; important choices can be made in a shifting and relativistic way. Well-defined Personal Values, on the other hand, are very challenging. Why? Because they stretch you to live a congruent life. When you have a well-understood Personal Value, they describe the real you and make sense of your life decisions.

Since this is a relationship book, I'm challenging you to know yourself and to articulate who you are in your Personal Values. Accurate self-knowledge is key. Discovering how you are intricately created will be the best thing you have to guide you in your relationship choices. Let's go to work on them!

Self-discovery using 21st century resources:
Spiritual gifts, personality profiles, talents and strengths

There are a myriad of self-assessments and tools out there, and although I have exposure to many of them, I really only use three. So let's discuss my recommended three tool selections. These assessments serve to better understand the roles you are wired to fulfill, or they will pinpoint the method and style, the amplifiers, by which you can best fill that role. You don't have the extra time to sort through the tools maze, so I have selected them for you. Take the assessments now, and you and I will move forward with a common language to accelerate our self-discovery. Look at the three tools in the figure below. See the stack of three? I want you to use them from the bottom up as they are depicted. Let me explain why. The bottom tool in the stack shows Spiritual Gifts Analyses. This tool is easy to take, it is usually inexpensive (or $0), and the results are easy to interpret. I've used a couple of these, but most recently I've used the analysis from Ephesians Four Ministries.[26] As with all of these tools, the benefit is supposed to be clear understanding of your specific gifts; to give you some insight as to how they work and how they work together. Don't let the terminology throw you off. A 'gift' is the description of a particular innate skill. You've heard the phrase, "She is a gifted speaker" or, "He is a gifted communicator." This test is particularly good at identifying your gift-based role and responsibility. Even if you are not spiritually oriented, I recommend you take this test so you can receive this very

---

[26] The next picture shows the tools with the URLs. The easiest way to access the online tools is to use your on-line search engine (e.g. with DISC as the entry) and numerous on-line options will pop-up.

important feedback. As you read the descriptions of the person with your similar gifts make-up, you will usually see familiarity with how you behave,

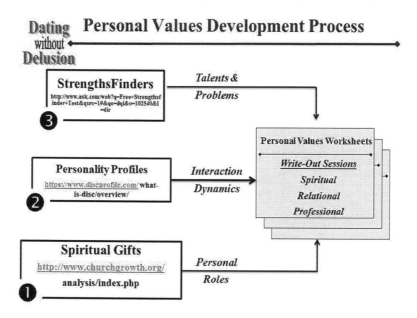

think, and react. These analyses provide the additional benefit of helping you see and understand the problems and challenges of the gift you have. I have the gift of 'Teaching,' which has specific benefits and specific challenges. It's very humiliating, very humbling, and also very important. The tool will show your propensity to twelve or so personal gifts, ranked and displayed on a bar scale report. For reference, I have extracted a pretty good extended list of gifts as the Bible catalogues them, which is shown in the next figure. The form you'll find online is not filled out along the bottom, so you can fill in your assessment results. I pulled together this list in the figure from a number of chapters and verses to provide you with a window on the diversity of gifts that are called out. At the bottom, you see my three top spiritual gifts and a short timeline on how I have used these gifts over the years. There is no one list of gifts that will be sufficient to describe God's design for you. If you are not a Christian, please be open-minded to receive the 'role' feedback from this resource. So get in there, take this assessment, and get your self-discovery going! It's a pretty easy first step, and it's important for anyone, but it is particularly important for Singles who must manage the vagaries of dating.

Here's a real-life story about gifts told in our home group. There is a man who has had great success speaking at evangelistic conferences. Many people have had spiritual conversions. Thousands of people have been positive-

Dating without Delusion

Gifts: _Given by God to Enable Your Personal Core Values_

The gifts in alphabetical order :

1. Administration
2. Apostleship
3. Craftsmanship
4. Creative Communication
5. Discernment
6. Encouragement*
7. Evangelism
8. Faith'
9. Giving
10. Healing
11. Helps (serving)
12. Hospitality
13. Intercession
14. Interpretation
15. Knowledge
16. Leadership*
17. Mercy
18. Miracles
19. Prophecy
20. Shepherding
21. Teaching*
22. Tongues
23. Wisdom

'I guess it was my reason for being...'
Charles Schultz

*Encouragement
*Leadership
*Teaching — Gifts

Teacher
Coach

Small Group Leader

Inspiring Singles' Ministry

Core Value →

ly affected. This man is clearly endowed with the gift of 'Evangelism.' A similar story recounts how a lady in our neighboring town hand-makes greeting cards, sells them, and uses the funds to support a couple of African orphans. I think she even went to Africa on one occasion to see and support these kids. She clearly had the gift of 'Mercy.'

The discussion goes on to validate both of these people, who had figured out how to use their gifts in significant ways. Is one better than the other? In my opinion, absolutely not. These people are 'being who they are.' Does Jay have the gift of Evangelism? No. Does Jay have the gift of Mercy? No. Does Jay think that God wants him to be Merciful, or to share Christ with someone on occasion? Absolutely. Here's the difference. These people should factor their test and life-validated gifts (roles) into their Personal Values, don't you think? And then, be quietly confident in the _role_ they are filling. On the other hand, if someone challenges me to go on an Africa aid and evangelism trip, you know what my answer will be: NO. Because I've figured out what my #1 role is! It's teaching!

Look at the markers in my life. I have taught at two schools. I have taught the Singles seminar for many, many years. I have been a sports coach on many occasions. I can't change or deny my primary role which is also a spiritual gift — it's teaching. If you ask me to do a Singles conference in France because France is seeing a growing population of Singles in their demographic, I'm probably going to go. I've made my best guess that this is the Lord's job for me. And Debra wants to see Paris! (James 1:17) It's also very good to realize I should *not* try to teach in every situation; sometimes it's appropriate to quietly let the situation unfold without my assistance. Don't ask me to do childcare, benevolence, therapy, and/or recovery-support. I might be able to stopgap those efforts but in the longer run, they are not me.

In the shaded box, you see a short quote from Charles Schulz. Remember him? The creator of the Peanuts cartoons. I'll guess that he had the gifts of Creative Communication, backed with a little Craftsmanship, and maybe even Administration, dealing with all those newspapers. Am I sure that these were his gifts? Absolutely not. But these kinds of insights form the basis for Personal Values, don't you think? The cartoons are fun, but I'll bet Charles had some pretty pervasive Personal Values. I'll guess Schulz's role was to encourage and entertain children. No doubt it gave him sheer delight. Also maybe it was something to do with enriching kid's lives... remember Charlie Brown's Christmas? Please get the point: roles supported by talents and strengths are the 'enablers' for life-defining Personal Values. They are the personal attributes that empower you to do the job God has designed for you. Try to be something or someone that you're not, and you will be one frustrated person. Charles Schulz knew it, too: "I guess it was my reason for being." So here is step #1: Get online and into Ephesians Four, and take the assessment. When the results come back, print them out and do a good slow read, highlighting as you go. Chances are the roles for which you are wired are revealed by the Ephesians Four results. Now, three-hole punch the results and put them in a binder.

The next layer up in the tools stack shows the next-most complex element, which is Personality Profiles. These more complex tools have more complex results. Backed by lots of research, the tools parse and sort your mix of four personality types. Unfortunately all, of these Personality Profile systems have developed their own unique language to describe your profile. See the problem? If you use a tool and get the results, I won't be able to easily understand you because the tool I use has different descriptor language. As a relationship guy, I might have to manage this problem. But don't you worry about it: your job is to do smart *self-discovery.*

Specifically, I have developed expertise in the DISC Profile (Dominance,

Influence, Steadiness, and Compliance), so it's the one I want you to use. This is a tool based on William Marston's research, and it's the one we used in my graduate studies at the University of San Diego (USD).[27] It uses a forced choice test — as do most of these tools — to determine your personality type. For the moment, please put this book down and go online to search for and take a DISC assessment.

The personality profile is essential because it will help you to comprehend the underlying responses and emotions you experience as you go through the day. For those of you who are interested, I am an I/D and my profile is Persuader.[28] My profile is not the issue. The tool is not the issue.[29] Getting you to use them is. The profile will show some very positive personal potential and some associated problem areas for your careful consideration. The Ephesians Four work is about you finding your possible roles.

The DiSC Profile

Dating
without
Delusion

D = Dominance

I = Influence

S = Steadiness

C = Compliance

The DISC work is about comprehending your personality disposition. These are the behavioral, emotional, and attitude components that are deep within your makeup. When you learn about yourself, you begin to see why you feel and react the way you do. You can reflect on the interchanges that preceded your feeling happy, sad, fulfilled, intimidated, and that self-knowledge will provide just enough insight to prevent some internal frustration. For Faith people, it is a queue to quietly pray for the peace that passes understanding without feeling beat-up and spiritually inadequate. As you continue to grow in your personal insight and emotional control, you will be able to better in-

---

[27] The MS in Executive Leadership (MSEL) uses the DISC methodology for self-insight and for creation and leadership of high performing teams.

[28] There is also a temperament tool from Keirsey: https://www.keirsey.com/. Another is the Meyers/Briggs MBTI assessment. These tools all tend to type you using combinations of four temperament/types.

[29] For personality assessments, another one of the primary tools is the Meyers/Briggs Type Indicator (MBTI). Here is one of many links (or just Google it): https://www.personalitypathways.com/MBTI_articles.html.

teract with others because you will see them as people who have to manage their internal 'stuff,' just like you do.

Debra (my wife, an S/I) has done a little work on this area, and she quickly saw one of the major benefits. Debra used to take other people's frustrations personally and feel as if she had to 'fix' the circumstances with her friends and family. She has seen and learned that it is not her role to fix circumstances largely out of her control — a part of her 'Steadiness' personality profile. She has learned that people can be frustrated for a whole host of reasons she couldn't see, much less understand...meaning another person's sour mood often had nothing to do with her.

Mark Twain

Dating without Delusion

"The two most important days of your life are the day you are born, and the day you find out why."

She concluded:

Their frustration, aggravation, and annoyance is not *always about me!*

And most of the time, she is right.

After you have taken the DISC Profile (sorry, it might have cost you a small fee), sit down with the profile results and spend some quality time reading the description. Most of the descriptions will resonate and be very familiar to you, but note the areas where you have some questions and uncertainty. Also pay close attention to the potential negative aspects of your personality profile. Remember, those vulnerability insights will be very important to know on your self-discovery journey.

Lastly, at the top of the stack is the talents and strengths analysis. The only tool with the depth and quality we need is *Strengthsfinders*. The people at Gallup tell me they are closing in on 30 million people who have used the assessment. In a nutshell, Strengthsfinders is an analysis tool administered by Gallup that identifies your signature themes/talents. Strengthsfinders people have been using this online tool in many business and church organizations to help leaders to lead, and for people (especially on teams) to interrelate more effectively. In my life, it has been absolutely critical for me to know my own signature themes. Using them, I have learned to adapt to interpersonal relationships by adjusting my behavior. I am able to use my insights to help

Dating *without* Delusion	**Strengthsfinders 34 Themes** *(The 3rd Assessment Tool)*		
	Achiever	Competition	Futuristic
	Activator	Connectedness	Harmony
	Adaptability	Context	Ideation
	Analytical	Deliberative	Inclusiveness
	Arranger	Developer	Individualization
	Belief	Discipline	Input
	Command	Empathy	Intellection
	Communication	Fairness	Learner
	Competition	Focus	Maximizer

people to better understand me (talents, strengths, weaknesses, and everything else). Strengthsfinders identifies these themes — which are the foundations for talents — which are really innate potentials. Adding knowledge and skill to a Theme produces a genuine strength. The equation:

Theme/Talent + Skill + Knowledge = Strength

Are you beginning to see how important this whole discipline of *self-discovery* is to your life relationships? One of my themes/strengths is 'Maximizer.' It causes me to look at any situation or person and start to envision all of the things they could do to make the situation, and even themselves, better. You can see how my strength in the seminar environment, combined with teaching, is a powerful combination. You can also see that letting this potent strength combination out of the classroom environment can cause great annoyance among my friends and associates. I have another signature theme called 'Individualization' that 'leads me to be intrigued by the unique qualities of each person.' I 'instinctively observe each person's style, each person's motivation, how each thinks, and how each builds relationships. Because I am a keen observer of other people's strengths, I can 'draw out the best in each person.' If you could see me in the seminar classroom, you would see me doing just that. I hate to see people immersed in the culture (the tool of our enemy) trying to be someone they are not. So your personal feelings will shed light on this theme (which has become a strength), combined with my teaching skill, I constantly call Singles to a higher standard of living. It is a high standard they intuitively *know* already exists within each of their minds, souls, and spirits. My Individualization/Maximizer Strength combination is a major reason why I am writing the book you're holding. Do you see how critical it is to forget the concept of self-creation ...in favor of self-discovery?

When you do the Strengthsfinders online assessment, the tool comes back with your top five signature themes. Invariably, at least in my experience, these theme descriptors are right on the mark. Looking at their theme descriptors, people feel as if they have 'opened the window' on their behaviors and deepest feelings. Describing these insights, you will have the ability to allow other people to more easily see in. Looking at your themes, you feel like, "Yes! Finally someone understands me!" and you can share this knowledge with the important people around you. From here, you are set up to think about your spiritual gifts, your Personality Profile, and your potential strengths. Your sharpened insight sets you up to work on integrating them into your Personal Values, to ensure that you've used your strengths to pro-

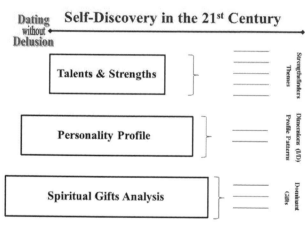

vide key amplifiers to the roles you are fulfilling. The individualized Personal Value descriptions you are creating will help you in *all* of your relationships. In Part Two, we will move on to using these insights dating relationships.

I realize that doing all of this work is not easy, but it is fun to learn about yourself (intrinsic learning). It's time-consuming and it will cost some money, but it will be well worth it. Also, please notice how you must interpret each gift/profile/talent in light of the others. You need to do the same. Each of your personal findings will shed light on your entire personal composition. Me? Teacher, Persuader, Strategic/Visionary, Individualization/Maximizer. Remember, these are *not* your values, but they will strongly influence your thinking when you move to your values worksheets. The combinations and perturbations are endless and unique, *as are you!* We'll combine your new personal insights with your very unique life background (childhood experiences and key life events or markers) to sharpen your understanding and articulation of your Personal Core Values. On the previous page is a summary worksheet to capture your newfound insights from your online self-assessments.

This self-discovery will also move you further along in the *belief* that you are unique. To move you to an even-deeper trust in your uniqueness, let's look at the three real-life examples for some encouragement, some instruction and, most of all, some validation.

Three real-life examples

The violinmaker's great-grandson

On a recent vacation to northern Idaho, we met an innkeeper who had a life experience of world travel, living in diverse cultures, and enjoying the people and their languages. One evening sitting around the hearth of a warming fireplace, we started a discussion about the innate abilities and strengths of a younger relative who fell in love with a young woman. As circumstances dictated, she accepted a post that took her out of the U.S. to Austria. Undaunted (or daunted as the case may be), he saddled up and

Khaleed Hosseeni

"It's now your duty to hone that talent, because a person who wastes his God-given talents is a donkey."

moved to Austria to be with his love. Not long after his arrival it became clear, for many reasons that he had to get a job. Pretty tough in a new country. I'm sure the job search had all the unpredictable twists and turns. The end result? He found a position as an assistant/apprentice to a violinmaker. Yes, it paid some bills but more interestingly, the young man found he not only loved his new job, but also that he was good at it. Fast forward many years and we find this same now-not-so-young man prospering in the violinmaking business. Using new technologies combined with the old-world violinmaking lessons learned in Austria, he had found his calling.

We all know how family relationships ebb and wane, how we stay in contact with some relatives and don't with others. Our young man had, for reasons I don't know, fallen out of touch with his great-grandfather. He didn't know his great-grandfather or his great-grandfather's profession. Yes, you guessed it; his great grandfather was a skilled violinmaker. So why do I tell you this story? ....which after all really wasn't that surprising to you. I share this story because this young man's parents weren't quacking at him, "You should be a violinmaker like your great grandfather." He didn't know *anything* about his great-grandfather. As a violin-ignorant person, I still know that violinmaking requires a certain very specific disposition, temperament, and skill set that you can't develop with just hard work. I'm sure that violinmakers see themselves as artists with a grasp of music history, and a keen sense of how the violin played a key role in historical sequences. They know how the violin has evolved over the centuries; they know the evolution of music and how the violin was essential in that timeline. Mostly, they know what makes a truly incredible violin.

Was the young violinmaker 'wired' from his DNA up to fill this role? Of course he was. Now perhaps the young man had brothers or sisters; it would not be surprising if *none* of them had any inclination toward violins.

Dating without Delusion

Parker J. Palmer

"Before I can tell my life all I want to do with it, I must listen to my life telling me who I am."

Think of the people you have known. Some were groomed by their parents to fill the roles their parents played. Some don't want to have anything to do with their parents' professions. "Son, you need to be ready to take over the business" has often fallen on deaf ears. Why, you ask. I honestly don't begin to be able to unravel that complexity. The point here is that if you *are* wired for a profession passed down through the generations, the sooner you figure it out, the better. On the other hand, all the parental pushing that goes on is pointless and frustrating if that young person is 'called' to be a missionary, a career military person, or a skilled and empathetic therapist. It is not about creating yourself...it *is* about self-discovery! Self-discovery is the foundation of good relationships. Do you remember the pyramid in the 40,000' introduction? Do you recall 'Don't look for Violinists at Rap concerts!'? Your Personal Values, at-best, will capture your specific 'wiring' and make it easy for other people to know and understand you. Now let's do a second real-life example.

King David's lifeline

Let's take a look back at David. Interestingly, I know much more about David, the king from ancient Judea, than I do about the twenty-first century violinmaker's great-grandson. The Bible is expansively revealing about David. We know his history and his heart. David lived in the period around 1030 BC. If you remember the story documented mostly in the Book of Samuel, David was the shepherd son of Jesse. The prophet Samuel was directed to go to Jesse's house to anoint the future king of Israel (1 Samuel chapter 16) to succeed Saul. (David eventually went on to reign for 40 years. He died in approximately 837 B.C.) When none of the sons was discerned to be 'the one,' Jesse replied that he had one more son who was in the field tending and defending the sheep. Let's look at the graphic on the next page. My argument is that the blueprint for David's life was built into him from the day he was born, just like the violinmaker's great-grandson. When Samuel arrived at Jesse's house, David was still in the field tending the sheep. As David was a young man doing his shepherd job, he was required to face lions and bears and all of the other natural elements that try to take down the flock. In the graphic, I'm pointing out 'Equipped Today' on the left-hand side of the slide. Samuel, of course, knew none of this. Samuel, the prophet, was following the Lord's direction in finding the right boy to anoint.

What Samuel also did *not* know was the 'wiring' that was in place in David's DNA that would take him all the way to the kingship of the country. Now, can I use the modern tools to describe David? Let's give it a try. He certainly was a gifted leader. Remember DISC (Dominance, Influence, Steadiness, Conscientious)? Read how David goes in to see Saul. The Israelite army is arrayed in front of the Philistines, and Goliath is badmouthing Israel and the God of Israel. Listen as David says: "For who is this uncircumcised Philistine, that he should taunt the armies of the living God?"[30] Later, David says to Saul, "The Lord who delivered me from the paw of the lion, and from the paw of the bear. He will deliver me from the hand of this Philistine" (1 Samuel 17v37).

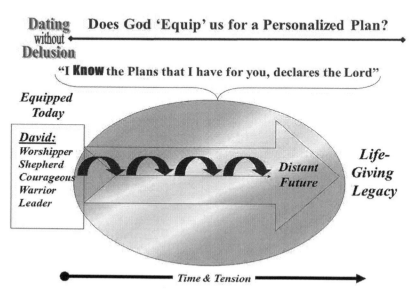

Do you see those Courageous, Warrior, Leader, Worshiper attributes coming to the forefront? Do you think David conjured those up, or do you think God purposefully built these strengths into David's very fiber? To me, the answer is an obvious yes to God's built-in design! My *guess* is that David had the Classical DISC Profile called 'Results-Oriented Pattern.' This pattern is very high in Dominance and also very strong in Influence (a D/I). Listen to the results-oriented description from the DISC Classic:

"Results-oriented people display self-confidence, which some interpret as arrogance. (Remember David's brothers confronting him?) *They actively seek opportunities that test and develop their abilities to accomplish results. Results-oriented people like difficult tasks, competitive situations, and unique assignments and 'important' positions.* (Does the Goliath challenge fit pretty well?) *"Results-oriented people undertake responsibilities with an air of self-importance and display self-satisfaction* (like Goliath's chopped-off head) *once they have finished"* (Parenthesis mine).

More from David's DISC profile:

---

[30] 1 Samuel 17 v 9; NASB.

"Results-oriented people tend to avoid constraining factors. They are forceful and direct. They prefer to work alone, they are quick thinkers, they take command of the situation whether or not they are in charge. They fear others will take advantage of them. They also fear slowness, especially in task activities."

Do I *know* that David fits this pattern? No... but it's a pretty good guess, don't you think? Over the years, I have been able to use DISC thinking more or less on the fly. It has helped me to better relate to my wife, the people I meet, and also all of my friends and relatives. If you lived in ancient Judea, and you wanted to create and sustain a relationship with David, how valuable do you think it would be to understand the insights from his personality profile? If you were in David's close circle of advisors, wouldn't it help if you knew your own profile so that you could better manage your relationship with the king... and perhaps with your own family? Even people high in Dominance (sometimes called 'Turbo Ds') can be intelligent and open-minded enough to learn about themselves.

So what were David's gifts and talents? I took a guess at his gifts, using layman's terms. See if they make sense to you. **Worshiper:** David must have had a strong orientation towards the creator Lord, looking out over God's fields and streams. Remember, he authored many of the Psalms. **Shepherd:** sheep need constant attention and oversight, just as the people of Israel would need that same attention. **Courageous:** think about bears and lions trying to attack the flock. Think about Goliath (9 feet tall?). **Warrior:** One-on-one battles are tough, and they are rugged preparation for leading armies. **Leader:** Courageous action against Goliath set the stage for David's leadership of the whole country.

Now, let's look at the cycles and seasons of David's life. After David took down the first big animal (bear or lion?), he must have realized his innate courage as well as his level of natural giftedness to be a warrior, don't you agree? But now as life and circumstance move forward, he is called to use those same gifts in expanding venues. Next, he is tasked to be a courier to his brothers, who were deployed in the Israelite army facing the Philistines. Saul then sends David out to face the giant... and so it goes, in expanding venue after venue. David's gifts were leveraged in increasingly more powerful ways. Shepherd becomes courier, becomes warrior, becomes general, becomes king.

At the end of the timeline arrow, you see David as the king of the nation. In the chart, you also see people who David was called to submit to and serve. It starts with his father Jesse and the sheep, moves to the prophet Samuel, then King Saul, the king's son Jonathan, and finally Jonathan's crippled son Mephibosheth. By itself, this spectrum of submission-to-service could be a book unto itself. Early on, David submitted to his father and Samuel. Always there was someone for David to show kindness and mercy. In his king's court he compassionately cared for Mephibosheth. Always, David was called to be a *servant* as well as a leader. I look at that sequence and often think it an order that *ascends* in leadership influence. Do you see it? Sheep-Brothers-Saul-Armies-Nation. Lastly, on the far right of the slide you see 'Life-Giving Legacy.' The premise for you to consider is this. Persistent use of your God-given gifts, disposition, and strengths will create your unique life-giving

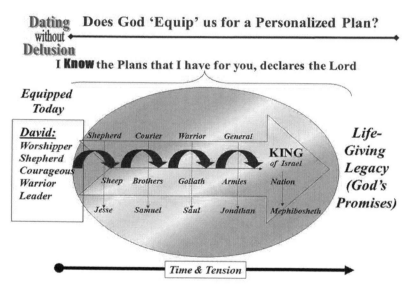

legacy. Gifts used over the long haul of a significant portion of your life; are these God's callings? You will be called to serve others. Isn't service the place where we find ourselves? The legacy that God wants to bless you with. The legacy that you will leave behind. The legacy that you will be remembered by. Don't try to be David; don't try to be Billy Graham. Be you.

Back in the twentieth century, you could argue that the urgency of life and the lack of scientifically sound psychological tools limited the amount of true self-discovery you could achieve. It was not true then and definitely not true today. There are so many good personal assessment tools, and they are available for such a small investment of time and money; the potential personal benefit is something you have to experience to understand. Each of the three selected tools will provide you with essential insights that build upon one another and provide insights for living out your Personal Values in a more effective manner. Remember the recommended three tools, in that specific order? Spiritual Gifts (Ephesians Four)...Personality Profile (DISC)... Talents and Strengths (Strengthsfinders).

Now, let's take a try at David once again, this time using Strengthsfinders to look back. Now I hope you better understand the Strengthsfinders language (Talents and Strengths, etc.) because you have taken the assessments. Here's my guess at David's top five talents/themes, and their order (which is less critical). I have excerpted some descriptor phrases from the Strengthsfinders themes text.[31]

Activator: 'When can we start? You are impatient for action. The bottom line is this: you know you will be judged not by what you say, not by what you think, but by what you get done.'

Command: 'Command leads you to take charge... Once your goal is set, you feel restless until you have aligned others with you...People are drawn toward those who take a stance and ask them to move in a certain direction. Therefore, people will be drawn to you. You have presence. You have Command.'

Belief: 'You have Core Values that are enduring...your Belief theme causes you to be family-oriented, altruistic, even spiritual, and to value responsibility and high ethics. Your Belief theme makes you easy to trust. It demands that you find work that meshes with your values. Your work must be meaningful, it must matter to you... guided by your Belief theme, it will matter only if it gives you a chance to live out your values.'

Self-Assurance: 'In the deepest part of you, you have faith in your strengths. You *know* that you are able — able to take risks, able to meet new challenges, able to stake claims, and most importantly, able to deliver. Blessed with the theme of Self-Assurance, you have confidence not only in your capabilities, but in your judgment... no matter what the situation you know what the right decision is.'

---

[31] Buckingham, Marcus and Donald O. Clifton , 2001. *Now Discover Your Strengths*. The Free Press, a division of Simon and Schuster. New York, N.Y. 10020.

Communication: 'You feel the need to bring (ideas) to life, to make them exciting and vivid. You take the dry idea and enliven it with images and examples and metaphors. This is what drives your hunt for the perfect phrase. This is what draws you toward dramatic words and powerful word combinations. This is why people like to listen to you. Your word pictures pique their interest, sharpen their world, and inspire them to act.'

Am I *absolutely* sure that these are David's signature themes? Absolutely not. Nevertheless, I can look back at the very well documented life of David and see these talents/strengths at work. If you haven't been in the Bible in a while, this is a very good opportunity for you to dig in and read some timeless and world-shaping stories. In the Strengthsfinders context, David's deeply ingrained personal themes must be matured to 'strengths.' This is achieved through experience (using and sharpening the talent) and through the acquisition of key complementing skills and knowledge. A simple example for David is to consider *how* he communicated his intense and very bumpy relationship with God. Through his vivid and dramatic experiences, from Goliath to Bathsheba. David learned to know God: His character, how to trust Him, and how to confess to Him. David's strength-building experiences are the subject of many volumes of analysis by theologians, pastors, and evangelists. I am none of those things but I do read the Psalms, and I know enough about David to see his strengths being finely sharpened over time. If you are so inclined, read some of David's Psalms and see if you can 'hear' his Belief; see if his Communication strength is powerful as he is drawn toward dramatic words and powerful word combinations.

Now, the previous graphic lays out David's strengths in layman's terms. Do these align with the Strengthsfinders terminologies? You bet. There is a nice correlation, and here it is:

Worshiper: David, as a 'man after God's own heart,' was living out his *Belief* strength (for example, his faith that God would deliver him from Goliath), and later he vividly communicated his faith, trust, and repentance as documented in the Psalms, exercising his gift of *Communication*.

Leader/Shepherd: God wanted a leader of Israel, who had the humility and care of a shepherd. But make no mistake: David was a full-throttle leader, exercising his gift of *Command*.

Warrior: Like a typical *Activator*, David was anxious to get into the fight. The Goliath story is a tangible example of this strength.

Courageous: For David, most of his life was an expression of his dependence on and trust in God. His confidence was often rock-solid because he was depending on God, not himself. So from the outside, David had the confident air of *Self-Assurance*. Listen again to the description of this strength: 'You *know* that you are able — able to take risks, able to meet new challenges, able to stake claims, and most important, able to deliver.' If he could speak to us today, David would say he knew that *God was able*. God's awesome care and protection were the underpinnings of David's *Self-Assurance*.

From our twenty-first century point of view, this discussion of David is upside-down. It's *inverted* because we are looking back at David through history. We're trying to discover and describe David long after his life was over and documented. David also had the nice advantage of having a prophet come to his house to announce his selection as the next king, and to anoint him with oil. So David had the insight of a supernatural selection. Chances are that you won't enjoy such a dramatic calling-out; but then again, you might. God's choice.

Looking *back* at David, we can make very good assessments about his natural personality profile, his giftings, his strengths, and his character. Do you see how I have 'intersected' the results from David's gifts assessment and his personality disposition with the estimates of his Strengthsfinders results? This book is about you doing the same thing for yourself. This is where the light can begin to shine for you. With these insights, you can begin to capsulize... to combine... to synthesize your insights into crisp Personal Value phrases. It's about *you* moving forward toward better relationships with a transparent understanding of who you are. We did this work with David (and the violinmaker's great-grandson) to encourage you to use these modern tools (spiritual gifts assessments, DISC personality profiles, and Strengthsfinders) to help you see how you are 'wired' and how you can move forward to your values, and then your personal legacy, with better self-understanding. Remember David's #1 Core Value? The one God directly provided? "A man after God's own heart".

A family story.

As always, a real-life applications help cement the concept, so here is a third story. This one is for my wife Debra and our former daughter-in-law Kristina. Back when our son Michael and Kristina had a baby girl, Marlie... the cutest baby I have ever seen. Many people laugh at me because they think I'm just being a gaga grandparent. No, she *is* the cutest baby I have ever seen! (OK, I'll drop it.) You can imagine how excited Debra was to finally have her first granddaughter. Now, Debra is a very experienced mom; she and many of her closest friends have shared motherhood with a lot of babies. So Debra intuitively felt that Kristina should afford Debra's baby-care advice some pretty hefty respect. Makes sense, don't you agree? Well, Kristina would listen to Debra, and then go online and pull up all of the latest baby-care research and guidelines to determine exactly how to handle whatever problem little Marlie was having. To a certain extent, this is a generational thing. Kristina's Millennial generation has been raised on the Internet. Still, Debra felt ever-so-slightly slighted because she wanted to be a great hands-on Nana whose contributions were highly respected. Then, Kristina took the Strengthsfinders on-line tool. One of her top talents, which I believe she has sharpened into a strength, is *Data Input.* Listen to excerpts from Strengthsfinders on *Data Input* (it used to be called Analytical[32]):

> 'You do not want to destroy other people's ideas, but you do insist that their theories be sound. You see yourself as objective and dispassionate. You like data because they are value-free. They have no agenda. Armed with these data, you search for patterns and connections. You want to understand how certain patterns affect one another. How do they combine? What is their outcome? Does this outcome fit with the theory being offered or the situation being confronted? These are your questions. You peel the layers back until gradually, the root cause or causes are revealed.'

When Debra understood Kristina's natural bent to research everything, she began to see that Kristina meant no disrespect to her, only that *Kristina was being who she is.* When problems of any kind emerge, Kristina wants — immediately — to get into the research and to extract the latest and best data to support any decisions about the best course of action.

---

[32] Buckingham, Marcus and Donald O. Clifton , 2001. *Now Discover Your Strengths.* The Free Press, a division of Simon and Schuster. New York, N.Y.10020. p.86.

After this realization, Debra could carefully offer advice, knowing that Kristina's strength was firing in her brain... and off into the research she would go, digging for clues and data. (This strength also makes Kristina a very good student.) Armed with these data, Kristina will take well-meant advice and carefully factor it into all of the research and information that she would 'mine.' How important is this to one of our most important family relationships? Very. Debra's feeling of being undervalued could have gone on and on, subtly degrading her feelings for Kristina. No more. Debra's understanding — and I would say wisdom — now factors Kristina's strengths into her Nana relational mindset... and things are fine.

The violinmaker's great-grandson, an Israelite king, and a grand mom's former daughter-in-law. I contend that all three had their giftings and strengths from the moment they were born and, if you take the Bible seriously, from the moment they were conceived and even from ages before time, back to Psalm 139. It is intense arrogance to take a hard stand and expect others to get to know me because "I am who I am." Not only does it take a lot of time, it is very imprecise and can create many affronts and hurts. Insults, misunderstandings, and wrong expectations are the stuff of an ambiguous life, don't you agree? These very nasty potentials can be covered up for a while in emotional dating. The price of this kind of superficial behavior in dating is severe; the cost is an ineffective life: a life hamstrung by broken relationships and divorce. Self-awareness and Personal Values, on the other hand, support good relationships that have the potential for great marriages.

Doing vs. believing

For you Faith people, here's an encouragement. In our twenty-first century world, there is incredible emphasis on getting things done fast, correctly, and inexpensively: all of what we sum up in the word _efficiently_. After all of our discussion about God's plan, I hope you are persuaded to work to find _your_ right direction: the one specifically intended for you. Like so many people in our society, you are going to be greatly challenged to get this self-analysis work done; hopefully I'll help you with that. Then you have sit, pray, and strategize: what changes are you going to make to steer your ship onto the right course? Just like companies and countries, you have to establish an inflection point. You were headed in a direction... you stopped and contemplated... then you changed direction. You sharpened your focus. I want to help you get on course for higher-level, more purposeful living. You shift your aim to higher level goals and objectives and, when we get done, I hope those will be expressed in your Personal Values. In the Bible, Paul talks about this change, comparing it to a change of clothes, like taking off an old jacket and putting on a new one. Consider:

> "Do not lie to one another, since you laid aside the old self with its evil practices, and have _put on_ the new self who is being renewed to a true knowledge according to the image of the One who created Him." Col 3: 9–10; NASB (underlines mine)

> "So as those who have been chosen of God, holy and beloved, _put on_ a heart of compassion, kindness, humility, gentleness and patience, bearing with one another, forgiving each other." Col 3:12–13; NASB (underline mine)

> "You were taught with regard to your former way of life, to _put off_ your old self which is being corrupted by its deceitful desires; _to be made new in the attitude of your minds_, and to put on _the new self, created to be like God in true righteousness and holiness._" Ephesians 4:22–24 NIV (underlines mine)

These verses remind that the only way we can make this course change — _to put off_ and to _put on_ — is to have a new mindset; _to be made new in the attitude of our minds._ Our culture manipulates our nature, and our nature is to rush past this decision point and to get busy doing the urgent but not the essential. Christians and most people in general fall into this trap (me included!).

Often, I use the phrase "stop messing around and get moving:" a reflection of my Navy days. This is not to say that we don't need activating, achieving, results-oriented people to move forward. It's just that a pause, a moment of reflection, for faith people a prayer, is always going to help set the course correctly. Do you remember the old analogy about course setting? Even a one or two-degree error at the start will result in a direction that is many miles off-target in end (see the 'Demise of PR-03' in Appendix B). So how do we set the course correctly? Personal Values are great course-setters, so we're working hard to get to those. If you are not a faith person, I am confident that you will find a fresh glimpse of God the Creator in your wiring and DNA, and in the values that emerge from your intelligent self-examination. For you Christians, I'd like to borrow some words from J.D. Greear as he talks about working for God:[33]

---

[33] _The Gospel._ p. 206

"What does a gospel-centered approach to the brokenness of the world look like? This is an important question to ask, because if we get it wrong, we'll either waste our lives in meaningless pursuits because we don't think we need to do anything for God; or we'll burn ourselves out carrying a load that Jesus never intended us to carry. But if we get it right, we will have the joy of leveraging our lives for Jesus as He leveraged His Son for us." (Underlines mine)

It's all about creating the inflection point, and then making sure we steer our lives in the right direction. J.D. talks about 'diagnosing' our condition: recognizing that we *all* need to do some course refinement. Then he talks about 'prognosis:' figuring out what to do about it.[34]

"Lovelessness, apathy, and habitual sin are diagnosis of spiritual death. We go desperately wrong when we think we can fix those things by correcting our behavior."

J.D. goes on to recall the gospel of John chapter 6; let's look there. Jesus has just fed the 5,000 with, no doubt, the best bread that has ever been eaten. Everybody wants more. He has walked on water, bringing the disciples to a safe landing and validating beyond a shadow of a doubt that He is God. So now, here comes the Type A question: "What must we do to accomplish the work that God requires?" (Verse 28) Jesus' answer:

"The work of God is this; to believe *in the One He has sent." (John 6:29)*

I summarize this intellectual/spiritual attitude with these three words:

Be quiet... behold... believe.

No 'get-out-there-and-do-it' Type A responses! You have seen the loaves and fishes; you have watched the instant deliverance from the storm; now sit back and contemplate the wonder and deliverance of God. In careful consideration — the Behold part — you can recognize God's greatness and His love for you. Beholding leads to a tangible faith. J.D. says in *The Gospel:* [35]

"Wow. Our most important 'doing' turns out to be 'believing.' When we have 'done' that of course we will naturally start doing the other stuff. Truly believing

---

[34] *The Gospel.* p. 245

[35] *The Gospel.* p. 245

the gospel produces in us a concern for the poor, a love of scripture, a desire to be in authentic community, a love for holiness and everything else that is a part of the Christian life."

At a recent Friday evening at church, one of the pastors was preaching on belief, using *The Gospel* as a resource. He recounted the story of the tightrope walker who is going to walk a tightrope over a raging river. Everyone loves the spectacle. The tightrope walker says, "And I'm going to tightrope-walk across this river with this wheelbarrow." The crowd is amazed. Then the pastor goes behind the stage and rolls out an actual full-size wheelbarrow. Continuing the story, the tightrope walker asks, "And who would like to get in the wheelbarrow and go across with me?" No volunteers. The pastor points out that getting in the wheelbarrow is an act of belief. In *our* heart of hearts there is often *a lack* of belief... not in the tightrope walker, but in God. And what do we do? We cover our non-belief with activity: getting it done for God. Why? Because we really don't *believe* that He is capable, without me. The bottom line message is this: you must Be Quiet... Behold... Believe all *before you do anything else.*

That particular evening, the worship band was in rare form, mixing in a little bluegrass with some of the old praise hymns. At the end, they did a quiet and introspective old piece, "Just Give Me Jesus." I didn't even sing; I just enjoyed some quiet listening, trying to remember and believe in God's purpose for me. I love Chris Tomlin's, "All my Fountains are in You." It reminds me that my source is the Lord: "Rain on me... Reign in me."

As you develop your values, you will continually think about getting out there and doing it, for the sake of your self-esteem, or to honor and be used by God... or both. Not simple, is it? With upcoming work on your Personal Values, the temptation is to get on the burnout treadmill and to start working for God. What Jesus, J.D., and our pastor are all saying is the *believing* part is first and most essential. When we get to that ever-so-important inflection point, that's exactly the time that we have to slow down and be quiet. It's like they say in sports: you work hard to get ready. Believe in God as a base for belief in yourself, and then let God bring the game come to you.

The 4C Model

Our goal here is for you to become a *Relationship Craftsman*. To do so, you need a go-to tool you can rely on: one you can remember no matter where you are in the dating/relationship process. Remember, a great tool that doesn't make it onto the job doesn't do you any good. We'll offer a number of additional

Dating **The '4C' Model**
without
Delusion

These four elements, in priority order, constitute the primary ingredients of a good relationship that should be developed:

Core Values   You *Understand, Appreciate, & Respect* **One Another's Spiritual, Relational, Occupational Values**

Commitment   **This Person Demonstrates the Ability to Commit:**
- Spiritually - Relationally -Professionally

Communication **Has <u>Some</u> Ability *and* is Willing to Learn (humility)**

Compatibility * **Shared Activities**
                   * **Personality Dispositions / Birth Order**
                   * **Sexuality (Physical Appearance)**

tools in Part Three, 'Tools for Singles.' On the other hand, the 4C Model is central; it's easy to use, and easy to remember. It also captures the whole spectrum of concepts in ***Dating without Delusion***. Over the years, people who have attended the seminar and the classes seem to retain this tool better than any other. When the heat and emotion of a dating relationship get going, a mental tool is worthless if you can't bring it to the front of your mind. So here are the 4C's, shown above and in order below:

Core Values · Commitment · Communication · Compatibility

Personal Values development is not my idea. Many, many people and organizations across the span of geography and time have recognized values as the central element of good behavior. Our discussion about the violinmaker's great grandson, King David, and my former daughter-in-law gave you a window on values development. I hope you will embrace the need to know who you are and to express your individuality in your Personal Values. Remember, your unique values are the way to find and articulate God's plan for you. Here we go.

Core Values: The foundation of personal integrity

Right after the word 'Love', the word 'Integrity' is probably the most misused and abused word in the English language. Remember the Webster definition? Integrity is 'firm adherence to a set of moral values.' Here's my modified definition for your consideration and application:

Personal integrity: Firm adherence to your *set of Personal Core Values*

In the early sessions of the dating seminar, when people are grappling with the personal ambiguity they see in their lives, 'honesty' is a one-word description they come up with. The 'Speed Meet' shown below is a good opening seminar exercise. After passing out this page to groups of three or four people, I ask each person to write down the names of the people at the table. Then we do a round robin, where each person has an opportunity to verbally describe just one of their central Personal Values. That's when the 'integrity' word often gets written down and discussed. When I ask what a seminar person is thinking about when they say integrity, the answer comes back: "Well, I guess it means honesty." Nice little circular reasoning. We all want hones-

Dating without Delusion	SPEED MEET Notes Page	
Names of the Persons at Your Table (*Be sure to Sit at the Same Table Next Week*)	**Strong/Succinct/Clear Personal Value**
-	-
-	-
-	-
-	-
-	-

ty from others; even if sometimes we ourselves are dishonest. Without values at the front of your mind, you might believe that you have Integrity, but based upon what? Then we go around the room and ask people to describe a good value they heard from *someone else* at their table. Remember, we haven't done any Core Value work yet, so you can envision the mushy responses. To experience this yourself, go ahead and speak one or two of *your own values* out loud, THIS MOMENT. (Yes, right now! Put down the book and go!)

Did you feel the confusion? Like you, people in the seminar are going to a mental place they haven't been to before, and I can feel their bewilderment. In the seminars, people talk about love and integrity and honesty. This exercise helps people see the values vacuum that they have been living in. The point is to help each person gear up intellectually to start really working on their Personal Core Values. Why? Because with clear Personal Values, you can build better relationships...and most people *do* want to have personal integrity. Lastly — maybe 'Firstly' — this is a book about dating. Married baby boomers with six grandkids are very busy living out grand-parenting responsibilities and 25+ year marriage commitments. They can get away with unspoken values. *Not so for you, my Single friend.* In dating relationships, Personal Values are essential. They can provide great guidance and an excellent source of clear communication. Without Personal Values and personal integrity, you can talk yourself into all kinds of delusional relationships and 'pragmatic' decisions. So here is a saying that you can tuck into your mind; I hope it is an encouragement:

"It is never too late...to start doing what is right" (Jay)

Not simply moral right, like honesty. *Personal* right choices, based upon who you are. Obvious right choices are right at your doorstep. "Really, Jay?" you say. "And just how exactly do you know that?" Here's a real-life story to explain. A young Christian woman is sitting in the seminar and we're discussing Personal Values. In this case, Relational Values. A young Single woman who is a mother of three little kids speaks up. "I hate being a mother" — and I knew exactly what she meant. She 'hated' the endless pressure coming from her kid's needs and wants. From the ignorant and abusive behavior of the father of those kids. Money issues; schedule issues; the list goes on and on. Nevertheless, the hard reality is that God, the Creator, allowed her to birth those kids. The role of mother has been given to her, regardless of her feelings about it today or tomorrow. As she struggles with the practicalities of daily living with her family, she has come to realize her role as a mother, and her 'call' to be a spiritually grounded and inspired mother. Her calling must supersede her feelings. Following the "I hate being a mother" comment, I asked this young woman to pray for direction and revelation regarding her circumstance. Making a long story very short, God pointed her at 1 Peter 1:7. She thought the Lord pinpointed this verse specifically for her. All Christians are somewhat unsure when these revelations happen (at least the ones I know). In her case, the church service she attended the following Sunday was centered on 1 Peter 1:7, which speaks about suffering in this life:

"These (trials) have come so that your faith — of greater worth than gold,

which perishes even though refined by fire — may be proved genuine, and
may result in praise glory and honor when Jesus Christ is revealed."

The message? Her suffering, tests, and trials during these early years with her kids are refining her faith, just like the refining of gold. Many would say that a good God would never allow this. Others would say that her situation is one she created through a string of bad choices (easy to be judgmental). Let's simply say in the midst of her difficult circumstances, she knows and is very clear on the fact that many of her situations are a direct result of her choices. Can God orchestrate the innumerable circumstances for good in her life? Easily. Her belief is that He will, despite the hopelessness all around her. Her call is to press on as a mother, despite the depressing circumstances which fill her daily routine. It is a call for her to trust God, knowing He will use these extreme circumstances, if she stays faithful. Easy to say, but very hard to do. Her Personal Value is a constant reminder of God's plan for her and her kids. A reminder of the fact that He has a plan which, at this juncture, is beyond her understanding. Her value?

I am God's daughter, chosen, seeking, and obeying in the trials of my faith.

Despite the devastation around her, there is a higher story.

Personal Integrity: What is it?

Language is a difficult thing. Just like love, so many words can be interpreted in so many ways. 'Integrity' is one of those words. Like love, which we have already discussed, Integrity gets used a lot, but with a strange ambiguity. When you say it, you're never really sure what the listener is thinking. When you hear it, it sounds like honesty with a righteous twist. It's a good slot-filler on the 'Speed Meet' exercise, but that's about it. One of Webster's definitions for integrity is 'firm adherence to a set of moral values.' To have some fun and to provoke critical thinking, I ask this question in the dating classes: "Do you think that Adolf Hitler had integrity?" Almost always, this question is debated with enthusiasm.

To keep up that critical thinking churn, I take the position that Adolf Hitler did have integrity. How? Well, he said that he believed the Germans were the master race, and he said that he hated the Jews. He then went on to enslave the Jews, to put them in forced labor camps, and to send them to termination camps like Dachau. Using the slide below, I argue that Adolf Hitler's beliefs and values were consistent with his actions; therefore, he *did* have integrity. Since many people confuse honesty with integrity, you can see how my point

Dating
without
Delusion

Integrity

Integrity: Firm adherence to a set of Moral Values ..... (*Webster*)

Integrity is a concept of <u>consistency of actions, values,</u> methods, measures, principles, expectations and outcomes. In western ethics, integrity is regarded as the quality of having an intuitive sense of honesty and truthfulness in regard to the motivations for one's actions. Integrity can be regarded as the opposite of hypocrisy ...... (*Wikipedia*)

is not so well taken. Hitler honestly communicated his hatred of the Jews, and the subsequent actions of the reign of the Third Reich were consistent with that belief. World War II historians certainly talk about the many lies and deceptions that Hitler perpetrated as he rose to power; that is what makes this debate so interesting. But you see the point: if you have clear values, *integrity demands that your actions be consistent with your words and your words be consistent with your values.*

Here's another interesting seminar drill we do. I ask everyone to stand up and recite the Pledge of Allegiance. Almost everyone in the class will be able to recite the Pledge of Allegiance word for word. Why? Because in grade school, most of us stood up at the beginning of the day and recited the Pledge of Allegiance. Kids wanted to learn the pledge because they are Americans. Now in the dating classes, most of the people are Christians. When I ask them to recite the 10 Commandments, many of the people have a general idea of what some of the Commandments are, but they don't know the specific order or the exact wording. You can see the problem. When someone says they are a Christian, they immediately tie into all of the religious issues we have experienced in organized churches. As we know, 'religion' has been responsible for some very serious bad behavior.

But what does the Bible say? Moses brought the 10 Commandments down from Mount Sinai. Speaking to the Israelites, God warned him to be careful to obey all of the Commandments. Before Joshua crossed the Jordan, God reminded him to be careful to keep all of the Commandments; to bind them around your neck; to be strong and courageous. And what did Jesus say? "If you love me, you will keep my commandments." Is this starting to become clear? *Before you do what is right, you must know what is right.* If you are a Christian, you must have the source of truth in your mind and heart. If you are not a Christian, the challenge is to be clear about what is right and what is wrong, based upon your Personal Values. In the noise and distraction of today's media-blasting society, this is not an easy thing to accomplish.

Consider what George Barna says about values: *"Let me state emphatically that determining your values is a necessary and important step in your personal development and maturity."* He then adds, "as a Christian" because his audience is largely church-based. The same is true for everyone, however. Barna continues to say:

> *"Until you can confidently state your Values, every philosophy, every behavior, and every desire known to humankind is a potential substitute. Your Values become the filter through which you determine right from wrong, value from worthlessness and importance from insignificance. If you do not specifically identify your values, they will be defined for you by the whims and the influences of the world. (That's the culture.) Values are the non-negotiable perspectives in your life. More often than not, people who do not intentionally set forth their Values in a clear and concise format waffle under pressure. When it comes to concern about consistency and backbone, Christians who do not have well defined sets of values run little danger of moral or ethical compromise because people who have no clear values have nothing to compromise. On the other hand people who specify their values are more likely to live in harmony with those core beliefs."* [36] *(Underlines mine)*

This brings us back to integrity. We all want to claim it for ourselves, and we often expect and demand it from others. It is very annoying if someone says one thing to you and then contradicts himself/herself with 'different' behavior. This is inevitable in our society because relativism is the underlying theme of the culture. Everything is relative to the extenuating circumstances, which allow us to waffle as we make our life choices. As you work to be clear

---

[36] Barna, George. *Turning Vision into Action.* Regal Books, A Division of Gospel Light. Ventura, CA. p. 91

about what you value and what your specific Core Values are, pay attention to the people around you, to see if they have any idea of what *their* Personal Values are. I usually get responses like, "I value love and honesty," or I get a

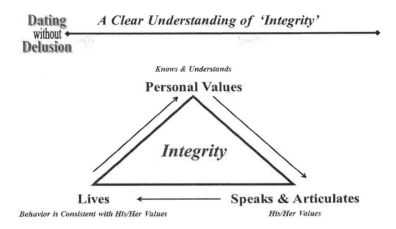

perplexed look and an uncomfortable silence. It really comes down to saying what we believe, and then behaving in a manner that is consistent. As the slide below depicts, it is the rare person who knows their Personal Values; who can succinctly articulate them; and whose behavior is aligned with their well-stated set of Personal Values. If you meet someone who can do these things, I contend they do have 'Integrity.' On the other hand, you have encountered many people — and many organizations — whose talk *and* walk change and morph with each new situation. A caution to you all: once you have clearly defined and articulated your Personal Core Values, they will hold you to a high standard. I find that I *fail* my Personal Values more often than I would like to admit. I also contend that a good Personal Values set will draw you higher, to better behavior, on a more consistent basis.

Hopefully, the values development and the self-assessments offered in this book will help you achieve added personal clarity. As the figure illustrates in the Integrity triangle, knowing values is the necessary first step to speaking values, all of which is the precursor to values-based *behavior*. The next step is to *use* your personal clarity to build your relationships in a more healthy and transparent fashion: what I have been calling *Personal Transparency*.

For the Single man, for the Single woman, the stakes are high, so do the relationship thing with *all* of your values in *all* of your relationships, every day. Use your values for all of your choices. When people question the why of your decisions, simply explain the stories and experiences underlying your Personal Value. Hopefully there is a limitlessly deep well of corroboration waiting for your values in the Bible. From personal experience, I can tell you that the verses which validate my values are a tremendously powerful source

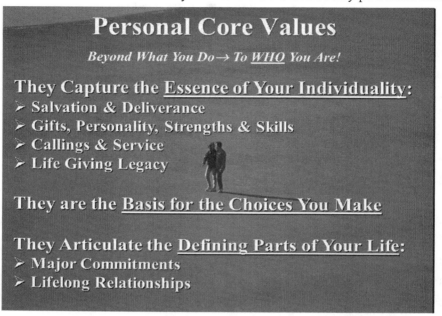

Personal Core Values
Beyond What You Do→ To __WHO__ You Are!

They Capture the __Essence of Your Individuality__:
➤ Salvation & Deliverance
➤ Gifts, Personality, Strengths & Skills
➤ Callings & Service
➤ Life Giving Legacy

They are the __Basis for the Choices You Make__

They Articulate the __Defining Parts of Your Life__:
➤ Major Commitments
➤ Lifelong Relationships

of encouragement. If you dig in, you no doubt will find affirmation...maybe adjustment...and maybe refinement...for your values. When you share your values with the verses, sayings, or beliefs that confirm them, listeners will understand faster and with better comprehension. They will understand you! Your friends and family will appreciate what you have discovered; they will enjoy your better personal clarity. You will learn from your new personal transparency. I don't hope — I *know* your values will be life-changers for you.

Spiritual, Relational, and Professional are the categories I suggest. But if you own a value that doesn't fit into these categories, don't sweat it. Just make sure you can articulate it and, if questioned, back it up with your real-life stories and learning.

Personal Core Values: Beyond what you do →
To WHO you are!

Let's take a look at the definition of Personal Core Values that I have used in the seminar. Often we call them just Core Values, like the first C. If there is one thing I wish we all could get right, this is it. Personal Values done well will Inspire, Influence, and Inform[37] every relationship in your life. So what is a Personal Core Value? The definition I use in the ***Dating without Delusion*** seminar is in the graphic on the previous page. Looking at the graphic, you see two people walking on the beach. Isn't that romantic? Activities and moments like this are memorable, but they really are about two people enjoying a shared activity. Shared activities are good things, but I contend that shared activities are good parts of Compatibility (the fourth C, not the first C). Good relationships have elements of Compatibility. So I say that Compatibility is necessary, but it is *not* sufficient. Core Values are the first and most important dynamic which has to exist in great relationships to sustain them for the long haul. We are infinitely complex creatures: each of us is a unique combination of body, mind, and spirit, and we all bring a myriad of life experiences along with our personas. A good Personal Core Value will — bullet one — 'Capture the essence of your individuality.' If you are a spiritual person, your defining relationship with God should take first place. If you are not spiritually oriented, there are still defining 'moments of a lifetime' which have shaped your life; what are they? What is the essence of your individuality? How has God 'intersected' your life? How do you use your gifts and skills to serve others, to give back? If you can sustain giving-back over the long haul, you will begin to see the roots of your personal legacy.

Many people balk at this point. "Me? Leave a legacy?" Perhaps you have seen this on a smaller (but important) scale when you watch excellent parents influence, inspire, and inform their own children and grandchildren. Move to the larger venue, gifted teachers, for example. Every day in the classroom, there's the teacher, pulling the kids out of the cultural muck and moving them, inspiring them to reach for their individual destinies. Think of the lives and foundations of true philanthropists. How much money did Warren Buffet give to the Bill Gates foundation?[38] Wealthy people — those who are wise — often come to the realization that either they give their money away, or it will slowly drive them crazy. The point here is that if you are going to leave a life-giving legacy, you must find where your callings and gifts are,

---

[37] Yep, you guessed it: there are the '3I's'. Inspire, Influence, Inform. If they help you explain the 'why of Core Values,' put them into your vernacular. If you're overloaded with **Dating *without* Delusion** acronyms and 'hooks,' then leave this one on the table.

[38] Answer: 30 billion dollars.

and then use them to serve others over the long haul. Only towards the end of the long haul will you find your personal legacy. Remember our example of King David? For Jay, there are elements of personal legacy in my marriage and extended families, and then there is the legacy to Singles I hope to leave when I'm done.

Next major point, and it's one worth repeating:

A value is not a value unless it drives your choices (Jay)

What good is a Personal Core Value if you don't use it for your own guidance? That would leave out the 'Lives' in the Knows, Speaks, and Lives sequence. An action that conflicts with one of our stated values is the essence of *low* personal integrity. Look around you. When people think they live by a set of values but they can't express them clearly, do you see the disconnect? Good values articulate the defining parts of your life. You will eventually see those in your lifelong relationships and major commitments.

Real-life values in action

To see how Personal Values in action work, a real-life story will be helpful, as always. In a recent class the Singles completely understood the importance of Personal Values — but as usual they were struggling with the actual process of writing them down on paper. We were having an extended discussion on the benefits of having a trusted and spiritual accountability partner. One of the gals says, "Well, I have the 'Gumbys!" She explains the details about her group of women who meet regularly and hold one another together with all kinds of support — prayer included. She explains the group label — Gumbys. "It's based on two verses from Isaiah chapter 64. Here's a quick excerpt from the Isaiah chapter, verses 8 & 9:

> *Yet O Lord you are our father. <u>We are the clay, you are the potter</u>; we are all the work of your hand. Do not be angry beyond measure O Lord: do not remember our sins forever. O look upon us we pray for we are all your people.*
> *(Underline mine)*

If you don't know the Gumby toy, he's the little twistable square-headed guy (with his little sidekick pony named Pokey). Little kids just love to carry Gumby and Pokey around and twist them into all kinds of weird shapes. The idea is the Gumby women want to be moldable-shapeable-in God's hands.

The aha moment for her (and me) was the fact these gals and this woman had some bedrock commitment to one another which was defining. "It's one of your values!" I practically yell at her. She may not want to use the Gumby label, but she sure wants to express this critical personal commitment to God and her group with some descriptors like 'Moldable' or 'Shapeable'... in God's hands. What a great Spiritual AND Relational value!

The Lord's woman...shapeable in His hands!

Does this Core Value drive her choices? You bet; every week when she faithfully joins her fellowship group. If one of the 'Gumbys' ran head first into a crisis, I'll guess these women would be there to help and encourage. So as we enjoyed this value revelation one of the other class members says "Now I get it I have been living some values — I just don't 'see' them!" This is exactly right. But here's the 'So What'. If you're Single in this culture and your values aren't front and center, you can talk yourself into all kinds of conflicted relationships with people who have no values and really don't want to know yours. Mr. or Ms. Single you need to have your values well-articulated and understood so you can date with integrity (remember our 'integrity' discussion?). One more quick story.

I know a Christian man who is working on his faith-based values. Encouragement and hospitality are his strengths ('Relator' in Strengthsfinders language), and he uses them well. Always a smile on his face; always genuinely glad to see you. No agenda behind the façade, just wants to share his latest experiences with you. But he also wants to hear you. He wants to build *you* up — not himself. Do you know someone like this? You see them coming and you immediately anticipate a little surge of encouragement, of appreciation. They appreciate you! I hope you have people like this in your life. Where would we be without them? Now, this Single man is working on articulating his values, on speaking them clearly. For the moment, the only other thing you need to know is that this man's faith is genuine and heartfelt — as far as I can tell. He's working on his commitment to God and building his serious faith in God, all of which is easy to say, much harder to do. So with that little background, here's the story.

You know how relationships go through an ebb and flow? Particularly man-woman relationships. For this man, he has known and dated an attractive woman intermittently over the past couple of years. The question is, should they reestablish this former dating relationship? The infatuation danger has subsided — at least a little bit — because they have known each other over an extended period. As he is working on rebuilding this relationship, he is having honest discussions with this woman, and they are starting to think about moving through the dating process towards the lifetime marriage commitment. I can imagine the discussion — perhaps sitting in a car? As Christians, they both agree that marriage should be for life. Perfect match, right? Not so fast. As he works to express the depth of commitment he is feeling to know and honor God, he notices her listening, but not really embracing, the reality of what he is saying. Does she argue, disagree, contradict? No. She just doesn't share his commitment level, or his enthusiasm, or his future relationship vision. She doesn't value his *values*. If they were in the midst of fluffy infatuation or sexual entanglement, it would be so easy to be deluded into believing this was *the* relationship. But in the clarity of his thinking he knows, in the long run, there is frustration and ineffectiveness waiting for him. He sees ahead and considers the deadness of a relationship without complimentary values, and he chooses to move on. Along with the decision comes a sense of freedom, of exhilaration. The rest of the story is yet to be determined. Relationships are a work in progress aren't they?

The challenge of faith-based decisions is the uncertainty ahead. Values-based decisions aren't easy. I became a Christian when I was 28 years old, and it was a definitive and dramatic moment for me. As I have continued, I know God has done specific and consistent things in my life to further define who I am. Saying "I am a Christian" is just a buzz phrase. Once again, I apologize for the popular connotations it may bring to your mind.[39] My key personal value, however, is to be a Spirit-abiding man of Christ. If you and I were sharing time and you were curious, I could tell you the intimate details of how God communicated this #1 value to me — and I'll briefly discuss this later on. But this book is not about me; it's about you! It's about you using your values in your relationships, making all your relationships better, and moving on to dating relationships when the time is right. Two marks of a good Personal Value.

---

[39] A recent study of 18-29 year olds who have grown up in the church yielded this: One quarter of them said Christians demonize everything outside the church and 23 percent said the church ignores the problems of the real world. Regrettably the culture's stereotype of Christians is often that we're a group of religious people mad about stuff. Mad about abortion, mad about gay rights, mad about America losing its moral footing. Steve Massey Spokesman Review, 2/15/14.

Personal Values are unique to you. You must 'own' them.
Personal Values reliably call you to a higher level of living

A good Core Value always will stretch you to live better, more consistently, and with reliable commitment. I find a good Personal Core Value has enough stretch in it so that I don't live up to it as well as I would like. In the Christian world, saying that you are a 'Spirit-abiding man of Christ' almost comes off as being arrogant, and I have to explain how God *directly* gave me that central Core Value. To do what this value suggests is an unreachable goal, but it's one that keeps me thinking upward. To some extent, I *fail* this value every day. I might wander around for two or three hours ignoring God, ignoring what He might be telling me, or being oblivious to the people in front of me who need support and encouragement. Fortunately, I know that His forgiveness is a five-second prayer away and I can move on. So my Personal Core Value still drives my choices on a daily basis and the result is tangible, make-a-difference behavior. My Core Value calls me higher. Your values can do the same for you. Let's get yours underway.

Unpacking your suitcase

Remember my claim that "a picture is worth ten thousand words"? So what does the picture tell you? Is he going to a job interview? Does he dress like this every day? Is he wealthy? Where does he get his money? Did he rent his suit? Pictures are powerful, but when it comes to people, there is a *lot* more complexity. Does he have ripped abs? What is his job? Is he a Greek tycoon?

Then, there is that little guy in the lower right corner. What is he doing? He's pasting up an image, that's what he is doing. This guy has worked to present a carefully crafted image. Maybe he has a financial degree and wants to be hired by a bank. Perhaps he never wears a tie ex-

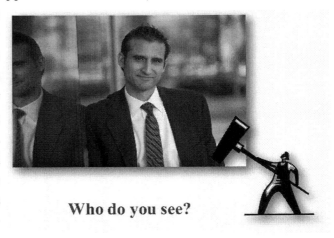

Who do you see?

cept at the bank. When you finally get to talk to him, all the 'impression' comes flowing out from the first words, the voice inflection and tone, and you get to hear what he says (content). Often the phrasing is so culturally driven that there is little surprise: it all sounds so familiar. "Really?" As I write this section, there is a TV show on where they are interviewing Rob Walters, a UK fashion plate. He looks like the guy in the picture above, without the ethnic edges. He wears a nice sports coat, but no tie. He has made millions as a male model. The talk show host questioned Rob about his future wife. "She must have a butt of epic proportions" and, "Yes, I'm truly looking for love." An epic butt to bolster his epic image.

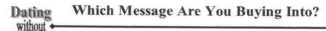

Heath L. Buckmaster

"Often it's not about becoming a new person, but becoming the person you were meant to be, and already are, but don't know how to be."

So here is the ongoing dilemma. The culture tells you that you can create yourself; you can craft and adapt your image. The culture tells you that

Which Message Are You Buying Into?

• Self-Directed
• Self-Focused
• Self-Centered
• Self-Determined
Self-*Deluded*

Or Will You Be:

Gen 24: 1-14

• **God-Directed**
• **God-Focused**
• **God-Centered**
• **God-Designed**

you can morph yourself on Facebook; that's what a lot of people use it for. I recently watched an older lady post a provocative picture of herself, in a bathing suit, on Facebook. To once again borrow a culturally relevant phrase, "Really?" The culture tells you that you must adapt to fit in. Look at our watch lady above. See the tiny little text below her picture? It says, "Who will you be in the next 24 hours?" As if changing your watch can change your entire persona. As if you can swap out personal beliefs and values for a new self at the drop of the hat. As you can see in the text I have dropped in, that is being *self-deluded*.

The picture on the right-hand side shows Isaac and Rachael. Remember the story? Isaac trusted God to select his wife from a distant tribe, trusting that the Lord would guide the selection. Now, I'm asking you to trust God in how he made you. There is a lot to discover. There are so many modern resources now, it's a little overwhelming. Isn't it nice that I've narrowed it down for you to three? My experience in the seminar tells me that most people haven't taken the time to use *any* of the resources. And knowing yourself, as you will see, is essential for better relationships.

Now, consider dating. It's about you having personal transparency, which by itself is a tough challenge. It's also about getting to honestly know someone else. *Personal Transparency* is tough. But how else can we create guitar-string purity in the 'notes' of our relationships?

Discovering the 'Baggage' in your suitcase?

I have struggled mightily trying to figure out where to put this suitcase section of our discussion. I put it here at the front end of the Personal Values section because your Values — without a doubt — will strongly be influenced by the 'stuff' coming out of your childhood. When you get to the Personal Values worksheets you need to be ready to factor in the learnings which come from an objective look at your child-hood. So here we go!

We all bring baggage. And not all baggage is bad. It is an integral part of who we are. One woman in a recent seminar said she had heard the saying, "God had packed our suitcases." Yes, the Bible is filled with many references to the fact that God has *equipped* us with gifts and abilities[40]. Hopefully, you have taken advantage of the three modern tools available to help you discover *your* talents and strengths, per-

---

[40] Romans 12; Ephesians 4, etc.

sonality disposition, and spiritual gifts. If you want an easier starter, go do Love Languages (which is a great way to start the process!). In Part One, I hope you embraced these first steps. On the other hand, you have also heard counselors and psychologists talk about the 'baggage' that we bring from the often-difficult circumstances in our childhoods. Yes, other 'stuff' besides gifts, talents, strengths, and callings are packed in your 'suitcase.'

The iceberg represents the complexity that is you. Have you heard that 90 percent of the 'berg' is underwater, out of view? That's the part that sunk the Titanic! So here we are, beginning the work that you need to do to increase your self-awareness, all of which is a big move forward toward self-transparency, what I have been calling personal transparency. Yes, you need to comprehend and embrace God's design for your life. Articulating your Personal Values is the critical first step. Knowing how you are pre-dispositioned for relationship problems is the second essential step.

Here, I would like to introduce you to Harville Hendrix, a long-time marriage therapist and author of one of the books I recommend for your Relationship Library, *Getting the Love You Want.* Harville asks you and me to recognize that during our childhood years, we all were impacted by the way we were raised. Harville makes the critical connection between how we were parented and what our romantic attractions are today, in our adult years. Many of you will say, "I didn't really have any parents" or, "I only had one parent, and it was tough!" As children, we had parental — and other — influences working subconsciously to drive the romantic attractions in our adult lives. He calls this the Phenomena of Recognition.

The chart on the next page summarizes Harville's proposition, which is the result of decades of work on his part as a professional therapist and counselor. You meet someone who triggers the subconscious recognition of traits and behavior we experienced during our childhood and BOOM! Hormones are released in our brains that create attractions which are both magnetic and powerful. As you see in the chart, these phenomena appear as intense feelings of familiarity. The familiarity is a precursor/predictor/symptom of romantic attraction. Listen to Harville describe the effect that he calls 'Imago' (I-MAH-go, Greek for Image):

> *"Many people have a hard time accepting the idea that they have searched for partners who resembled their caretakers. On a conscious level, they were looking*

for people with only positive traits — people who were, among other things, kind, loving, good-looking, intelligent, and creative. In fact, if they had an unhappy childhood, they may have deliberately searched for people who were radically different from their caretakers. They told themselves, "I'll never marry a drunkard like my father," or "There's no way I'm going to marry a tyrant like my mother." But, no matter what their conscious intentions, most people are attracted to mates who have their caretakers' positive and negative traits, and, typically, <u>the negative traits are more influential.</u> I came to this sobering conclusion only after listening to hundreds of couples talk about their partners. At some point during the course of therapy, just about every person would turn angrily to his or her pause and say, "You treat me just the way my mother did!" Or "You make me feel just as helpless and frustrated as my stepfather did!" (Underline mine)

Dating without Delusion   'The Universal Language of Love' Harville Hendrix ←——————→

Phenomenon	***Sounds Like.......***
* **Phenomenon of Recognition**	* **'I Feel As If I Already Know You....'**
* **Phenomenon of Timelessness**	* **'I Can't Remember When I Didn't Know You....'**
* **Phenomenon of Reunification**	* **'When I'm With You, I Feel Complete!'**
* **Phenomenon of Necessity**	* **'I Can't Live Without You....'**

'Bells & Whistles' may be your hormone-induced warning signal!

And here is his conclusion: *"With few exceptions the traits that matched up the most closely were the negative traits! Why do negative traits have such an appeal? If people chose mates on a logical basis, they would look for partners who compensated for their parents' inadequacies, rather than duplicated them. If your parents wounded you by being unreliable, for example, the sensible course of action would be to marry a dependable person, someone who would help you overcome your fear of abandonment. If your parents wounded you by being overprotective, the practical solution would be to look for someone who allowed you plenty of psychic space so that you could overcome your fear of absorption. The part of your brain that directed your search for a mate,* *however, was not your logical, orderly new brain; it was your time-Locked, myopic old brain. <u>And what your old brain was trying to do was re-create the conditions of your upbringing, in order to correct them.</u> Having received enough nurturing to survive but not enough to feel satisfied, it was attempting to return to the scene of your original frustration so that you could resolve your unfinished business." (Underline mine)*

Getting the Love You Want is a solid effort by a gifted therapist to help people create harmony and understanding in marriage, thereby enabling them to build a more 'Open Marriage' (his term). I bring you to Harville's work now, *while you are Single,* so that you might become aware of what's going on in your mind and emotions. You *can* be equipped to manage that attraction through honest self-evaluation, personal awareness and, I would add, prayer. Unfortunately, in the dating seminars and in life in general, I see many people attracted to the same flawed personality type over and over again. Then, they wonder why they can't keep a relationship together or why they have serial relationships with the same kinds of dysfunctional partners. Haven't you known and seen some of your friends fail in multiple relationships with people with nearly the same dysfunctions, over and over again? From your standpoint, you think that one failed relationship/marriage should be enough to learn from. But you and I underestimate the power of these deep psychological challenges.

This effect is what I hear people refer to as all of those 'feelings.' "I *feel* as if I already know you." "When I'm with you, I *feel* complete." In the very front of Harville's book he cites the story of Maggie, who meets a man named Victor. When she first meets Victor she says,

"I had the strangest reaction. My legs wanted to carry me to him, but my head was telling me to stay away. The feelings were so strong that I felt faint and had to sit down."[41]

Put that entire emotional surge together with compatibility — like a common activity or Interest — and you've got trouble... potentially BIG trouble, simply because the attraction and the person you are — as described in your Personal Values — may be at odds with one another. You find that you love true and deep honesty, so much so that it has become one of your Personal Values. And you discover that you have a magnetic attraction to people who are chronic exaggerators, gossips, or outright liars. Red alert! Call it the *Infat-*

---

[41] *Getting the Love You Want,* p. 3

uation/Values Disconnect.

Is strong attraction good? Well, maybe. And yes, compatibility is a good thing; but combine that compatibility with the 'evil little twin' of infatuation and you can quickly become convinced this person is the one that "I can't live without." Compatibility and the 'evil little twin' can combine to send people into a near swoon, down the emotional slide to spontaneously hurtful relationships and anemic-at-best marriages. More probably, the slide will end in a crippling divorce.

All of the above is why I am very critical of the concept of a 'soul mate.' I've seen the most romantically inclined/emotionally intense couples think they had 'found the one.' Reality is that every successful married couple will have to learn all of the relationship, communication, and forgiveness skills, just like everyone else who is going to have a stable marriage.

More validation? Here's Laura Schlesinger from *10 Stupid Mistakes:*

THE "BUT I LOVE HIM" FOLLIES[42]. *When my caller Jody pleaded, "But I love him..." I suggested that her idea of love — from what she'd described to me — had gotten her into trouble so many times before and was getting her into trouble again. My advice was emphatically not to use those feelings she calls love to make a relationship decision. Since they inevitably led her to the wrong decision, she would do better to tough it out now and spare herself the endless anguish she might otherwise be setting herself up for.*

THE LOVE STUFF ISN'T A DIVINE DIRECTIVE. *Women like Jody must learn that hormones and heart are not necessarily our best leaders. This love stuff is not an omen or divine directive — so stop wallowing in it! If you find your rational sense being overridden by mushy feelings ... know that you are probably on the wrong track! Stop with the "Oh, I know he's (fill in the blank with abusive... mean...cold... uncommunicative... negative... bullying or violent... addicted... controlling, workaholic, jealous, etc.), but I love him." The "I love him" does not erase what came before!*

MY ACID TEST FOR GENUINE LOVE. *I feel certain that what many women call love, under so many obviously ugly, hurtful, and sometimes downright dangerous situations, is more about passion and promise and fantasies and desperate dependencies and fears about taking on alternatives. Real love is a long marination of qualities having to do with respect, admiration, appreciation, character, affection, cooperation,*

---

[42] Schlesinger, Laura. *10 Stupid Things Women do to Mess Up Their Lives,* p. 54; Stupid Devotion

honor, and sacrifice. I ask all these "I love him" women the same question: "If you were a parent, would you introduce this kind of guy–or even this guy – to your daughter?" Funny how the answer is always an emphatic No!

More validation? Back in the '90s, this suitcase concept was also nicely captured in the *San Diego Union Tribune*. 'The Relationship Radar' idea is succinctly presented in the short articled that I have scanned for you below. The 'Homing in on the 'Mr. Bad-for-Me Guy' article is one more documentation of the Imago concept drawn out in detail in *Getting the Love You Want*. This

article offers two encouraging points:

1) We can be aware and begin to change patterns, and

2) We can rather quickly and effectively change our self-esteem.

3) Number two is not so easy, as you will see.

To begin your 'Unpacking Your Suitcase' work, I have adapted two of Harville's awareness tools for introduction in the seminar. My experience is that this kind of self-awareness only comes from real effort over a longer period of time. So don't disregard or put off this essential self-examination. The sooner you start, the sooner you will be able to combine your new self-awareness with your Personal Values to start the sometimes lonely road to comprehending yourself — and achieving personal transparency.

Let's look at the first tool adapted from *Getting the Love You Want*. The idea of this chart is for you to very briefly list in the circle the Positive Traits (in the B section) and the Negative Traits (in the A section) of your primary caretakers.[43] Part C asks, "What I wanted most as a child and didn't get was_____." Part D asks, "As a child, I had these negative feelings over and over again: _____." In my experience, people in the seminar can very quickly point out one or two key pieces of information, and quickly fill

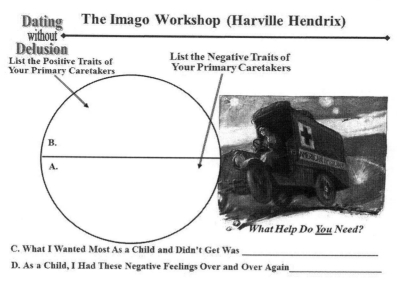

Dating without Delusion

The Imago Workshop (Harville Hendrix)

List the Positive Traits of Your Primary Caretakers

List the Negative Traits of Your Primary Caretakers

B.

A.

What Help Do You Need?

C. What I Wanted Most As a Child and Didn't Get Was _____

D. As a Child, I Had These Negative Feelings Over and Over Again _____

in the blanks. So what, you ask? Using myself as an example, I'll recount my childhood with my father and stepmother. It was beyond volatile; it was often violent. I experienced dramatic screaming. The full-blown violence included police response and full neighborhood disruption. As dozens of people congregated in the street to gawk at what was going on, I remember one of my neighborhood friends offering me a cigarette to ease my whatever. At the time, that struck me as odd: I never thought of cigarettes as a calming solution. The whole scene was surreal. So what did I want that I never had? A normal, peaceful home. What negative feelings did I have? I felt that I would never have the nurturing and peaceful home that I saw my friends enjoying. And sure enough, I didn't ever get it. After the inevitable divorce, my father asked one of the neighborhood families to take me in, which they

---

[43] *Getting the Love You Want*, p. 211

did. Fortunately, that family was very healthy: a saving blessing that gave me respite from the turmoil. The next year, I went off to preparatory school in New Hampshire. Compared to what I had experienced at home, the school was a model of predictability and stability. It really did save me in many ways.

But oh, how the repercussions rolled, and I still deal with them today. Like what? you ask. Even today, one of my need-to-haves is a stable home and household. And Debra seemed to fit the mold, with her Harmonizing, Hospitality skills and very warm disposition. Little did I know that in her childhood was a distinct kind of volatility that she experienced as her mom and dad screamed at each other over the household budget, or over the next tax return. Please remember, though, I never heard those stories until after we were married.

Let's hear the quote from Harville Hendrix:

"If your parents wounded you by being unstable and volatile, the practical solution would be to look for someone who allowed you plenty of psychic relationship space so that you could overcome your fear of instability. The part of your brain that directed your search for a mate, however, was not your logical, orderly new brain; it was your time-locked, myopic old brain. And what your old brain was trying to do was re-create the conditions of your upbringing, in order to correct them. Having received enough nurturing to survive but not enough to feel satisfied, it was attempting to return to the scene of your original frustration so that you could resolve your unfinished business." (Underline mine).

Sure enough, my brain picked out Debra, who in some ways was a person with who I could 'return to the original scene of the frustration.' That was parents arguing. In the seminars, people use these little Harville Hendrix excerpts to begin their own self-examination. All because we are trying to foster relationships having an inherent stability, not the other way around.

So how to deal with this? First and foremost is *recognition;* Harville's tool does that for me, and hopefully for you too. During this entire discussion, if you have alarming moments or flashes of doubt and fear, please remember to take advantage of professional help. The next step is honest discussion. As you can guess, I had to explain to Debra that screaming/yelling were really a problem for me. Yes, I could be provoked to angry responses — just like I learned in my childhood. In Part Three, there are also some key relationship resources (see 'Stopping the Four Horsemen' in the Tools section) that are designed for couples to exercise conflict resolution and experience better, more forthright and timely communication. Lastly/firstly there is prayer, which Debra and I exercise regularly and which provokes us to humility and gentleness... as opposed to the other way around... which would be pride and arrogance.

Let's look at another tool, which is the complementary Imago tool from Harville Hendrix. This one uses the information from the previous chart. Look back at the A, C, D entries on the Imago chart, the one with the ambulance on it. As you can see above, the A, C, and D entries are the sources of *frustration* in the Frustration/Response sequence. Now that you are familiar with my crazy childhood, you are also familiar with the frustrations and disappointments I experienced as a young boy. So the question is, *how did I respond* to that frustration? The answer? I would get on my bike and head over to my friend's house. Yep, the friend with the stable family, nicely manicured lawn, and basketball hoop over the garage door. Not surprised, are you? My

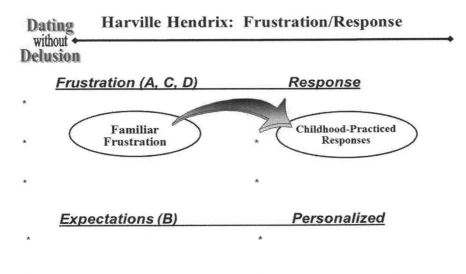

response was to *escape*. So I don't have to tell you that my practiced response is the one that I'll naturally and immaturely revert to when a screaming episode begins. So if I pick a screaming partner, which I am predisposed to do, I'll repeat the very unhealthy response of escaping: a form of the no-communication stonewalling response. Here's Harville in *Getting the Love You Want*:

> *"It is especially easy for people to transfer their feelings about their parents onto their partners, because, through a process of unconscious selection, they have chosen part-*

ners who resemble their caretakers. All they have to do is exaggerate the similarities between them and diminish the differences." (Hendrix p. 49)

Thank God, Debra has learned not to go into high-pitched, out-of-control accusations, which helps me very tangibly. It also gives me the space to work on more normal and rational communication. She understands, because we have had some open discussions about my childhood and the difficulties I experienced as a child. Ask her and she'll tell you that there are plenty of times that she feels like screaming at me for my poor listening/relating skills. She

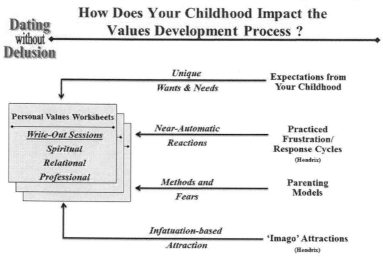

would also tell you that God gives her an extra measure of patience during these times, and it all is grounded in her better understanding of me... and of God.

On the flip side, if you had the time and energy, I could recount all of the similarities that I shared with her dad. Her dad was a service veteran, her dad was an aviator, her dad loved cars, and so on. Her dad had a propensity towards anger, just like I picked up from my dad. These very familiar, subconsciously selected traits significantly and subtly influenced her attraction to me. As Harville says, the *process of unconscious selection* was in full-swing operation, whether we recognized it or not. On a positive note, Debra's mom and dad also had a no-divorce, lifetime commitment-kind of marriage. Debra got to see real commitment lived out in her parents' marriage: a very good thing. In today's world, a very rare thing.

So as you see in the chart above it is very important for you to do your childhood investigation work (guided by Harville Hendrix's self-examination tools), and then go back and take another look at your Personal Values development worksheets. How will this Imago-based insight influence your Personal Values? It's almost unpredictable until you take the time to do it.

Do you see that dating and marriage based upon these subtle and powerful attractions, like feelings of 'completeness,' are very, very tenuous? Meaning: unstable! It's almost like we are predisposed to hurt each other as we were hurt in our childhoods. This is why people go into marriage, get hurt in predictable ways, get divorced, and then go out and do it again, with the same kind of partners that they subconsciously 'selected.' All of this is particularly true for people who are more severely impacted by dysfunctional childhoods. Depending on the depth of the dysfunction in your childhood, the depth and intensity of your attractions to the bad boys/bad girls may be *very* intense. As Jeff Herring said in the *San Diego Union Tribune* article, "Homing in on the Mr. Bad-for-Me Guy" is a real deal. It lurks beneath many of the infatuations you've seen and experienced. The 'evil little twin' hooks up with a little Compatibility and the race to marriage — and a divorce — is on.

Having this discussion in a class is a great place to get this out in the open because I'm usually talking to people who want to get off the infatuation merry-go-round. There are always at least two or three people in the class who are doing this kind of infatuation loop, so when they see what is happening, the light bulb goes on. They nod their heads in knowing agreement because for the first time they are starting to understand *why* they have been having such trouble in dating relationships. Now, if you still don't totally agree with my emphasis on Personal Values, please reconsider. Using values as a filter for *who* you date and a basis for *how* you date gives you some tangible relationship 'space' to work with.

One last point on the Harville Hendrix slide. Our childhood may have some great, positive, uplifting, and memorable elements to it. When a growing-up experience is good, it shouldn't be surprising that we want to recreate those good experiences and good feelings. Please remember that the person you are dating may have never experienced anything like the warmth and love that you felt as a kid. So explain it to them. They may have never had close and caring moments like you did with your parents. Help your dating partner by being very open about your expectations and needs. Certainly by the time you are dating exclusively, these are important facts to share.

Meet the parents?!

If you have taken my advice to use the Harville Hendrix tools, you are gaining some valuable self-awareness. The worse your childhood, the more urgent this task is for you. Now, let's look forward to dating. When we get into the dating process in Part Two, I'm not going to ask you to trot out your deeply felt childhood hurts in the early dating process. Instead, be relentlessly transparent with your Personal Values. Don't fall into the trap of over self-exposure in the early phases of dating. You can continue the depth of your honesty as your relationship grows and matures over time. Once you make a commitment to date someone exclusively, *then* I am going to ask you to continue this discussion in earnest. When you get to exclusive dating stage, having done this self-assessment, you will be ready for some careful dialogue with your dating partner. The problem is, he may not have *any* understanding of his difficult, probably marred-by-divorce childhood. She may not have really considered how her addicted and absentee father has driven a fear of abandonment into her mind and spirit. These kinds of discussions are not easy and they are not flattering; I recommend that you undertake these conversations with someone you trust — like your accountability partner — before you dive into self-exposure with someone you are dating.

When you do make the essential transition to exclusive dating — as you will see in Part Two — it is then essential to be ever more open with the person that someday might be your husband or wife. So what's the deal about 'meeting the parents'? Remember, we talked about 'Connecting' the person you are dating to the life domains where you live out your key commitments. Invite the person you are dating to come with you to the 'Growing spiritually' class...to the benevolence food bank...to the VA hospital...to your spiritually based home group. Why? Because you want them to know you better by seeing you in your values elements. You get the benefit of seeing how that person reacts to one of your values-based activities. If they experience a gut-level discomfort — it may tell you a lot.

The same thing is true for meeting the parents. At some point, you can benefit from see-

Mitch Album

Dating without Delusion

"All parents damage their children. It cannot be helped. Youth like pristine glass, absorbs the prints of its handlers. Some parents smudge, others crack, a few shatter childhoods completely into jagged little pieces, beyond repair."

ing the real-life relationship of your dating partner with his or her parents. Particularly watch the relationship between him and his mother, or her and her father. I'm not asking you to be a psychologist. I am asking you to be wise in understanding that he experienced a whole childhood with that parent relationship, whether they were there or not. Absence is also a huge influencer. She developed frustrations that she learned to cope with. He had deep desires in his childhood that weren't met, for whatever reason. We all have had to adapt to difficult circumstances, we all have been affected by those circumstances, and we all have 'adapted.' So should you meet the parents? If it doesn't mean re-opening family rifts or re-creating a family upheaval — I say yes. These personal insights are a backdrop to the development of your values. They also provide essential insight you will need when you decide to date someone intentionally and exclusively. As far as Mitch Album's quote — which is mostly true — the 'beyond repair' thought does not take into account God's healing capacity. With that said, let's move on to the values-worksheets.

Your spiritual domain (and a Worksheet)

I am giving you a Personal Core Value system that you can follow to discover your essential ingredients. It's step-by-step. You already started the process when you did your online work with the self-assessments, and with the little exercises brought to us by Harville Hendrix in _Getting the Love You Want._ You no doubt discovered some very important things about yourself. All this happens as you look back at yourself through the lens of the tools.

I divide values into three distinct areas: Spiritual, Relational, and Professional. If you have another area to add, go ahead and do it! Just remember, to be effective, you probably are not going to develop and apply more than six or seven quality Core Values. The one area where there sometimes is better understanding is in the area of family relationships. In the instances where people talk about their work values, they often revert to talking about _what_ they do as opposed to _who_ they are at work. So watch out for that pitfall.

From this point, we move on to discuss what a value is and what kind of personal clarity it provides. To accomplish this, we work on worksheets designed to pull out key life experiences, beliefs, and relationships. You have taken the online assessments. I hope you've been honest about the contents of your 'suitcase.' Now, the discussion turns to why and how those are definitive. Here I provide you with three worksheets: one is designed for spiritual values, one for family and relational values, and one for professional/occu-

Personal Core Values Worksheet
Spiritual Domain

Dating without Delusion

How has God Revealed Himself to You?:_____
(an Event, a Deliverance, an 'Impossible' Occurrence)

How did You Receive Christ?: _____
(Key new Life-changing belief, the Location, the Circumstance, the Effects)

What are Your Spiritual Gifts?:_____
(From Ephesians Four or other testing source)

What is Your Personality Profile:_____
(From DiSC, MBTI, or Kiersy/Bates or ?)

What are Your Top 5 Talents/Strengths:_____
(From Strengthsfinders)

How do You Serve (Give back)? _____
(Charitable or Church Commitments)

What are Your Best Worship Habits/Disciplines?_____

Describe a Defining Moment with God:_____

What is Your Favorite Bible Verse?:_____

What is Your Favorite Bible Story? Why?:_____

What Problem Tendencies Do You Now See?_____

pational values. Let's look at the spiritual values worksheet first. When you complete the three worksheets, I'll ask you to sit back and succinctly summarize what you have been reminded of about yourself. On the left-hand side of the worksheet are fill-in-the-blank areas for spiritual input. I share my experiences because that is what I have. I only use these as examples, knowing that you have a rich life databank of your own unique experiences. Let's start at the top, and then discuss each entry as we move down the page.

How has God revealed himself to you? God has dramatically intersected your life, and you know those circumstances; what are they? If you are not yet a faith person, you probably can still recall improbable circumstances where you skirted disaster or received an unexpected reprieve. When I was dating Debra, we went to a wedding ceremony as a couple. One of the rituals I really dislike is the garter toss, and I was trying to avoid this one by retreating to the corner of the room. Just before the toss happened, a chant started, "Jay, Jay, Jay." Thanks a lot, guys; so much for avoiding the hated pagan ritual. I went to the lineup, where there were about 12 guys waiting for the groom to slingshot the garter in our direction. They did a drum roll, the groom aimed the garter in our direction, and then faked the shot as the drum roll reached a crescendo. I thought, "I *really* hate this thing," and he did the whole faking the shot again. "How stupid can this get?" I thought. The third time he went through this routine, the groom was really going to shoot the garter. Standing on the far right of the Single-guy lineup, I elevated my hands to waist-height, palms up, and closed my eyes. The garter flew through the air, crossing the 25 feet between us and the groom. It somehow avoided the jumping-in-the-air Single guys trying to intercept it and landed perfectly into my upturned left palm — remember, my eyes were shut tight. I felt the thing hit my palm, and snapped open my eyes in total disbelief. Needless to say, the crowd thought this was pretty funny. To this day, I still marvel at God's sense of humor *and* the statistical impossibility of what happened. I had plenty of real reasons to doubt the wisdom of marrying Debra, and I needed something dramatic from the Lord — that is divine revelation — to help with that decision. Guess I got it. You'll see how this experience is incorporated into my Personal Core Values at the conclusion of this segment.

I contend that everyone has been 'intersected' by God. It may be that He saved you from a car accident. A good friend's dad is an USMC veteran who fought at Iwo Jima, among other Pacific theaters. In the heat of the conflict, he had a mortar round hit the ground right between his legs (he was sitting down). The mortar didn't explode and he lived to tell the tale. That was a faith moment for him, and he thanked God for the rescue. What about you? Perhaps He orchestrated an amazing set of circumstances to deliver you from personal ruin, or to turn the tide on an illness or injury. It would be low-integrity for you not to recall, to remember the situation. Write it down.

How did you receive Christ? Let's continue down the left-hand side of the worksheet. For Christians, the buzz term is your 'testimony.' If you have not had this experience and you are not in this place of belief, please just move on. I believe for every person, there is a major objection to the concept of Christianity because they have seen so many Christians live flawed lives, and they accept the negative image of the church and religion as a whole. As with most people, I had an intellectual barrier that was the basis of my objection. Personally, I objected to what I perceived as a religious cookie-cutter mentality in the Christian community. It seemed to me that Christians tried to talk alike, to dress alike, to behave alike: to 'toe the line' that was broadcast to them each week at church. That kind of 'mindless conformity' — my perception — was *not* for me. This was a huge block, a barrier that was very repulsive to me. The Bible calls these 'arguments and pretensions' that set themselves up against the knowledge of God.[44] My adopted brother-and then roommate-challenged me to attend a nearby Bible study "if you say you're so open-minded, Jay." As I attended the Bible study with my commitment to be open-minded, the leader began to unpack the New Testament book of Galatians, where Paul addresses this human tendency to 'work for God.' You know how it goes: "I'm working hard for God, shouldn't you?" or, "This is the way to work for God; let me show you how." This very fine teacher in Newport, Rhode Island carefully but powerfully blew up this notion. Yes, we are individuals who are not earning salvation, but accepting it as a gift. Our belief is the linchpin, as summarized in Galatians 3:5:

> "...does God give you His Spirit and work miracles among you by the works of the law, or by your _believing_ what you hear?" (Underline mine)

When I heard this explanation, I came to the realization that God _did_ make me unique and he didn't want any works-based imitations. My big intellectual objection came crashing to the ground. It is God who has carefully crafted a plan for my life, and it's my job to find that unique plan. No puppet shows, though. A real, unique, and tangible plan waited for me in my belief. That evening, I became a Christian. So now I believe 'God has a Plan'.

It's that definitive moment when you received Jesus' sacrifice for your sin — at the Cross-crucifixion event. After the moment, there should be some dramatic change in your life; personally, I think this change is different for every one of us. When the Creator of the universe invades your life,[45] the changes should be life-altering and ultimately memorable, don't you think? For me, it happened at that little Bible study in Newport, Rhode Island. From that moment, profanity dropped from me like dead weight and the next time I opened the Bible, the words exploded off the page to me. Are you getting the idea of this worksheet? In this slot, I simply write 'Newport Bible study, 1977.' If you can't nail down that moment, take the time right now to acknowledge Jesus' love and sacrifice for you, accept Him again, and then why not ask Him for some dramatic affirmation? We often don't receive because we don't ask.

---

[44] 2 Corinthians 10:5

[45] The doctrine of the Holy Spirit is well documented in many Bible passages, most notably Acts 2. _The Holman Study Bible_ says, "When Jesus is Lord, the Spirit is at work. The major work of the Spirit is to pour God's love into the hearts of people so that they begin to love God and to love one another." (Holman _Disciples Study Bible Summary of the Doctrine of the Holy Spirit;_ p. 1669).

The short entry on your worksheet is a cue to an essential experience that has contributed to your entire spiritual makeup.

What are your spiritual gifts? This is simply a summary of your test-validated gifts. Whether it is from the spiritual gifts inventory in Ephesians Four Ministries or from some other reputable source, get the results on paper as a reminder. Look back at the summary sheet you filled out to capture your assessment results.

What is your personality profile? Remember, I use DISC; you may have experience with another tool. Here, write down the learning that best describes your profile with its summarized characteristics. Some of the best tools will also alert you to problem tendencies of your personal disposition.

What are your top five talents/strengths? Please take Strengthsfinders, if you haven't already, and take the time to understand its results. Remember our analyses of King David? That rich databank of information about yourself is waiting for you.

How do you serve (give back)? This is the way that you are giving back, from you to the world. Giving money is good. Giving of yourself through church, an established charity, or some other focused service organization is better. I have friends that work with the leukemia organizations; I have friends who work hard for the USO; I have friends who work on service for veterans — all great service commitments. If you are a church member, how has God fit you into the church as a whole, allowing you to make your unique contribution to the larger body of Christians — remember 1 Corinthians 12? Ideally, you have a good grasp on your gifts and strengths, and you're using them to give back on a weekly basis. My personal entry here is Singles ministry; later on, you'll see it as one of my key Personal Values: 'To inspire Singles to become the people that God has made them to be.' This value uses my teaching gift, Individualization, and Maximizer strengths; I do it through the seminar and now through this book. How do you use your gifts to serve? Write it down.

What are your best worship habits and disciplines? How do you do your best to stay connected to God and to acknowledge all He does for you. To thank Him for how much He loves you. Most of all, it's *how* you do it. My key Core Value came from God through my adopted mom. She started a process that took over a year by asking me to read a book called *The Vine and the Branch* (Bruce Wilkerson). All the principles are drawn from the gospel of John chapter 15 where Jesus says, "I am the Vine, you are the branch. Abide in me and you will bear much fruit, but apart from me you can do nothing." There are many parallels drawn out in this gospel that are taken out of life in the vineyard. Abiding is the concept that could take a thesis to unpack, and that could be another book in and of itself; nevertheless, bear with me. As it turns out, this entry has become my #1, tie-breaking value, so I'll share the whole story with you.

Later that year, after DeDe (my adopted mom) gave me the Wilkerson book, a couple who had gone to the seminar and applied many of the seminar processes to their relationship[46] asked me to do a reading in their wedding. "Absolutely! What do want me to read?" "Why John 15, of course." Now, wasn't that a funny little 'coincidence'? I often tongue-in-cheek say, wasn't that a nice little 'co-inky-dinky'? Really, I'm making fun of people who observe these divine intersections and then write them off to chance. Fast forward to the fall of that year. A church called me to do a seminar series for their Singles. The seminar went well, I met many wonderful people, and I learned a lot from them and the whole experience. The last day of the seminar, we had a little celebration with cake and all of the accoutrements. To the side of the buffet there was a big wide and flat package with a ribbon and bow on it. "Thank you, Jay. Open it up!" I tore off the wrapping paper and there it was, a framed watercolor of a big bowl of red grapes with the indented inscription below: 'I am the Vine...you are the branch.' Admittedly, I am a slow learner — one of the flip-sides of Strategic/Visionary — but I do learn. In this case, the Lord was telling me, *"This is who I want you to be."*

So how do I try to live up to that value? First and foremost, I try to create a dynamic and daily relationship with the Bible. I have decided that the Bible is God's revelation to us, meaning that He is speaking to us. I have decided that the Bible is *not* 40+ hallucinators writing about what they 'think' God is like. I read, I memorize verses and chapters; I apply the concepts to daily choices and problem areas. Example: I have inherited a propensity towards anger — recall my Harville Hendrix work? I apply a verse from the book of

---

[46] This man also did some very fine values work, writing down his values, redoing my format, and generally becoming clear on who he is.

James that causes me to pause before I blurt out a verbal stupidity: "But let everyone be quick to hear, slow to speak, and slow to anger; for the anger of man does not achieve the righteousness of God." (James 1:19–20; NASB). While I am recalling the scripture I am also hesitating, and listening, and my anger is cooling. If you have taken the time to crack the Bible and check my reference, look down to verse 21. Right there is the principle that I believe is so essential to my Core Value. It says to do this you must "receive the Word _implanted_ which is able to save your souls." (Italics mine).

The ancient monks (don't worry, I have no aspirations for monkhood) are described by Robert Benson in his book, _Living Prayer._ He talks about _lectio, meditatio, contemplatio._ A short translation would be _read, meditate, contemplate._ Bear with me as I extract the descriptions:

> "In **lectio** you begin by reading a scripture passage, slowly, aloud perhaps once or twice or three times. Then you imagine yourself in the setting of the scripture itself. You see yourself as the different characters in the story or the setting, you listen to the sounds that emanate from it, touch the textures, smell its smells, feel its tensions. Then you begin to listen for what it is saying to you, making notes if you think to, not making notes if you do not want to. Journal against it or not. Paint pictures if you like. Or simply sit and say a phrase over to yourself, the phrase that catches your eye and quickens your heart this day. The hearing is prayer itself. The hearing is the beginning of being 'shaped by the Word' as Mulholland calls it."[47]

Do you see it? Take the James phrase above, "receive the Word implanted" (verse 21). Is the Word implanted in me? That's what my Personal Value is calling for. To be honest, _lectio_ continues to stretch me, as the distractions of the morning and day clamor for attention in place of the Word of God.

Once I have engrafted the Word through reading and memorization, then the spiritual process goes to the next level. Again from Robert Benson:

> "That practice is called meditatio, meditation. It is here that the material that you have read and begins to reverse the hold. It starts to work on you rather than you on it. Your imagination begins to move along where it will, and you let it run. It wanders back into the details of your own life, and you follow, letting yourself be taken to a place where the Word wants to take you this day. You do it

---

[47] Benson, Robert. _Living Prayer._ Tarcher/Putnam 375 Hudson Street, NY, NY. 1999. pp. 110,111.

with your heart rather than with your mind."[48] (Underline mine)

'Reverse its hold' is very counter-cultural. It's saying that God is beginning to work on you. It's the opposite of the cultural call — the LIE — to be whoever you want to be. It's also the opposite of you deciding how you are going to work for God. At this point, I hope I have convinced you that the 'be whatever you want to be' idea is an evil lie. We Christians are very vocal about our commitment to the Bible. The reality, for many of us, is the Bible is an afterthought in our daily schedule — me included. Every so often, however, I run into a person who is totally animated and excited. "God is teaching me _____ and I never knew this, I never understood this before!" In our smugness, we dismiss that person as being spiritually immature. Really, *I* am the one who is spiritually uppity and irrelevant. When God reveals something to you, you *should* be excited! The truth may be that our friend may be experiencing a circumstance which injects the truth of scripture into his life and consciousness. Truth is getting traction. Maybe this person has been intersected by the Scriptures, and by the Lord. Maybe this person has taken the time to let the Word 'reverse its hold on him' — *meditatio.*

I contend that memorization is a foundation for meditation. In our accelerating lives, how can we possibly take the time to let the word reverse its hold on us? Memorization helps. You can be driving to the next event and simultaneously mulling over the Word that you have received implanted. I pack my 3x5 cards around, mostly — but not always — forgetting to pull them out for an impromptu review. I'm struggling now with Ephesians chapter 4. I'm struggling with the concepts of unity and maturity, knowing that God wants both from us. I'm struggling with the concept of discipleship and what the word implanted is telling us about it — finding that it defies simple definition. Every time that God intersects all this thinking and struggling, I am always surprised and excited. When I share my excitement about what the Lord of the universe has been revealing to me, my Christian friends look at me with a puzzled look. I'm reminded I feel similar puzzlement when someone shares some important learning with me. Maybe it's because we have been to a place where we have 'contemplated' (*contemplatio*) and received what God wanted to reveal to us? Listening to Robert Benson one last time:

---

[48] Benson, Robert. *Living Prayer.* Tarcher/Putnam 375 Hudson Street, NY, NY. 1999. p. 112

"In two thousand years of devotion even the most saintly of the saints are united on two things about it. Contemplation is the most desirable stage of prayer, and it is also the one no one can explain very well. It is not so much you praying to God, but God praying in you. It is not about supernatural phenomena, although such things can be a part of it from time to time. It often begins with a conscious thought but you cannot predictably think your way into it. It is not something that happens very often, not even for the saints. It may last a few moments or a few hours, so we are told. It is a place that you cannot seek, it will come and find you. But it is the communion of the highest order that we can know here, the closest we can come to union with God."[49] (Underline mine)

As I reread Benson's description of contemplatio, I once again recognize *this* is the place God wants to me to visit, at least on occasion. He knows I have too much of the world in me to stay there very long. But I know how to begin the interchange. "Be still — cease striving — and know that I am God" (Psalm 46:10). It's physical, intellectual, and finally spiritual quiet. Quiet allowing me to listen, to abide. As I sit here rereading what I have written, I feel a repentance that calls me back to dependence on God for this book. That this book might be a blessing to you. So I write on the sheet, 'Bible Memory.' I also add 10C's (10 Commandments) because I have had a good experience trying to live those. Please flip ahead to my filled-out worksheet (pg. 156) to see my simple entries. I spend a lot of effort describing them to you because those simple entries have formed the foundation for my #1 Personal Value — which you'll eventually see on my Personal Values summary sheet. It was relatively easy to look at this entry and see how God has shaped my mind and thinking. To this day, I am still trying to live up to this #1 Personal Core Value, and in true fashion for a good Core value, this is the one I fall short of on a daily basis. But it *never* fails to call me higher: *'Spirit-Abiding Man of Christ.'*

Describe a defining moment with God. I was involved in a Navy aircraft accident in 1972, and at that time I had forgotten church and my faith. The 'wake-up call' experience put me back on the trail to find the God who saved me from drowning. Debra says the story is a lot like the front part of Laura Hildebrand's *Unbroken* — Louie Zamporini — only a shorter version. If you're interested in the details, the complete story is tucked in Appendix B: 'The

---

[49] Benson, Robert. *Living Prayer.* Tarcher/Putnam 375 Hudson Street, NY, NY. 1999. pp. 112, 113.

Demise of PR-03.' I've asked you, on the worksheet, to recall the time — or times — when God delivered you. This was one very dramatic time, of a few, that God rescued me. So on my Spiritual Core Values worksheet — see the graphic — I simply put Navy Aircraft Accident (PR-03 was the call sign of the plane we jumped out of). You can be sure I believe God answered my frantic pre-bailout prayer with saving deliverance. I *know* that if I had not regained consciousness in time to do the essential water entry preparation, I would have drowned — without a doubt. When did God answer one of your urgent 'Save Me' prayers? Write it down.

Let me share one very much more recent personal experience with you. Debra and I used to go to church on Friday evenings. The church is so big they prefer to have some of the members come on Friday evening to ease the crunch on Sunday morning. For us, there is a distinct contemplative atmosphere to the evening service, which we both like. It also frees up Sunday morning to be a truly relaxing day of rest. So there we are at the evening service, which is not so crowded. At some point in the service, I looked around. There was a young guy who I knew was going through a divorce, sitting by himself. There were four or five Single women, sitting by themselves. There was a Single mom with her young son. I could almost tangibly 'feel' their loneliness and emotional hurt. Do I really know any of them personally? No. Did I know their unique and painful circumstances — widowed, divorced, abandoned, separated? No. But that evening, I felt their pain in a very connected way. These people, in the midst of their personally draining circumstances, had made it to church to seek a moment of respite from their 'stuff.' Watching them, I experienced a 'fellowship of suffering:' a deep, heartfelt compassion for each of them in their loneliness. If you asked any one of them, they would no doubt freely own — to honestly admit — the relationship blunders that brought them to this lonely place. Thankfully, they were seeking comfort in church, where we can find the Great Comforter. This experience of 'Godly sorrow' reminded me of who I am: a man with God's call to serve Singles. I could put this more recent experience on my values sheet because it is a fresh reminder.

What is your favorite Bible verse? Or your favorite philosophical saying? It's surprising to see how many Christians have not selected one definitive verse to help them through the day, month, and year. Mine is Colossians 3:17:

"Whatever you do in word or in deed, do all in the name of the Lord Jesus Christ, giving thanks through Him back to God the Father."[50] I love this verse for a number of reasons, perhaps first and foremost because it fits with my Maximizer strength: to always try to make things better. It also helps me fight through nasty jobs and my tendency to be lazy. The verse also talks to the theology of the Trinity — at least two parts of it: the Father and the Son. It talks to the priesthood of Jesus: the idea that we gain access and give our thanks *through* Jesus back to the Father. About His intercession on our behalf. So to keep this verse front and center in my mind, I have put it in my email address: *jparker317@gmail.com*. I put C317 as a little notation on those name tags they ask you to wear at church. Don't be limited by my ideas; get on with it. What's your verse? What's your defining quote or saying? Write it down.

What is your favorite Bible story? Or what is your favorite real-life story? The story I love is the time that Jesus went to the Pharisee's house for dinner (Luke 7) and the prostitute comes in and weeps her tears on His feet, and wipes them with her hair. Simon the Pharisee is amazed; doesn't He know who she is? Jesus takes him aside and tells him a little story. There were two debtors; one owes 50 denarii and the other debtor owes 500 denarii. The debt-holder forgives them both. "Who will love the debt-forgiver more?" asks Jesus. Simon the Pharisee answers, "The debtor who owed the 500 denarii." "You have judged correctly," says Jesus. Turning toward the woman, He says to Simon the Pharisee, "Do you see this woman? I entered your house and you gave me no water for my feet, but she has wet my feet with her tears and wiped them with her hair. You gave me no kiss, but since the time she came in she has not ceased to kiss my feet. You did not anoint my head with oil but she anointed my feet with perfume. For this reason I say to you, her sins, which are many, have been forgiven for she loved much, but he who is for-given little loves little." Then Jesus says to her, "Your sins have been forgiv-en." Those who were reclining at table with Him began to say to themselves, "Who is this man who even forgives sins?" And He said to the woman, "Your faith has saved you. Go in peace."

She receives big forgiveness from God on earth, and her love overflows. In accordance with the little story, Simon the Pharisee feels that he needs little forgiveness — because he, after all, is a priest — consequently he loves (and

---

[50] *New American Standard Bible.*

loves Jesus) very little. For me the message is powerful, clear, and critical: *don't underestimate your sin.* In confessing it and then receiving forgiveness for it, your love for the Lord will increase proportionately. What Bible story do you love? Write it down.

What problem tendencies do you now see? "Problem tendencies? Oh no, not in me!" Yes, in me and in you. Here's the catch: your inclination to err — or, as we would say in the Christian vernacular, to sin — is very unique to you. On our own, we can become experts at disguising our gnarly little bad features. We become very adept at rationalizing them and giving ourselves some slack: "After all, I'm just human!" You probably do it and so do I; when we see ourselves being ourselves, to someone else's offense and discomfort, we are experts at ignoring our problem. So for Jay, his gift of teaching can be very offensive on the golf course, where Jay is not such a good golfer. Jay's Strategic-Visionary thing is really out of place and not-so-needed when the 'whirlwind'[51] of getting the job done today really has to be the top priority. Jay's need for verbal compliments — a love language called 'Words of Affirmation' — is something he needs to acknowledge and get past. My Personal Values work has opened the window of my personal makeup so I can become more genuine and honest. Honest about what I am called to do and honest about the areas where I tend to overdo it. Most of all honest about who I am. Remember one of our early goals in this book? *Personal transparency*! Remember Devil's Ping-Pong? This is one of the ways you *get off the Ping-Pong table*! Combine these 'awarenesses' with a crisp understanding of my Personal Values and callings and I can relate to *everyone*, including God, better.

Now, I'll share my completed spiritual values worksheet (next page). It's a strange mix of history, recalling the past parts of my life. Of God 'intersecting' my life. Of my internal wiring, which I wish I understood better earlier in my life. Of confession, recalling how I am offensive even to the closest people around me. And most importantly, it's a window to see God's calling for me.

In our six-week class schedule, I have asked people to start their Personal Values worksheets at the beginning of each class simply because it is so absolutely foundational to building better relationships. Some people might be bugged because I put off the dating process all the way to week four. Then there are those people who get it. They bring in their worksheets with coffee

---

[51] The Four Disciplines of Execution defines this term.

stains and the marks left over from their peanut butter sandwich. The sheets are crumpled. Notes are scrawled in the margin. They have started to write values statements on multiple pages of yellow notepaper. They are serious, and they are working it. Watching that activity gives me great hope.

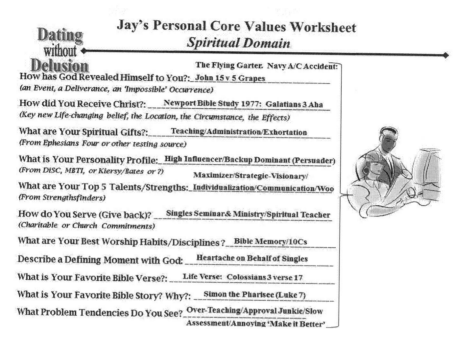

Dating *without* Delusion

Jay's Personal Core Values Worksheet
Spiritual Domain

How has God Revealed Himself to You?: The Flying Garter. Navy A/C Accident: John 15 v 5 Grapes
(an Event, a Deliverance, an 'Impossible' Occurrence)

How did You Receive Christ?: Newport Bible Study 1977: Galatians 3 Aha
(Key new Life-changing belief, the Location, the Circumstance, the Effects)

What are Your Spiritual Gifts?: Teaching/Administration/Exhortation
(From Ephesians Four or other testing source)

What is Your Personality Profile: High Influencer/Backup Dominant (Persuader)
(From DISC, MBTI, or Kiersy/Bates or ?) Maximizer/Strategic-Visionary/

What are Your Top 5 Talents/Strengths: Individualization/Communication/Woo
(From Strengthsfinders)

How do You Serve (Give back)? Singles Seminar& Ministry/Spiritual Teacher
(Charitable or Church Commitments)

What are Your Best Worship Habits/Disciplines? Bible Memory/10Cs

Describe a Defining Moment with God: Heartache on Behalf of Singles

What is Your Favorite Bible Verse?: Life Verse: Colossians 3 verse 17

What is Your Favorite Bible Story? Why?: Simon the Pharisee (Luke 7)

What Problem Tendencies Do You See? Over-Teaching/Approval Junkie/Slow
Assessment/Annoying 'Make it Better'

Is prayer one of your Core Values?

'You're in my prayers...' Someone loses a close friend or family member. A tragedy strikes. Someone loses a job or has a serious illness or accident... and then you hear it: 'You're in my prayers'. Some people really mean it; and others use it as almost a cliché'. The people who mean it have developed a *Lifestyle of Worship*, and you can tell who they are. These people want to have an everyday overflowing relationship with God. Those are the people who you want to pray for you — because they will! For them a relationship with God is not about going to church on Sunday, although they would feel cheated if they didn't get to worship on Sunday. It isn't about going to Wednesday small group, although once again they look forward to sharing time with people who are 'closer than a brother'. It's what the Bible talks about when it refers to 'praying without ceasing'. It's what spiritually serious people are referring to when they use the term, 'my walk with the Lord'. This begs the question 'Is this one of your Core Values?' The National Day of Prayer in 2001 showed this picture of George Washington and a very young man. Both of them faced crises of different sorts no doubt. But the poster is clear: *The face of prayer has changed. The need for prayer has not.* So I'll ask you again, is this one of your Core Values? It might fit on the 'Worship habits and disciplines line'

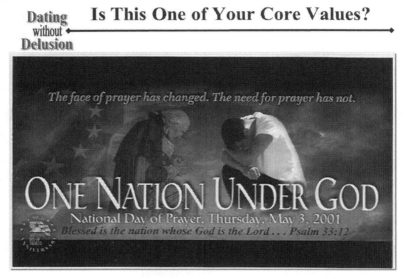

Dating without Delusion

Is This One of Your Core Values?

on the worksheet. Or it might be a defining Personal Value which you adopt and begin to exercise on a regular basis. Be ready to share your new value commitment, and it may begin to really shape your life and relationships.

Your relationship domain (and a Worksheet)

Let's take a look at the next worksheet: the relationship worksheet (below). If you stop and think about it, some relationships are 'defining', meaning that they strongly influence your articulated Personal Values. Once again, remember:

A value is not a value unless it drives your choices.

You can easily see that some relationships *do* drive your choices and some do not. This area is for you to think about your defining personal relationships. Because the Bible is so explicit about honoring your father and mother — in the Fifth Commandment — please start with that.

Your relationship domain should be triggered by the questions, but please don't be limited by those. Use the answers as a good starting point. Let's start with Best Parent Relation. At your best, what kind of son or daughter do you want to be? Even for those of us who are coming out of divorced households, there is an internal desire to honor at least one of our parents. The commandment suggests we honor them both. Then there is Parenting: as a father, as a mother, how do you want to lead your children? Go see the 'Power of

Dating without Delusion

Personal Core Values Worksheet
Relationship Domain

Describe Your Commitments to Your Parent(s): _____
(Father, Mother, or Other Caretaker)

What Kind of Parent do You Want to Be?: _____
(Spiritually, Intellectually, Emotionally...Remember the 'Target Zone')

Do You Have other Defining Family Relationships?: _____
(Uncles, Aunts, Other Relatives, Sisters, Brothers, Cousins)

Do You Have High-Value Friendships?: _____
(People Who You Will Sacrifice for; and Vice Versa)

How do You Relate to Your Accountability Partner?: _____

Do You have Other Defining Relationships?: _____
(Mentors, Pastors, Employers, Counselors, Coaches, Teachers)

Influence' in the Part Three Tools section. By being a whole and values-functioning person, you can have a strong impact on your kids. This value has the added benefit of communicating one of the key roles in your life. A good friend recently lost his wife to cancer, and he has two kids. When he gets through the healing time, he will emerge as a dad who is committed to his kids but with a whole different perspective on future relationships. Anyone who wants to have a relationship with him must clearly understand one of his major life commitments as a Single parent. This value statement should introduce people to an essential part of his life.

Once again, let's look at the top left of the blank Worksheet:

Describe your commitment to your parent(s). So what is your best parent relationship? Are you one of the few fortunate people who grew up in a functional, whole family? Write down your father and mother. For me, my last set of parents — father and second step-mom — passed away in the early 1980's. In their place, DeDe and Pappy unwittingly (but graciously) adopted me, I think because they are the parents of my 'adopted' brothers. As dedicated Christians, they accepted me I say unwittingly because they had no idea of the length and duration of their unspoken commitment to me. Keeping our story short, DeDe and Pappy stood up at the ceremony when I married Debra. They had a pretty big fight the day of the wedding because we were serving wine and beer at the reception, and they were very unsure of how to handle that. (They had quit all alcohol after seeing its effects on military personnel, when Pappy was an Air Force senior officer.) So here I would put down DeDe and Pappy, even though my father loved me intensely and sacrificed a lot to get me through college and onto a Navy career. My father accepted Christ when he was 74 — a dramatic conversion. He passed away when he was 76. As you can see, this is not a math exercise, is it? Relationships are messy, and mine are no exception. When we write this stuff down, do you see what is happening? You start to carve out the defining parts of your life in this segment through your family/personal relationships. You are starting to see where you have been committed to maintain and grow those into even better relationships.

I like to watch college basketball. I get caught on the horns of a dilemma when USD — my graduate school — plays Gonzaga because in the Spokane area, we all pull hard for the Zags. In the Pacific Northwest/Spokane area, this is a tremendous spectacle. The arena holds ~6,000 fans, many of whom are screaming students. In 2012, I got to go with a friend to see the Zags play Notre Dame. With no exaggeration, the Zags handed them a true beat-down. After the game, the Notre Dame coach commented in the newspaper that his guys "weren't ready for that," referring to the electric atmosphere. I also like to watch other college teams, as well. The other night on TV, I saw this point guard with a tattoo, which is not at all remarkable because this generation is going to great lengths to define themselves using every means possible. Facebook and tattoos are just a fraction of the self-creation effort. This tattoo was a full-face shot of a very attractive woman. I have no idea if this was his mother or his girlfriend. (I hope not). So if he is really, really grateful for all that his mom did for him, I can see the basis for a really great Personal Core Value. A Personal Value about his gratefulness for her commitment, her sacrifice, her steadfast support for his school and basketball career.

Do you see the point? His tattoo may start a conversation, but it's the values-based gratefulness this young man wants to express — and he needs to be succinct and clear about why she means so much to him. Remember

Know, Speak, and Live your Personal Values? Sooner or later, he will face a tough circumstance and he better have the strength of commitment to step up to help his mom. That's what relationship values are all about. Is he a deeply grateful son? A great value will remind him to walk the talk for his mom in very specific ways. He'll be lining up with the 5th Commandment, so he should be claiming its promises. On the other hand, if that's his girlfriend indelibly inked onto his arm, uh-oh — guess just I'll say, "No comment."

What kind of parent do you want to be? If you are a parent, I know in the depths of your being, you want to be a wonderful parent. I read somewhere that when you become a parent, you don't get an instruction manual along with the baby. Actually, you get the Bible, which is loaded with parenting instruction, and you also get thousands of how-to books, each one holding the secret to parenting success. And you don't have time to read any of it. If you are Single and a parent — which many, many Singles are — you're really strapped. Strapped for resources, strapped for time. Out of patience, often depressed, and overly reactive to the latest crisis. Nevertheless, you are what you are: a parent to that kid or those kids. What kind of parent do you *want* to be, at your very best? I didn't ask you what kind of parent you are; see the difference? Once again go see the good tool in the tools section entitled 'The Parenting Target Zone'. It may be a great reminder for you. Knowing, Speaking, and Living your Core Values as a model for your kids is the central idea. Check it out. I know you want to be the best parent possible for your kids; what does that sound like? Say it. Write it down.

Other family relations. Over my life, some great families 'took me in' while I was going through difficult life transitions. These families are ones, like DeDe and Pappy, who cared for me with self-less love and acceptance. I enjoyed being a part of a family in Anaheim and sharing life with them as their kids married, grandkids were born, and life rolled itself out. Perhaps you had a grandparent or uncle who cared for you, who sacrificed for you, who provided spiritual stability in your life when everything else was going sideways. You want to acknowledge them. Would you be there for them in crisis? Write down their names.

Best friendship(s). I always say that every relationship has a 'best outcome.' Some friendships are for a season, some friendships are for a particular job or challenge, and some friendships are for life. When we moved to the great

Northwest, we reconnected with people that we had known from many years in San Diego. We're connected with people I knew from many years in Fullerton. Today, we spend time with them regularly, always enjoying the common ground of our pasts and the resolve to move forward to the future, with all of its unknowns. You know it, you feel it: these are friendships for life. Past friendships are all important. But for this entry, I want you to think about the friendships that, for unsearchable reasons, are friendships for life.

Mark, who you got to know in the book intro, and his family fall into the 'for life' category. He was the pastor who led the church I attended for 20 years. I was on his elder board — three times! His youngest daughter is our goddaughter (she is in my will). He has the gift/strength of Ideation. He is always available to *think* about challenges, to *think* about who God is and what He is doing. When ***Dating without Delusion*** was in its infancy, Mark not only encouraged but also dedicated church resources to develop and conduct those seminars. And we had some great ones. At one point we had actors — Mark and Ilona — doing short skits to dramatize relationship principles. Funny...poignant... good. When God 'told' me to write this book, Mark was one who provided important affirmation and encouragement. At a minimum, I write down Mark's family name. Are there others? Of course, but you get the idea. Write down those names.

Back in that era, Debra and I were in a weekly home group that we'd attended for over eight years. With seven couples, we'd come to know one another very personally. I liked to say that we loved each other "because of, and in spite of." *Because* we know the very best things about each other as spiritual people, as parents, as friends sharing life challenges and celebrations. *In spite of* the gnarly personal issues we each face. When Jay leads our weekly study, he teaches too much: the little Yadro disaster, his incessant car-leasing stratagem. One of the couples moved to Palm Springs: no worries. Through care and contact, we still feel connected to them, we still pray for them, and we look forward to seeing them when the time is right — many are the plans on a person's heart! Though they are distant geographically, they are on our minds and hearts and we talk about them, and about seeing them, constantly. By acknowledging these relationships on this work sheet, you'll be reminding yourself to be there for them when they need it. The reverse is also true. *They will be there for you.*

Accountability partner. Since I am married, I really feel my accountability is provided by Debra. Most of the time, she does it with restraint and graciousness. If, on the other hand, you are Single, your same-gender accountability partner is someone who is critical in your life. Back in the 'Tools' section of this book is a nice little tool called 'Your Accountability Partner: Who Should You Choose?' Many seminar people have reiterated how important it is to have sound and wise accountability in their lives. If you have someone like this, write down their name. If you don't, then use the tool to think about building one of your key friendships in that direction.

On this worksheet, you're looking for relationships that, in a sense, define *who you are.* Are you an honoring son? Are you thankful for the examples of spiritual insight and patience your mother never failed to provide? Write them down. If you are not a Christian, modify the worksheet to make it user-friendly for you. It's thought-provoking because it asks you to *own* your relationship beliefs and to articulate those in tight value phrases. Write down those names. [52]

Your occupational/professional domain (and a Worksheet)

This is the third and last of the worksheets. This is the area where you try to nail down *how* you exercise your Personal Values and gifts at work. It's the one where you ask yourself the question: how do I fit in at work? Or perhaps, why do I have the same problems at work repeatedly? Over and over again? If you are armed with the intrinsic insights from spiritual gifts, from DISC, and from Strengthsfinders, you have a lot of insight to work with. My hope for you is that your self-discovery has already enabled you to see why you are effective in certain situations, and why you struggle in others. In the very best outcomes, you have learned how to sidestep difficult scenarios, and how to leverage your best strengths in the roles you fill with the responsibilities which are yours to own.

On the other hand, if you have reached this point in the book and you have not taken the assessments, guess what? You will be frustrated with whole process I'm asking you to do. You still have the self-discovery challenge, which will help you in *every* relationship opportunity. How powerful is it when you are able to engage more effectively in relationships *at work*?

---

[52] For brevity, I'll skip showing you my filled out Relationship values worksheet. It is the most straightforward of the three worksheets.

For Christians, the additional question is, "How do I live out my faith in this work environment?'" If you have 'unpacked your suitcase' and used some of the tools — like Strengthsfinders — you have a good idea of what I'm talking about.

For the professional domain, let's start with one simple example from my experience. As I have told you, I'm Strategic/Visionary. I contemplate all of the variables in a situation and *usually* I'm able to sense the one correct direction for the enterprise to pursue. Strategic/Visionaries can't leave the job and go home. I continually think about all of the possible combinations and perturbations. I roll them over in my mind; I think about them in the shower; I wake up in the middle of the night and think about all of the implications and ramifications. Strengthsfinders people know a talent that has been refined into a strength *cannot* be switched off. I wander around the house, cleaning the toilets and thinking about the next chapter of ***Dating without Delusion***. It is the essence of what people mean when they say, "That's the way he is wired."

Dating without Delusion

Personal Core Values Worksheet
Occupational/Professional Domain

How do You Use Your Gifts at Work?_____
(Spiritual Gifts, Profile, & Strengths on the Job)

How do Your Gifts Influence Your Work & Leadership?_____
(Fitting Your Gifts & Strengths into your Role)

What are Your Flip-Side Weaknesses that Call for 'Adjustment'?
(Teachers over-teach, Strategic Persons require Thinking Time etc.)

How do You Adjust at Work with Christ-like Attitudes?
(Response to employees, employers, co-workers: See Ephesians 6 :5-9 Galatians 5:22)

One evening at the seminar, a lady who had just taken Strengthsfinders came up to me and said that she tested out with Strategic/Visionary as one of her top themes /talents/strengths. We shared our common experiences of wandering around doing mundane what-evers, and thinking over and over about some significant challenge that we could not get out of our minds. Thinking about all the aspects of the challenge, refining the direction for a problem solution. I am also a Maximizer: always trying to make good things better and better things great. As a business consultant, I am brought on-board because I am 'wired' to take a good company and encourage them to drive for the next level of excellence. That's what most CEO's want. So it starts to become clear for me how I should use my 'Gifts at Work,' and exactly when I should challenge and lead to the next level. Let's look at the Professional Values worksheet (previous page).

How do you use your gifts at work? For me, it's a matter of taking the time to contemplate the details of a work situation and help figure out the best path for improvement. That's Strategic/Visionary thinking-Maximizer helps me figure out the best improvement path. Then I use the Teaching gift to communicate the improvement strategy to the company organizational leaders. *But* I've learned to contain my Maximizer/Teaching to the right place and the right time. Otherwise, it becomes annoying. When I am asked to come into a company, these suggestions are very well received because I offer a quality of thinking that provides a new perspective. I communicate to the company leaders: "Here's a new vision, and here's how to go after it!" Very essential information. At this juncture, the Achieving company leaders should take the vision and develop smart action plans to make it an improved reality. Time for me to revert to a support role. Recently, a business leader that I supported described this as migration into a 'coaching role,' and that is exactly what I try to do.

You took those assessments and did all that work online to figure out your own wiring. Now, can you write a paragraph like the one above — about yourself?

How do your gifts influence your work leadership? Left to our own habit-based behavior, we'll see how we can be effective in one specific circumstance, and then try to behave and interact the same way in every circumstance. How smart is that? Like everyone else, I am prone to this same mistake. Think back over your professional/work career, about the times you stormed out of the room, or left feeling insulted and emotionally damaged. How much of that friction was due to our lack of flexibility and our very immature understanding of the evolving circumstance going on around us? Conversely, the person who knows themselves well can adapt and react in very careful and responsible ways. Encouraging others. Stepping into obvious gaps. Stepping aside to enable the person with the right skill set to get engaged.

What are your flip-side weaknesses that call for adjustment? The simple downside of the Love Language 'Words of Affirmation' is that I need people to validate me with compliments and kudos. As I look at this need objectively, I see it's a sneaky way to boost my ego, to inflate my pride. What's your Love Language? What are its downsides? One very astute guy that I worked for once said to me, "Jay, everything is not a strategy." I also know Teachers teach too much. Communicators can't shut up. Achievers do too much at the wrong time. Highly Interactive people bounce around the room, not even remembering the name of the person they just met. *If* you have taken all of these assessments as I have asked, *if* you have learned about yourself though an honest look at your past, then you have the rare ability to see and understand yourself. Complex and 'fearfully and wonderfully made.' Damaged and sensitive from past hurts. Know thyself.

Christ at work. For me, this means being humble and gentle — once again, difficult for me — bearing with the other teammates as we reach for the next goal. Those could be buzz phrases, so let's dig a little deeper. I have learned that being Strategic/Visionary means that I am a slow thinker. It takes thinking time to wander around the house and clean those toilets. People approach me and pile on new information, and expect an immediate response. Usually, I have to take time to process that information. It might be 24–48 hours (two days!) before I can give them the well-thought-out answer they wanted in two minutes. Being humble and gentle means asking for patience from that person. It means explaining to them about Visionary thinking. If I don't do this, they will think I am rude or ignoring them. Not true! How about Maximizer? I'll try to guess how LeBron James could be a better basketball player because I have this bent to enable me to see how something great can go to the next level.

Two misunderstandings can arise. First, it may seem that I'm saying *I* could perform at that next level. Usually I'm figuring out process improvements to help the larger enterprise. Secondly, if I 'Maximize' too quickly, it may seem I'm ignoring all of the sweat and blood that went into getting the team to where it is today. I have to very deliberately NOT do that. It's all about an 'Others-Focused' attitude. Now that you are learning a lot about me, you'll be able to see how I do the entries in the Professional/Occupational Domain of the worksheet (next page).

Jay's Personal Core Values Worksheet
Occupational/Professional Domain

Dating without Delusion

How do You Use Your Gifts at Work? Strategic/Visionary: Business Process Teacher → Build the Team
(Spiritual Gifts, Profile, & Strengths on the Job)

How do Your Gifts Influence Your Work & Leadership? Maximizer 'Coach'
(Fitting Your Gifts & Strengths into your Role)

What are Your Flip-Side Weaknesses that Call for 'Adjustment'?
(Teachers over-teach, Strategic Persons require Thinking Time etc.)

Teach and Coach only in the right circumstances

Always appreciate the 'sweat' which got us here

Realize that *Change* takes time
How do You Adjust at Work with Christ-like Attitudes?
(Response to employees, employers, co-workers: See Ephesians 6 :5-9 Galatians 5:22)

My Boss's Priorities always in first place

Think first...think second.....then talk (Proverbs)

None of us is as smart as All of us

Above is my actual worksheet with all of the occupational/professional elements filled in. The people who have been successful with Personal Values discovery and articulation have one thing in common: they work on it. They work hard on it.

One woman who attended a recent series of singles classes took the blank worksheet home and started her journey. Write down, add, cross out, erase, write sideways in the margins. Coffee stained, folded in half, frayed on the edges, she brought that worksheet to class after class. I have to believe that she prayed for the Lord's help while she was doing this. Prayer, a lot of quiet introspection, thinking back, writing down. I've given you this worksheet tool, as a part of the 'system.' I wish it were easier. I wish you could put in the worksheet elements, turn the crank, and have wonderful succinct value statements pop out. It's just not that easy. You *are* fearfully and wonderfully made. Chances are you've also been shaped and damaged; great values will wonderfully weave all of this together.

Personal Core Value Summary

Spiritual

Relational

Professional

I have looked at previously published values-development efforts and choose not to adopt them, for important reasons. Some of these efforts, to me, seemed too cookie-cutter. You know that you want your Personal Core Values to be intensely personal *and* intensely accurate. So when you arrive at a Core Value, it may *seem* simple but you're ready (if anyone asks you) to offer all of the living that went into the ownership of that value (remember my 'Sprit Abiding Man of Christ' story?).

The second reason is that many of these values-development efforts resulted in values statements that literally went on for two and three pages. Are you kidding? I have seen many employees and church members struggle with just the organization mission and vision statements, and there are just two of those. Thinking you are going to able to apply three pages of value statements to any situation is, at best, going to be a hit-and-miss thing. You could carry them around in your purse or your back pocket, and you still wouldn't get the rubber to hit the road. This is like taking a 500-pound sledgehammer to a knife fight. No; five or six sharp (using the knife analogy) and crisp values is all you're going to effectively be able to incorporate into the flow of your daily life.

The Final Leap (to your Core Value statements)

We started with the 3 assessments: Spiritual Gifts, DISC, and Strengthsfinders. Pull out the summary sheet for those and put it on the left side of your desk. You used the Imago sheets from Harville Hendrix. Put them on the left side of your desk. Now you have completed 3 Core Values Worksheets; put those on the right side of your desk. Now take the Core Value Summary sheet and put it directly in the center — see the Core Value summary sheet (previous page).

Watch carefully as one gal did the last step. With the filled out Spiritual, Relational and Professional worksheets sitting in front of her on one side with the Imago worksheet and her self-assessment from Gifts, DISC, and Strengthsfinders on the other, she started to think and pray. Then she took some blank pages and started to write down Single sentences aimed at clearly describing her life commitments. Some of these had deeper roots in the past; some represented her life commitments going forward. In her case, she had about three pages filled with written-down thinking about the specifics she wanted to incorporate. So now we have her values worksheets and her written-down values thinking. The last and most essential step is synthesis of that thinking into those short, precise Personal Value phrases — see her final sheet below.

I (Jay) am an 'over-committer:' "Sure, I'll help you. Sure, I'll write the book. Sure, I'll work your Strengthsfinders. Sure, we'll get together." My 'Persuader' profile (from DISC) is underneath all that. Why? Because I want you to like me and I am afraid of losing your approval. In the case of our seminar woman, however, I was not going to let her down. I challenged everyone to get moving and get their values work done, *and she did it*. OK Jay, time to kick in that Maximizer/Individualization thinking and support this sincere woman's work to become who God wants her to be. So she did another round of values refinement, and then sent me two pages to work with. My job was to take her well-thought-out Personal Core Values statements and synthesize them into sharp, precise values phrases in the Spiritual, Relational, and Occupational domains. Without further ado, here they (anonymously, with a fictitious name):

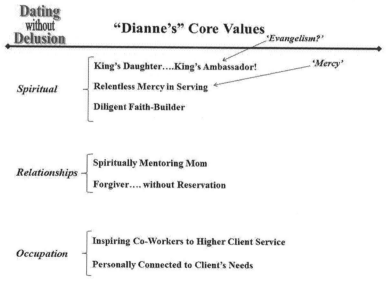

Dating without Delusion

"Dianne's" Core Values

'Evangelism?'

Spiritual
- King's Daughter....King's Ambassador!
- Relentless Mercy in Serving ← *'Mercy'*
- Diligent Faith-Builder

Relationships
- Spiritually Mentoring Mom
- Forgiver.... without Reservation

Occupation
- Inspiring Co-Workers to Higher Client Service
- Personally Connected to Client's Needs

Summarizing who you are in Personal Core Values is an imperfect process; nevertheless, it is a *powerful* process. Share your Core Values with someone and you will soon discover how interested they are in you. If they are *not* interested in your values, you've discovered how really *not* interested they are in you. Speaking your Personal Core Values holds you to the 'integrity' of keeping those values. Now let's see the impact of just one of Dianne's Core Values — *Forgiver Without*

Reservation. I don't know all of Dianne's life detail, but consider how important it is for her to use this value to move on from past relationships. Is she divorced? Yes, and she needs to avoid relationships which might be repeat 'bad for me' scenarios. At the same time she must forgive her former spouse and move on to a values-based life. How about the love definition from 1 Corinthians 13? Isn't this Core Value a reminder to 'not take into account a wrong suffered'? Doesn't love forgive? What did Jesus say about forgiving — seventy times seven! The Bible is chock full of phrases like '...forgiving one another, loving one another, just as God in Christ loves you'. From past wrongs suffered....to moment by moment daily interactions 'Dianne's' Core Value will have continuous impact — *If* she can bring it to mind. In the class when we discussed this Personal Value we talked extensively about the three steps — *Forgive* (the choice) — *Forgiving* (the process) — *Forgiven* (the end result). Now 'Dianne' (in many circumstances we don't know) has seen the devastation which holding a grudge has done to her life. She wants to leave a spiteful, grudge-holding life behind. She knows God wants this attitude in her life. If you could meet her and ask her, she would gladly recount the pain of carrying a grudge — and the freedom of exercising forgiveness. We could write a whole book (and there are already many out there) on the healing treasure called 'forgiveness'. Do you have bitterness and resentment dragging you down? I suggest you adopt 'Dianne's' Personal Value, I'm absolutely sure she wouldn't mind. It will be life-changing for you. Dianne now has her Seven Core Values. You can see why they have life-changing potential for her — and we have discussed just one!

When your words and your life choices start to align, your whole life can make more sense. If you could talk to 'Dianne' she would remember the hurt of making value-less choices, and the blessings of thinking and living using Core Value choices. With Core Values, your life can take on a congruity that is rare in this world. With Core Values you can achieve *Congruity* and *Integrity* in your life. Your Core Values are now working 24/7, setting you apart.

Another woman attending the seminar was inspired to write down her values, but once again her thinking rambled over 3 or 4 pages.[53] I did the work of synthesizing her too-many words into a values summary. Let's call this woman 'Susan'. Her values, summarized into the three areas, are summarized in the slide above. Note that Susan also has the gift of Evangelism, and

[53] If possible do your 'rambling 'on the worksheets. You have enough paper just using those.

the outgoing personality (high 'I') to back it up. Her commitment to spend time with Jesus refers to her commitment to have dedicated prayer time and time set aside for reading the Bible. No doubt these are challenging concepts, and I'm sure she found that knowing and speaking her values was a great move ahead, but it is the better *living* of her values that she is after. See the reference to her gift of 'Mercy' (one of those the spiritual Gifts test will bring

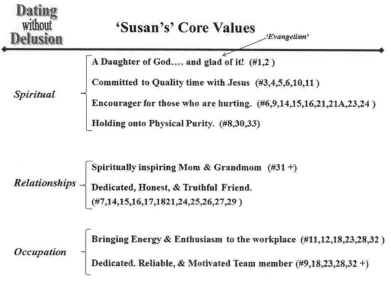

'Susan's' Core Values

Evangelism

Spiritual
- A Daughter of God.... and glad of it! (#1,2)
- Committed to Quality time with Jesus (#3,4,5,6,10,11)
- Encourager for those who are hurting. (#6,9,14,15,16,21,21A,23,24)
- Holding onto Physical Purity. (#8,30,33)

Relationships
- Spiritually inspiring Mom & Grandmom (#31 +)
- Dedicated, Honest, & Truthful Friend. (#7,14,15,16,17,1821,24,25,26,27,29)

Occupation
- Bringing Energy & Enthusiasm to the workplace (#11,12,18,23,28,32)
- Dedicated. Reliable, & Motivated Team member (#9,18,23,28,32 +)

out). Susan had that gift. Not only was she not put off by hurting and needy people, she actually gravitated towards them, willing to hear their personal stories laced with all kinds of life tragedy

Finally, I share my Personal Values sheet with you (next page). It is no better or worse than Dianne's or Susan's. In fact, *no two sets of Personal Values will look anything alike.* This diversity is a simple reflection of our individual uniqueness. It's is also a reflection of the infinite variety of personality, emotion, intellect, and perhaps most importantly, callings for each of us. For my Core Values I've offered some supporting Bible references for each of my values — something you might consider if you are a Faith-thinker. God's plan for Jay is for me alone. I have to continually ask myself, "Am I living the life God has designed for me?"

I hope to meet you someday, perhaps at a seminar? God willing I will be living out my values, and re-discovering and affirming God's callings for me. As I write this, a **Dating *without* Delusion** seminar is underway and we are at the halfway point. As always I am learning at every juncture as people share their lives and challenges with me and the rest of the class. They enjoy learning about themselves. Many of them are rejuvenated because they have a new way to see and build relationships. The challenges remain the same for us all:

It is never too late to start doing what is right... and

A value is not a value, unless it drives your choices.

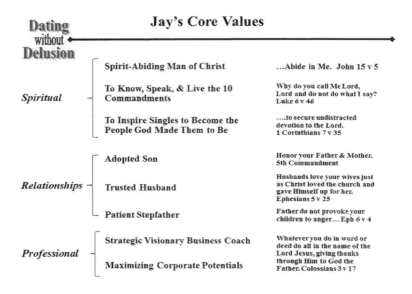

The Second C: Commitment, the mortar of your character

Core Values are the first C, but closely behind is the second C: Commitment. Personal Core Values are tested by time and circumstance, but it requires personal commitment to keep a value and to make choices using it. It takes Commitment for people to hold a job, to face difficult circumstances with their families, to serve others in charitable and ministry organizations, to trust God in the tough situations. Commitment means you and your values are clear, reliable, steadfast, predictable, dependable... add your own amplifier. Every day, your values will be tested. But isn't this also true for the people you know and may be considering for a personal relationship — like a date? So as they struggle to articulate who they are, they will also have the opportunity to demonstrate their Commitment to their values. Commitment is worth a quote:

> *"Until one is committed there is hesitancy, the chance to draw back, always ineffectiveness. Concerning all acts of initiative (and creation), there is one elementary truth, the ignorance of which kills countless ideas and splendid plans: that the moment one definitely commits oneself, then providence moves too. All sorts of things occur to help one that would never otherwise have occurred. A whole stream of events issues from the decision, raising in one's favor all manner of unforeseen incidents and meetings and material assistance, which no man could have dreamt would have come his way. I have learned a deep respect for one of Goethe's couplets: "Whatever you can do, or dream you can, begin it. Boldness has genius, power, and magic in it."* — W.H. Murray

Murray led the Scottish Himalayan expedition, and you can bet that leading an expedition successfully requires big commitment. What about you? What are you committed to? Here's a dramatization of the obvious, to the below. Can you see why having a mushy or confused understanding of your values also undermines your ability to commit? I fully share this challenge with you. I have been committed to work with Singles for many years, yet I am just now writing this book. That's soft commitment. Like you, I have to keep reminding myself of *who* I am (through my values) and recommitting to them every day. Let's go to the conclusion. If people are not able to commit to personal principles in their daily lives, will they be able to be committed to a realtionship with you? Probably not. Do they really have even the slightest idea

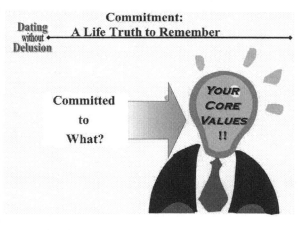

of what personal integrity is? Better find out during your dating journey.

If you think about it, every recognition or award, or every moment of true self-satisfaction, has come to you *after* you applied yourself to a worthwhile effort. Many things have come into your life that are good, and those things come from other people. For example, my father sacrificed a substantial amount of money and effort so I could go to college; a very good thing which came into my life through my dad's commitment. As a result of my commitment in college, I was able to complete a degree in physics. Though my fellow classmates had intelligence which greatly exceeded mine, that commitment has had a lasting impact.[54] For Christians, what about salvation? Our salvation has come to us because Jesus was committed to the plan His Father in heaven predestined for Him. Remember in the gospel of Luke where it says He was called to deny himself and take up his cross? That commitment was made for us so we might have eternal life. The challenge is to know and appreciate a life-changing blessing from someone else. The challenge is to know *what you* are committed to for the long haul. Here's a saying worth remembering:

> *Everything good that has ever come into your life has come as a*
> *result of commitment: either your commitment to someone or*
> *someone else's commitment to you. (Jay)*

The major challenge is to know *what* to commit to. Herky-Jerky quickly changing commitments are not commitments at all. This is the challenge we all face. If you did the math, you quickly figured out that I am a member of the baby boomer generation. Anyone who looks at today's newspapers will see the sociological analysis describing the baby boomer generation with a very full menu of self-centered dysfunctions. We had all kinds of material excess, we had all kinds of relationship dysfunction, and we certainly impacted the children of our generation in a serious way. The children of our generation — Gen Xers and Millennials — mostly think we are irrelevant and because they do, they fall back on defining themselves; I've been calling it 'self-creation.' Most of this book is dedicated to tearing down the self-creation *delusion*. In the center of our souls we want to Commit. Commit to what? — is the question. The second C, Commitment: is essential, and it is incredibly frustrating to commit to the wrong purpose or goal. Values give you the aiming points for your Commitment.

---

[54] The Physics professors at Bates College helped me struggle often-times just to earn a 'C'.

The Third C: Communication
the 'what-to-communicate-when' during dating

As a career businessperson, I saw problems caused by poor communication between the various parts of an organization (internally) or between companies trying to work together (externally). Interpersonal relationships are challenged the same way. Early on, we did all of that work to achieve an understanding of your values. The second C talks about the 'magic' of Commitment. We also talked about the complexities of man-woman relationships and communication. Now, let's look at how your values can help 'between-gender' communication. You know when you are attracted to someone, your communication skills go to a faraway place. Possibly Infatuation has tied your tongue? You over-think, blurt out, and second-guess everything you say. Guys revert to the strong and silent persona; gals start chattering about a random relationship they have with their girlfriends. When this relationship vagary comes out and you are forced back to depending on the emotional surge and physical attractiveness you felt when you first saw this person, you can easily ask, "How reliable is that?" Here's an alternative way to change and continually improve your communication mindset. Think of two primary elements of the third C, Communication:

Communication: Content and Technique

Content and technique. It's like saying you have to know *what* you want to communicate when, and then understand *how* to communicate it to be best received by the listener, meaning the person you are potentially dating. Ken Blanchard — one of my graduate school mentors — talks about the 'Platinum Rule': "Do unto others as they would have done unto them." Remember the simple example using love languages? If someone needs quality time, don't give them just a few words of affirmation because that's what *you* long for. Communicate what they need. Encourage them in *their* Core Value journey. Give them the content that will best help them.

Without a doubt, the most important Content advice I can give is this: *Communicate your values!* You may say, "Jay; that's so redundant!" When I'm trying to communicate to an infatuated person, repetition of values based content is the simple course of communication. If your values are clear, you always can talk about how they challenge you, how they have inspired you, how you have refined them and, most of all, how you have failed them and then learned from the failing. Being honest about your values-based living has a great second benefit: it eventually allows you to ask the other person about themselves and to ask about *their* Personal Values. Values discussions in early dating relationships can sustain good dialogue, and overcome infatuation-based silences and limit the meaningless chit chat.

Once you decide to date someone, the depth and quality of your communication needs to steadily improve. When you first meet someone, leaning on your practiced articulation of your six or seven Personal Core Values is good quality interchange...and there is plenty to talk about. So as dating progresses through the three stages in Part Two, I'll be asking you to think about deeper and more personal information content, particularly as you move into a **C**ommitment to date exclusively.

Let's do one key learning on Content before we move on. It deals with expectations. Sometimes they are appropriate, sometimes not, but one thing is sure: the *Relationship Ripper* tears up relationships. Uncommunicated expectations. If you have a childhood that is loaded with traditions you think are 'normal', or if you've learned to expect men to offer certain dating courtesies or women to behave

Dating without Delusion

The Relationship Ripper

Expectations Created...

....but NOT Communicated

within certain boundaries, you'd better get your head out of the sand. You have to communicate those expectations clearly, so that the people who you are dating, or might date, have a chance to be understood without unnecessarily messing up a potentially good relationship.

John Gray Tips

Let's look at a couple of important Communication techniques. These have been adapted from John Gray in the very famous book, *Men Are from Mars, Women Are from Venus*. They're designed to open your awareness to some of the challenges of inter-gender communication. The best relationships increase the quality of the dialogue as the relationship progresses. That's one of the earmarks of a growing relationship. As the relationship progresses (as we will see in Part Two), the quality of the dialog should increase also. Why? Because the level of Commitment is increasing. More Commitment... More

Communication!

These *Men are from Mars* principles expose the difficulties of man-woman communication for *most* men, and for the *majority* of women. The first is, 'Women are like Waves' (see below). Women are remarkable, with remarkable resilience, capacity, and perseverance. Some of Debra's finest moments

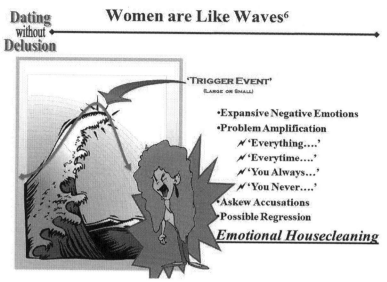

Women are Like Waves[6]

- •Expansive Negative Emotions
- •Problem Amplification
  - ✗ 'Everything....'
  - ✗ 'Everytime....'
  - ✗ 'You Always...'
  - ✗ 'You Never....'
- •Askew Accusations
- •Possible Regression

Emotional Housecleaning

'TRIGGER EVENT' (LARGE OR SMALL)

have come in the face of adversity. We men often accept this as the norm for the women we are close to, and we often take that resilience and capacity for granted when we are in a marriage relationship. As life unfolds, difficult circumstance upon difficult circumstance sometimes show up, subtly — or not so subtly — increasing the pressure. The next thing may be a small annoyance or just a misspoken word. That's the 'Trigger Event' shown in the slide. Then, with cataclysmic emotional response, the woman 'crashes' like a wave. All of a sudden she is accusing, attacking, blaming (this is as different as women are different). She is using phrases such as "you never support me," "you're always making excuses for them." Of course in our logical mindsets, we men take issue with the use of 'always' and 'never.' The natural male response is to now start reciting the last time we *did* support her: predictable male ignorance.

John Gray contends that women, on occasion, have to do some 'emotional housecleaning.' Many years ago after reading *Men are from Mars,* I remember Debra had an emotional housecleaning event. In my prior ignorance, I would have responded: with stupid rebuttals. This time, however, was different. I thought, "AHA! I know what this is!" And I followed John Gray's advice, which is to empathetically affirm her at every accusational turn (be sure to intersperse with very subtle grunts of agreement). Communication is very gender oriented, isn't it? Now, is every woman exactly like this? Obviously not. But I will tell you that when I teach this concept, the men in the class/seminar are usually amazed while the women subtly smile in agreement. Guys, I hope the graphics are memorable.

Now, what about men? Here's the parallel concept from John Gray. 'Men are like Rubberbands' — see above. OK, I'm giving my gender the benefit of the doubt here. After all, how many men are 'fully relational'? Maybe I should have said 'minimally relational.' But you get the idea; sometimes we men can be open and conversational, with good interaction skills. When a problem shows up, however, that kind of open/relational behavior gets truncated. Why? Because many of us have to think about that nasty problem — whatever it is — and consider all of the solution options.

Dating without Delusion

Men Are Like Rubberbands[6]

- Fully Relational (?)
- Open Emotionally (?)
- Expressive/Interactive
- Capable
- Respect Inspiring
- Responsive

Usually there are many options to weigh. Where does all this happen? In the Cave — see the right side of the next graphic. That black hole on the right of the slide is like a bear's den, and it's like that because men want solitude as they mull over the options and solutions to the problem at hand. Think about how many men behave this way when facing an issue. They want the ability to think; they'll be polite, but also very short and curt with their answers. They're 'working it out.'

In a marriage relationship, the wife of a man who is retreating to the cave might chase him in there to fill her need for feedback, dialogue, and interaction. Do you see the problem? In this case, she would be denying him the very thing he needs to solve an important problem: solitude. A woman has to understand and exercise some trust; in time, he will come out of the cave and return to normal interactions with her. The Rubberband's effect will pull him back. If women understand this concept, they will more likely be patient to allow some time for him to work it out. Women, I hope the graphic below is memorable.

Are all men exactly like this? Absolutely not. Like the 'Wave' phenomena, the 'Cave' phenomenon bears understanding — on the woman's part — to enable a better quality of relationship. A better quality of relationship?!!?? Isn't that what we all want? But remember that John Gray is talking (at this point) about marriage relationships...and this is a book about dating! So let's shift our focus to dating. This is difficult at this point in our **_Dating without Delusion_** saga because we haven't yet talked about the dating timeline and the phases of dating. Early in a dating interaction, when the infatuation quotient is high, these behaviors — Wave and Cave — are going to be perceived

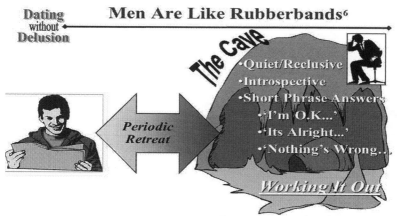

The Basement, TV, a Hobby....

by the opposite gender much differently than later on in the relationship, when there is spoken commitment between two people who are trying to mature their relationship.

So let's start with an early dating, low-commitment, low-expectation relationship. The man knows this woman only from limited interactions; certainly he is attracted to her, and hopefully he has a good idea of her Personal Values. Suppose she has a wave episode? If he is uneducated about man/woman communication, he might conclude that this person is volatile to the point where he might end the relationship with her right then and there — "I could never live with that!". His reaction might end a potentially great relationship. My advice to women: control the crash; vent and emote to your accountability partner or a close sister, not the man you have recently started to date. Men: you'd better realize that this is a feminine reality.

Suppose the man faces a difficult problem that requires focus and, yes, seclusion to work it out. If it's early in the dating timeline and he goes many days/weeks without making contact, what is she to think? She thinks he is not interested or that he's rude... and who would blame her? A wise man will communicate his needed involvement in creating a problem solution — business, parental, whatever — he's going to be busy! If he is wise, he will communicate the situation to her in order to stop all of the inevitable speculation on her part. Otherwise, a woman who thinks she has initiated a promising relationship will be damaged /insulted/confused. Men, do you understand? It would be insulting and irresponsible on your part to do otherwise.

When we tackle the dating process and timeline in Part Two, remember this discussion. You, the Single person, will be dating with purpose and sensitivity — hopefully. If the person you are dating has one of these cave or wave episodes, are you going to jettison the whole relationship because of your lack of understanding? Realize, please, that we all are humans and we all are a work in progress. Communication is the third C. The right content at the right time, with the right technique.

The Fourth C: Compatibility... with an 'evil little twin'

Compatibility — the fourth C of the four C's — is what many of the dating sites rely on. Do you like to hike, do you like to bike; do you like to dance in the rain? If you are doing a service like working with kids' ministries, you are living out a key Core Value. That's NOT what I'm talking about. I'm talking about recreational lifestyles and activities, walking on the beach, going to movies, participating in a shared sport. Lifestyles and activities held in common are good, but those change as we grow and get older. Remember the gray divorce couple? In the 'compatibility realm,' I prefer to focus on the personality aspects you can discover through testing, like DISC. These will affect daily interactions and have a strong impact on the quality of your relationship. So is this fourth C important? Sure it is, but unlike a Core Value, do not hang your hopes on it. The lie is that when we find Compatibility, and we feel the emotional surge of Infatuation, we will have found our soul mate, or at least someone who complements our living and lifestyle. *Here's the powerful lie:*

Compatibility + Infatuation = 'soul mate'

The good fourth C plus the 'evil little twin' of infatuation have sent many good people down the rapids of relationship disillusionment. When I was Single for those many years, I spent a lot of time playing and enjoying tennis. People who knew me said, "Jay needs to meet a tennis player." Can you see how shallow that is? Core Values based upon my faith, my essential relationships, or my professional career were not even mentioned or thought of by the pundits. So when I met Debra — who very recreationally enjoyed a very little tennis — the common reaction was, "That relationship will never work." Of course, many of those people also didn't believe that Debra had accepted Christ. Let's deal with realities.

The reality is that two people — _any_ two people, no matter how compatible they are — are sooner or later going to have significant differences of opinion, differences in lifestyle choices, and differences in life decisions. This is true even for you and your friends you only see intermittently. When they see life differently than you, it pretty easy to 'take a break' and have fewer intellectual/interpersonal interactions with them, or spend less time with them. In marriage, taking a break is not so easy, however. I contend that in exclusive dating, taking a break is also very problematic. Here's the root problem: compatibility will not help you if you have deep spiritual beliefs that don't cause conflict now, but are setting you up for a collision later on. Example: You want to pass on your faith values to your kids through the school they attend, and your partner is a devoted humanist who wants faith to be left out of the classroom at all costs. See the values disconnect? These examples could go on and on, but you get the idea. This disconnect is the culprit behind the many gray divorces (people over 50 getting divorced; see the section on culture), which is an escalating statistic in our postmodern world.

Opposites attract?

You've heard this before, haven't you? Do you think it's true? Now that you have taken a serious look at yourself through the lenses of the three assessment tools and Harville Hendrix's Imago exercise you have a level of wisdom that surpasses these cute little sayings. But let's look at this one.

You now know yourself from a gifts, personality disposition, and talents and strengths viewpoint. Do you think you should find someone with opposite values? Absolutely not. Do you think you should find someone with opposite gifts, or how about opposite Talents/Strengths? Again not such a good idea. So now we've narrowed it down to the area where 'opposites attract' might have some meaning and relevance — it's in the Personality Disposition realm (DISC). Consider the first DISC element: D for Dominance. Can you imagine two people high in dominance having consistently good interactions? Both people would try to take control and grab the reins on every decision. See the potential daily conflict? A high S might be a better fit for that high D, don't you think? Is a D the opposite of a high S? Well not exactly, but you can at least see how the 'opposites attract' saying gets a little traction. At this point you're beyond the little anecdotal sayings.

Say goodbye to the 'Unhooked' culture

Now, let's jump way ahead by looking at the kind of dating relationship worth targeting, and compare it to the kind of dysfunctional relationship that is the norm in today's culture. The effect is a 'STOP/GO' comparison of different re-

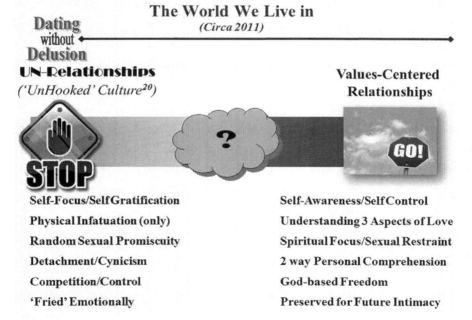

The World We Live in
(Circa 2011)

Dating without Delusion

UN-Relationships
(*'UnHooked' Culture*[20])

Values-Centered Relationships

Self-Focus/Self Gratification

Physical Infatuation (only)

Random Sexual Promiscuity

Detachment/Cynicism

Competition/Control

'Fried' Emotionally

Self-Awareness/Self Control

Understanding 3 Aspects of Love

Spiritual Focus/Sexual Restraint

2 way Personal Comprehension

God-based Freedom

Preserved for Future Intimacy

lationship types. The 'STOP' relationship is roughly described on the left side of the slide above. If you are involved in a superficial relationship like this, the red light should come on. The type of dating relationship I am going to recommend to you is described by the 'GO' green light on the right side of the slide. This is 'beginning with the end in mind' (Covey) because we're targeting the good relationship that you've developed using the thinking embedded in this book starting here in Part One and going to the end of the dating process as described in Part Two. So this chart is worth spending some time on. Look at the relationships around you — particularly the 'modern' culture-based relationships. When we redefine the 'date' in Part Two of the book, you will have the basis for developing healthy relationships, but you will be developing them in a counter-cultural way. As usual, the ridicule will come in various subtle forms, so be ready.

The phenomena of 'unhooked behavior' comes from Laura Sessions Stepp introduced earlier in the discussion on Culture. Reminder: she is the author of a recent book titled, *Unhooked: How Young Women Pursue Sex, Delay Love, and Lose Both*. Laura has done the hard work and spent the research time to delve into the modern university world and how young women are behaving in it. It may be easy to sit back and pontificate about relationships, and how your grandmother and grandfather did it in the old days; it's quite another to see what's really happening in the real world. I very much appreciate Laura for two reasons: 1) She is a researcher who spends the time and retains the objectivity to write an unbiased description of the young female world, and 2) She has real empathy and draws a few poignant conclusions, all of which expose the emotional damage that is being done around us.

The slide references Laura's findings as the 'Unhooked Culture.' For parents who have children getting ready to go away to school, this is a revealing must-read. The 'STOP' column — what I call UN-Relationships — are self-centered, emotionally turbulent, competitive, and extremely physical/sexual. I can't forget Laura Stepp's description of young women keeping Excel spreadsheets to track the number of guys they've had sex with. The culture promotes these random hook-up/rejections as a form of personal freedom. The end result, however, is women (and I would argue young men) who are emotionally fried. The idea is that the Culture 'blocks' or stands in the way of developing stable relationships. In the long-term these young people are undermining their capacity to commit to long-term, stable marriages. Single reader if you are tangled in one of these 'STOP' relationships, I urge you to free yourself as soon as possible.

Look at the 'GO" side of the slide: the Values-Centered side. The huge gap shown in the figure attempts to depict the difference between the culture-based emotionally/physically charged relationships so prevalent today and the Values-Centered relationships which can create lasting, best-outcome relationships — relationships with lifelong capacity (on the right in the figure). The Unhooked Culture is expanding its impact on young people. ***Dating <u>without</u> Delusion*** is one small effort to encourage you to be genuinely self-aware; understanding what truly constitutes genuine love and exercising physical restraint. Spiritual and personal freedom is the objective of this book. I hope you can make the exchange for the Green Light 'Go' relationship! The idea is to make sure that the person you might marry understands and appreciates your deeply held values, and respects and supports them in many different ways.

Part Two:
Dating Relationship Phases

Dating phases: Three key decision points

Counselors often talk about 'building' a relationship, 'growing' a relationship, or 'maturing' a relationship. All these are the opposite of destroying or compromising a relationship. Can you see that dating has to be about growing and building relationships, *even if that relationship evolves into a friendship?* We men often can't think beyond the sexual attraction of the moment; there is no denying the destructive power that pornography has unleashed in this world. But every relationship you have in life has a 'best outcome,' and if you believe the life-is-about-relationships tenant (Part One), then you want each of your relationships to grow in the proper direction. Family, friends, mentors, professional associates, spiritual groups, sports teams: each relationship has a proper outcome. The idea is to find that result. Dating also *should be* about finding the right result, even in the mind-numbing, romantically charged atmosphere of our party culture. Since you have taken the time to pick up this book, I know you have that higher calling in you.

So how do you find the best outcome in a dating relationship? By thinking in terms of phases. By knowing which phase of the relationship you are in, and then behaving and communicating appropriately *for that phase.* No matter where you are on the relationship timeline, heavy-duty sexual activity is inappropriate: it results in clinging expectations and possessiveness. It will blind you to unfortunate relationship realities. Dumping all of your past hurts and failures on another person is inappropriate. Assuming that there are big relationship and time commitments is inappropriate. These reminders are obvious but they bear repeating, mostly because we all have a tendency to err in one direction or another. Usually in the throes of infatuation, people want to move way too fast. So phases can help, and they can help you slow down. At the last seminar all of the participants observed the same thing. In today's culture everyone is moving too fast. Moving fast from initial dates to exclusive, not going to see anyone else, relationships. Lots of expectations about exclusivity — lots of unspoken expectations and assumptions. All trying to get to a meaningful relationship in a great big hurry.

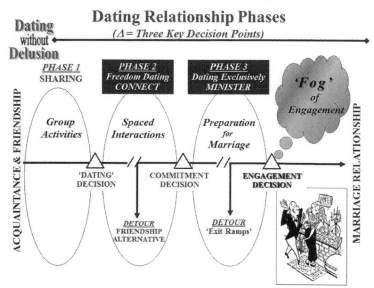

In **_Dating without Delusion,_** there are three simple phases[55] that are punctuated by three key decision points (see above). When the pressure mounts and confusion reigns, if you can remember the three key decision points, you will have the intellectual basis for making good relationship decisions. The three key decision points are shown at the triangles △. Each phase is punctuated by the simple decision: "Do I move on to the next phase, or not?" The first decision, moving from Phase 1 is, "To date or not to date?"

In Phase 2, we talk a lot about 'Freedom Dating' (which might enable non-exclusivity). No doubt this is very challenging skill. We talk about the Friendship Alternative: the _art_ of 'detouring' a dating relationship into a true friendship. Art is the appropriate word because doing this will require lots of clear, sensitive, and creative communication on your part. In the Phase 2 dating phase,[56] we discuss the problems of premature sexual involvement and the benefits of keeping your sexual impulses under control, understand-

[55] Phases are the right answer: Joshua Harris in _I Kissed Dating Goodbye_ recommends Casual Friendship–Deeper Friendship–Purposeful Intimacy with Integrity–Engagement (p. 205). John Gray in _Mars and Venus on a Date_ recommends: Attraction–Uncertainty–Exclusivity–Intimacy–Engagement (cover)

[56] Romans 12 v 1 is key. "Present your bodies as a living and holy sacrifice acceptable to God which is your spiritual service of worship."

ing why it is essential to keep your body under control. Even if you have had past failures-like me-get up, dust yourself off, and prepare yourself to think and live differently.

The second decision point is when you must decide whether this relationship is one that warrants _exclusivity_. If you decide that this relationship does warrant exclusivity, it is a relationship which needs to move forward; and moving forward means moving toward deep and honest understanding of yourself and the other person. With transparent understanding of each other, you can move forward to deeper personal commitment, and onto engagement. Therefore, it makes ultimate sense that a committed relationship like this should grow purposefully towards marriage. This is a life-changing decision which today's culture wants to you to rush past. It's a decision built on a commitment in which two people work to clearly communicate and understand. I suggest this phase have some clear objectives, mainly so that you and your now 'significant other' can begin to appreciate and understand each other for who you really are.

If an exclusive relationship is growing like this, two intelligent people can decide if their relationship has the substance to move into the last phase: Engagement. Look in the slide where the goofy little guy is proposing in front of the fireplace. I call this the phase the 'Fog of Engagement' because once the engagement decision is made, the marriage preparation often becomes frenetic, not really allowing any further quality relationship development. This is where counselors and pastors initiate compatibility testing. Perhaps this testing, built upon great research and refinement, can be used in Phase 3, before the engagement decision is made? That's what Debra and I did.

An evolution of communication and behavior

So beginning with the end in mind, I want to show you a slide (next page) that delineates the key differences and activities in each phase. This slide serves as a precursor to the rest of our dating discussion, progressing from _Sharing_[57] in the 'Not Dating' phase all the way to the life-changing decision to get engaged. This concept should help you to see that great relationships evolve

[57] This is extracted from the Share-Connect-Minister-Disciple (SCMD) process developed by Real Life Ministries in Post Falls, Idaho (where Jay and Debra went to church). The fourth phase, 'Disciple,' is a relationship term often used in church venues. Discipleship in marriage is briefly discussed at the end of the exclusive dating phase.

from stage to stage. As you move from left to right, the depth of interpersonal understanding and relationship clarity should always increase.

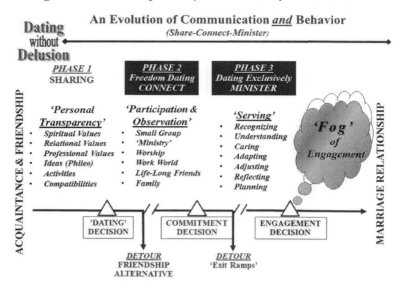

Please recognize that when you have just met someone, you *do not* really know them, no matter what your hormones and infatuations tell you. Having done all of your values development, you now have the ability to be transparent and honest about who you are. In Phase 1 (NOT DATING), your job is to *share* your self-understanding. Doing this well is *your* responsibility. Unfortunately, you will quickly find that the person you're thinking about dating most likely will not have done the same level of quality thinking. So the hard work of sharing who you are is an avenue toward discovering who that other person might really be — under the surface. This is the essence of the NOT DATING phase. Find safe venues (group events, picnics, or coffee shop discussions)[58] to initiate honest communication about the WHO of who you are. Is this the time to start uncovering your past hurts and failures? NO! This is the time to talk about values, how you are wired, and how your God-given values are going to get you to where you're going. Remember our discussion about Communication the third 'C'? Content & Technique. As a relationship grows the content will become more personal, and in depth — but that will take some time to develop a beginning level of trust. For now in early relationships focus your content on *Sharing* your Core Values.

---

[58] In recent Singles Fellowship gatherings we have descibed these low pressure coffee shop discussions as 'The Starbucks Alternative.'

How should the relationship change when you have made a sensible decision to date this new person? You move from talking about your values to carefully inviting the person you are now dating to *Connect* to some of those values-based activities. For example, you have the gift of mercy. You love to work in the benevolence ministry. You have the innate ability to inspire people who are down and out to get up and get moving — to use their God-given talents — to live effectively in this broken world. Your new relationship person needs to see you in action in that values-oriented venue. As you Connect them to your values-based life, watch to see how they appreciate, or are provoked to discomfort, by the life you live and the choices you make. Deep appreciation of *who you are* is powerful. Persistent discomfort also tells you all that you need to know. One of the Singles home groups I visit on occasion is comprised of mostly spiritually mature people who care deeply for one another. When inevitable life crises hit hard, these people close ranks and provide situational, emotional, and spiritual support for the person in crisis. These people 'love'[59] one another in a tangible, quality way. I really doubt that any one of them would choose to date someone who would not feel naturally comfortable in their home group venue. The same thing is true for you. Connecting a person that you have decided to date to these kinds of defining activities will give you all of the insight you need to move on... or not.

We're talking real life, right? Here's what often happens. A Single person has a quality network of relationships and activities. Then infatuation hits, and she is not able to convince her new dating relationship person to participate in any of her defining activities. What happens? She drops out of the spiritually and intellectually essential groups she has faithfully participated in. People say, "What happened to Madeline? I haven't seen her for weeks. Do you know what she is doing?" It's the opposite of 'Connecting:' it's disconnecting. I contend that the relationship for which Madeline is sacrificing her value-based activities will be a brief flare-up, leading to a painful breakup or divorce. The message? If you can't convince the person you have decided to date to *Connect* to your values-based life, STOP that relationship now. The sooner the better. Dragging out this decision will only make the pain worse later on.

---

[59] Now that we have a better understanding of 'Love' from Part One, I hope you appreciate my use of the word here. These relationships are mostly devoid of infatuation-based and emotionally unstable interaction.

Quality 'Connecting' during the early days of the dating phase is a great sign of relationship potential. She should connect with parts of his values-based life. He should see and enjoy participating in the values-based parts of her life. Remember, biking and hiking are fun — but small compatibilities like this are superficial. How telling is it when someone you are dating meets, appreciates, and encourages your relationship with your accountability partner? Powerful. Then you have the potential to hear honest feedback from one of the people on this earth who knows you best; your accountability partner. *Connect* — it's an essential concept for early dating.

Now, let's talk briefly about the exclusive dating phase. When someone knows and truly appreciates you, they will want to enable — in the most positive sense of the word — you to do what you value and do best. In the chart, I have labeled this activity as 'Minister,' which is a way of saying that the person you have chosen to date exclusively really loves to see you being your best, doing what you do best. *They want to serve you so that you can serve others*. If you have chosen this person to be in an exclusive, high-integrity relationship with you, you should feel the same way. You should want to enable your exclusive dating relationship person. You should want that person to be their values-based best in the venues where they meet the needs of others. Listen to Gary Thomas from *Sacred Search*:

> You have no idea how much kingdom time is wasted on ill-matched people trying to make their marriages a little less insufferable. I want you to gain a positive picture — a vision for how much kingdom work could be accomplished by two well-matched people working in harmony to seek the kingdom of God, grow in righteousness, and fulfill their unique calling to Christ.[60]

What is 'kingdom time'? It's a phrase referring to the time you *could* be using to serve others. If you don't relate to the spiritual jargon, you can simply remember that the most fulfilled and committed people are the people who serve others. A sense of purpose, well-being, and direction is theirs. Isn't this kind of life focus that you want in your life? On the other hand, when poorly connected marriages — or even exclusive dating relationships — fall apart, the two people barely have the time and energy to manage the chaos.

Check out the Catherine Marshall quote below. I hope you have been en-

---

[60] Thomas, Gary, *The Sacred Search*. David C. Cook publisher, 2013. Colorado Springs, CO 80918. p. 250.

joying the little quotes and excerpts from authors and philosophers. Usually they are in strong agreement with the principles I've been sharing with you. And I strongly agree with this excerpt to the right with one small exception. It's that word 'happiness'. It's when the Culture tells you to do 'whatever makes you happy'. A lot of emphasis on the extrinsic stuff. For example surfing might 'make you happy', but it will never come close to the feeling you get when you teach a downs kid to paddle and catch a little wave. Do you see the difference? It's what Marshall is talking about when she says 'above and beyond ourselves'. In place of the word happiness I wish she would have used the word 'joy'. To me joy is the word which describes

Dating
without
Delusion

Catherine Marshall

"When we become absorbed in something demanding and worthwhile, above and beyond ourselves, happiness seems to be there as a by-product of the self-giving."

the feeling when you give back. It runs deep within you, because you know you have done something well and without self-motive or selfishness — you have done it for someone else. It's when you recognize the part of your life designed to give back....and you actually do it. It's a part of what your Personal Values describe, and it's the best part.[61] So how does this selfless serving apply to the exclusive dating phase? In this phase you should really be learning about the *other* person, and how you can help them as they work to achieve their values, and you should enjoy doing it!. So back to dating exclusively....

We'll see extensively in the exclusive dating phase you not only are learning how to do this positive enabling, you should also be learning how to communicate most effectively with that very important person. Know them; know how to avoid their hot buttons, understand how they can best hear you. This is a relationship undergirded by exclusive commitment. You can carefully adapt your communication so the other person can really understand you. Ideally, as you continue building the depth and growth of this relationship,

---

[61] For my faith friends, please consider Hebrew 12 v 2: "...for the joy set before Him He endured the cross, scorning its shame, and sat down at the right hand of God". This reference illustrates the meaning of joy, because Jesus' joy came in fulfilling the Father's plan for Him in the face of the crucifixion trials.

they are doing the same on your behalf. After all, in this phase you will be looking (hopefully) forward to a well-built, long-lasting marriage. When we talk about having a vision for a great marriage at the tail end of this book, we'll discuss some concepts for operating in the ideal relationship dynamic (what faith-based people call discipleship). Operating in each dating phase is discussed next.

Decision Point #1:
To date or not to date?

OK, you're lonely, bored, and disillusioned. Please use some of the tools in the Part Three 'Toolbox'. In particular, look at the 'Loneliness' tool. Whatever you do, don't jump into a relationship to ease your emotional strain. You know what your Core Values are, right? Keep communicating them, keep being committed to them, and keep spending your time being true to who you are. Lean on your best relationships. Trust your accountability partner. Serve others. Don't hyperventilate and obsess over a potential relationship (easy for me to say). In short, this is the 'Date or Don't Date Phase' (the shaded oval in the slide below). You have to remember who YOU are in order to make the big decision.

When you meet someone who is tripping your emotional hot buttons (remember the 'Phenomena of Recognition' from Harville Hendrix?), and Dopamine and Serotonin and other brain hormones are firing in your head, be very careful. You 'feel' magnetically drawn to a new person. What are you going to do? The key is to find out *who they are*. Recite your 4C's! To do that, you first have to communicate clearly *who you*

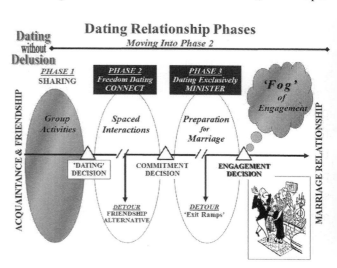

are! Your honesty about yourself *earns* the emotional space to ask the other person, "Who are you?" Do this over coffee, at the community picnic, in a class, at the party of a mutual friend; get the idea? Seek a safe environment. I call Phase 1 the Sharing Phase. So the obvious question is, sharing what? At this point, you know your Personal Values, so share them! Through your values, share how you have learned to know God; how you pray (or maybe you don't); how you worship; how you serve others; about your best, most important relationships; how you excel at work. It's about transparent information flow. Here's a 'sharing' starter list for you:

- Share your Personal Core Values (with all the stories and history that brought you to those values)

- Explain why and how your values are unique to you.

- Talk about the commitments your values have inspired.

- Talk about your spiritual gifts, your personality profile, your strengths and talents.

- Talk about your family, and what you love about it.

- Talk about your close friends and your accountability partner.

- Do you go to a home group? Talk about how you have been encouraged there.

- Talk about your service activities, and why you love to do them.

- Explain how serving brings you joy (even happiness).

- Do you have a short testimony (or maybe past hurts from the church)? Briefly share that experience.

Do you see that sharing these kinds of personal insights really should be pretty easy? You're a 4C person! Particularly if you have done some quality thinking about your life and how you are uniquely wired. Most importantly, these kinds of conversations should always be two-way. When you share key parts of your life, you *earn* the emotional/interpersonal space to ask that person about the key elements of *their* life. At the most fundamental level, you are *sharing* information about your life so you can hear values information about the other person's life... all to make sure you have an idea of what their values are. Enter Cardinal Rule #1 (next page). Why is this so important? Simply because no matter what you think or feel at this moment, a first date encounter might be the beginning of a long roller coaster of a ride. As it says on the slide: 'A decision to date represents a decision to take the first step towards marriage.' You've seen it happen to other people, and so have I. Don't

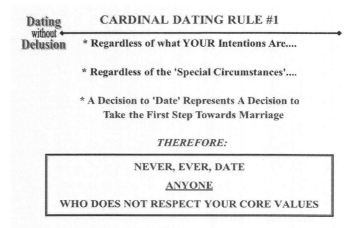

take the risk of getting entangled with someone who doesn't understand and respect your Personal Values. Make sure they have values of their own: values that are 'values-similar' to yours.

10 fatal flaws

If you are not a Christian, you may be tiring of my recurring Bible dependence. So here is another tool for your consideration. It comes from Barbara DeAngelis, a Ph.D. psychologist who has a number of published works and gives informative relationship seminars. The '10 Fatal Flaws' comes from her book, *Are You the One for Me?* Sure, there are more than 10 fatal relationship flaws, but this list gives you a great set of issues to be aware of. During the seminar, I try to make light of this very serious list. For you faith thinkers, you can imagine there's a lot of scripture validation and backup for every one of these flaws. Let's look at Barbara's list.

Addictions: Check out the first bullet down, for example (I add the comments in parentheses). Addictions are life-breakers; we all have known people who have been trapped in the jaws of an addiction. To keep the seminar atmosphere light, I use a Gary Larson cartoon that shows a commentator — who is a dog — with a panel of anonymous dogs behind a curtain. The caption reads, "Dogs who lick the toilet bowl, next!" Real addictions are not funny however, and they are relationship killers. If you are in a relationship with someone trapped in an addiction, the thought that they will change — someday — or that you can help them change — is not realistic. You have to be sure they have already made the change and committed to it on their own. You have to be sure that they have safeguards in place to fight a relapse. Remember way the back in the introduction, we talked about the only person

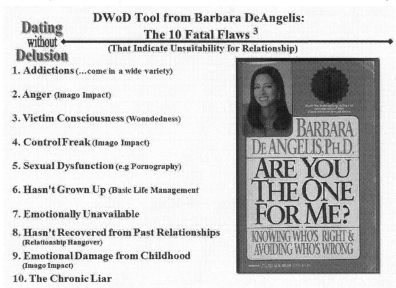

Dating without Delusion

DWoD Tool from Barbara DeAngelis:
The 10 Fatal Flaws [3]
(That Indicate Unsuitability for Relationship)

1. **Addictions** (...come in a wide variety)

2. **Anger** (Imago Impact)

3. **Victim Consciousness** (Woundedness)

4. **Control Freak** (Imago Impact)

5. **Sexual Dysfunction** (e.g Pornography)

6. **Hasn't Grown Up** (Basic Life Management

7. **Emotionally Unavailable**

8. **Hasn't Recovered from Past Relationships** (Relationship Hangover)

9. **Emotional Damage from Childhood** (Imago Impact)

10. **The Chronic Liar**

who you are going to change is you. If *you* are the person with the addiction, getting help from God and from professionals is your #1 priority. Please leave dating relationships alone while you do your personal change work.

Anger: Let's briefly talk briefly about bullet #2: Anger. I picked up this problem from my father's anger, and it's been with me my entire life. Remember Imago from Harville Hendrix? Anger was modeled for me all during my formative years, and unfortunately — and predictably — I picked it up. Consequently, anger management is very important for me; I use every tool that the Bible gives me to manage anger whenever it shows up. People with varying degrees of repressed anger are going to have difficulty in dating relationships. Seeing a person in the whole spectrum of life's situations to find out how they deal with anger is one of the reasons I ask you to freedom date — non-exclusively. It's a lot safer.

Victim consciousness:[62] I hope it is clear that you cannot look for new dating

---

[62] Victim Consciousness is an acknowledged psychological phenomenon. A Google search will give all you need (and more) to understand it.

relationships when you are recovering from the emotional hurricane coming from the dissolution of a former relationship. Some people are persistently aware of how they have been wounded in past relationships. And they always are suspect....the world and everyone in it is trying to take advantage of them. This is a real condition which requires professional counseling. These people hold onto the emotional damage which comes from life's inevitable downturns. For these people, healing time is essential. You should recognize people in this state of mind are not ready for a new relationship; time, healing, prayer, and counseling are the answer.

Control freak: The person who thinks they control your life because you started dating....much more dangerous if you compromised sexually. The Control Freak could never allow freedom in dating, and you'll find that out shortly after the first date — if you get that far. You've seen and perhaps experienced the persistent directives coming from that often-dominant personality: wanting to know every move, every circumstance in your life, even when it is not appropriate. Counselors often see this relationship as one that can easily become abusive in the long run.

Sexual dysfunction: For the purpose of this discussion, I'm going to home in on pornography because it is so widespread and infused into our culture. Women, as you get to know a man, you must be alert to the presence of pornography in his life. This is very easy to keep undercover in the early phases of a relationship, and it is a big problem. Women, suffice it to say that you can never compete with the evil of porn; during dating, it is reason enough to break off the relationship.

Hasn't grown up yet: For seminar discussion, I zero in on Money, House, Food. Does this person have the basic ability to manage money; to maintain their living space; to feed themselves? Remember my admonition in the very beginning of the book: "The only person you're going to change is yourself!" These are issues that a person must deal with on their own terms with help from their circle of family and friends... not you.

Emotional unavailability: Does their unavailability stem from distant issues in childhood? Does it connect directly to a recent relationship? Suffice it to say that healthy relationships are emotionally open. In healthy dating, people must be able to share personal feelings at an appropriate level, at the appropriate time. Women: if you think his persistent silence is going to improve, you may be deceiving yourselves. Men like this can easily become expert stonewallers, frustrating you with punishing silences. Don't hold out hope for people to magically become emotionally open and honest.

Hasn't recovered from past relationships: Remember the Part Two discussion on exclusive dating? I asked you to make sure that you both have recovered and matured from serious past break-ups. If either of you is still in the recovery process, exclusive dating is way too premature. If you're dragging around regrets and sadness from a past relationship, should you be dating at all? Maybe not.

The chronic liar: Let's skip down to the last bullet, #10. Many people have learned to lie, to conceal, to exaggerate the truth...and that kills relationships because it absolutely undermines trust. This book doesn't have enough pages to talk about the problems created by lying. Remember the man who fudged on his actual height on his on-line profile? He was insecure. Does that mean he is a chronic liar? Maybe not. Lies are serious because they usually cover up a deeper problem; lying is a weak attempt to cover up something else. One of the essential reasons for intelligent dating is to experience communication and commitment with that other person. A lie, a deception, or perhaps heavy exaggeration...they all are warning signals that justify ending that dating relationship. If you try to refer that person to counselors and psychologists who are trained to deal with this kind of issue, you'll probably get blown off. The bottom line? It's the Ninth Commandment for a reason! Lying is a great rationale to say "no" to dating or further dating that person. And, as I have coached you before, the "no" can be accompanied by this very valid reason.

Looking at lists like this one and talking about these relationship tools in general is important to do in the bright light of day, before you get on the relationship rollercoaster. As a Single, once the relationship emotions start to get intense, you probably won't be reading any of these relationship books but maybe you can remember key red flags that you've learned. When you tell someone forthrightly that they have an issue to work through, you're blessing them with honesty and an opportunity. You're suggesting that this is an opportunity for them to change _themselves_. As you look at these lists and tools, perhaps you see an issue that *you* have. So I recommend this 'tool' for your toolbox. It may even help you as you work on being the best you can be... now.

If you appreciate this approach to avoiding problem relationships, Barbara has plenty more. How about 'Compatibility Time Bombs' or '10 qualities to look for in a mate'. How about '10 types of relationships that won't work'? These and more are in her books and articles. But I know Singles driven by infatuation won't be looking at many lists. I hope that Singles in the midst of dating will remember the Personal Values they worked so hard to refine.

Cardinal Rule #1: Redefining the date

So let's look at what a date might, or might not, be. If you can be personally transparent, and if you can see some synergy with that other person, you are ready to answer the first big question: "To date or not to date?" It's the first triangle on the timeline. This is the first decision point. Rule #1 answers the "To date, or not to date?" question. Remember, we didn't do all that Personal Values work for nothing! Once again, if you compromise and go out with someone who doesn't respect and understand your values, you may be on the road to a marriage pre-set for failure. Remember the gray divorce phenomena! We all know people who dated, thinking there wasn't any long-term prospect; the next thing you know, the couple is 'an item.' Engagement (and probably an inevitable divorce) is very predictable. But you have your well-articulated Personal Values. You have close friends who know you, and you have your accountability partner. *Remember Rule #1!* When I say the word 'date' or 'dating' to Singles, they often roll their eyes towards the ceiling and chuckle nervously. All by itself, the word seems to tap into a whole range of emotions and painful histories many people would just as soon forget. The modern culture has pretty much disregarded the 'date' word. I now hear young people talk about 'being with' someone — inappropriately and unfortunately noted on the Facebook page.

Because sex is often an assumption in today's relationships, the negative impact of being 'with' someone is magnified many times over. The statisticians and researchers say that living together is often a precursor to big problems in marriage, if marriage happens at all. If you have done your values work and you're in a reasonably normal season of life, potential relationships can come your way — often when you least expect it.

What are you going to do? Let's do the date redefinition first. Please look at the slide below. Many other people will have many different concepts for what 'date' means, but you can be much more precise. Other people's dating

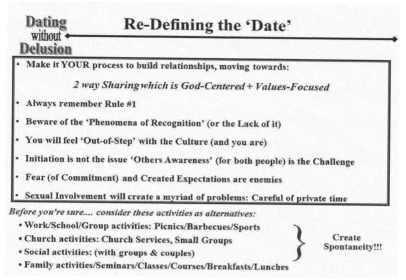

concepts and ideas of relationships are usually very vague, and often are just reflections of 'how I feel.' That's OK; with your values, you can work to be personally transparent and to discover the essentials of that other person. Instead of just compatibility, you can look for *values compatibility* (not the other fluffy stuff). Otherwise, before you know it, you may find yourself experiencing a divorce at the 18 month mark — if you make it that long. When you develop a giving (Agape), interesting (Phileo) relationship, you create the foundation for an emotionally controlled relationship (Eros). You're aiming for a relationship positioned to potentially grow in Commitment (the second C). The idea of growing the relationship is a concept that must be clear and unambiguous. The italics in the slide are the key→ *2 way sharing that is God-centered and values-focused.*

If you are a Christian, you must work to keep God in the center of your relationship development, and you both must keep working at clear communication of your Personal Values. Repeating Rule #1 (second bullet down): 'Never, ever date anyone who does not respect/appreciate/understand your Core Values.' Do your values have to be exactly the same? NO. Do they have to work with yours? Absolutely.

Remember the Three-Part Love discussion in Part One? If you elect to date someone, you better know their values and make sure they understand yours! There is a hilarious Gary Larson cartoon that shows a totally unkempt slob in a stained wife-beater T-shirt. He is sitting in a tattered overstuffed chair in front of a TV. Banana peels and empty beer cans litter the floor. Food is all over the place, including on his unshaven face. The caption: 'Giorgio Armani at home.' The message is subtle, or maybe not so subtle: 'Appearances can be very deceiving.' Or how about, 'People can put on airs.' Or how about, 'He is not what he seems to be.' The deceptive ruse is easy to pull off if you're meeting her in an over-packed bar. Deception is proving to be pretty easy over the Internet. The over-packed bar is the perfect storm of emotional attraction, physical sexual compromise, and no real communication. That's why people go to bars.

But remember, this is **Dating _without_ Delusion**. You want to date someone who respects, understands, and maybe even shares some of your Personal Core Values. Do you think you can communicate your values in the over-packed bar? Do you think someone you meet in a bar is ready to discuss Personal Values? NOT. So work to spend time sharing and communicating before you make the dating decision. Once again, I suggest the key dating definition:

Two-way sharing that is God-centered and values-focused.

Maybe you're not a Christian. Then replace the God-centered (hard for me to recommend) with something else like honest, high-integrity, transparent, or some other key element that you deeply appreciate. An example might be: "Dating is my process to build values-transparent relationships moving towards _____." You fill in the blank. Here's another dating definition for you to consider: "Dating (for me) is the process by which I build a relationship with deep inter-personal understanding as the basis for a life-long marriage relationship."

Beware of the phenomena of recognition (or lack of it). The third bullet down recalls Harville Hendrix's teaching. Remember those brain stimulators released when you encounter someone with dysfunctions similar to those you experienced in childhood? That might be intense infatuation firing. Be careful. Think. Look for those red flags that have been tucked into your persona from childhood. The opposite is also true. If you meet someone who loves to serve and give in a way similar to you DO NOT turn down that relationship just because 'bells and whistles' aren't going off in your head.

You will feel out of step with the culture (and you are). Slow paced in-control dating is absolutely the opposite of what this culture promotes. The fourth bullet down suggests that. You may get subtle disrespect, demeaning attitudes, and low-key verbal abuse, about your relationship choice — usually from the people who have no values and are interested in random hook-ups. Gossip will try to bring you down. People will assume, because you went on one date you have established an exclusive dating relationship. They will assume you abandoned your moral standards and had sex. You must meet these innuendos and suggestions with a clear explanation of your altruistic goals and intentions. Be ready. Be on your guard.

Initiation is not the issue. Others Awareness (for both people) is the challenge. Singles spend a lot of time discussing who-should-ask-who to do a date. Old school traditions mandate that the man step forward and ask the woman to go out. Traditions have faded, haven't they? Why not spend a nice 30 minutes at Starbucks over a cup of coffee, discussing real life values and you'll know why a date makes sense — or not. I say spend some good quality communication time with a person of character, and the question of going out on a date, treating it as the special occasion will naturally resolve itself.

Fear of Commitment and Created Expectations are Enemies. Does one date signal to the world that you are a committed couple? The gossip will try to suggest you are; and knowing how you will be attacked by the whisperers is very scary. You must hold onto your reality that one date does not define you as being 'with someone'. Some people carry around expectations from just one-date which are mysterious and camouflaged. These are tough challenges which your excellent communication skills (?) will have to face head-on.

Sexual Involvement will create a myriad of problems. Careful of private time. All the complications of sexual involvement are ever-present. We will discuss them in detail. Here is one more reminder to stay in 'safe' environments.

Now that we have spent half of the book working on your Personal Core Values, this next point should be obvious. Once you share your values with someone you are attracted to, how do they react? Recently, there was a mature woman in a ***Dating without Delusion*** seminar; like everyone else, she was struggling to define/refine her Core Values. She still had her parents, who she loved and deeply respected. Unfortunately, for a number of medical and financial reasons, she had to move them into her house. Now, she was providing their caretaking. One seminar night we were discussing Core Values, and I was using one of my Core Values as an example. It's my Core Value to: "Know, Speak, and Live the 10 Commandments." If you are a Christian, you know these are the bedrock basics of life. Given to Moses by God and validated for us many times by Jesus saying, "If you love Me, keep My Commandments." Commandment #5 is the one regarding parents. "Honor your Father and Mother, which is the first Commandment with a promise, that it may go well with you and you may live long on the earth." Do you remember the discussion on values from Part 1?

A value is not a value unless it drives your choices. (Jay)

Now you know your choice to date or not to date (remember to use the Starbucks Alternative as a before-dating option)) should be driven by your values. Seems logical, but it's hard to do because of infatuation. Well, this woman was living out the Fifth Commandment — any man who wanted to have a quality relationship with her had better understand her commitment to her parents (and to God). Now, imagine a man meets this attractive and vibrant woman, and wants to initiate a relationship with her. He should understand the depth of commitment she has made to her parents. First, however, it is her responsibility to clearly articulate her personal commitment. It is *not*, "Oh, by the way, my parents live with me." Let's say it again: it is *her* responsibility, as a mature adult who takes personal responsibility for her choices, to clearly articulate this value as a defining part of her life.

A decision to date is the first step towards marriage, so it is a BIG decision. The person you are going to date should understand who you are, and vice versa. Now, imagine that she does her part: she articulates clearly and succinctly that "I am committed to care for my parents in xyz ways," and he blows it off. "Sure, I'll meet them sometime." He doesn't respect her Core Value; he doesn't understand her commitment to her Core Value, and he doesn't even begin to understand that a relationship with her is going to entail a resulting relationship with her parents. Cardinal points on the compass start with north; true north for dating relationships is essential. It's so important,

I'll repeat it again:

> *Never, ever date anyone who does not understand, respect, and appreciate your Core Values.*

A man who demonstrates disregard for one of this woman's defining values has given her the clear *reason* she will not date him, and she can articulate her choice not to date him exactly that way. Here's a concluding dating thought:

> *The idea is to know yourself, to be known as yourself, and to use your understanding to build relationships with others.*

Women: Never say "NO"?

When you meet someone for the first time, most people are a bit nervous and self-conscious. That goes double or triple when you meet someone you are attracted to, and when it's someone you might date. Obviously there are slick players who can conjure up all kinds of nonchalance, but there are many more 'normal' people in the world: people with natural anxieties and doubts. During the seminars, I go to great lengths to explain how, for most men, it is an act of courage to ask a woman to date him. I also explain that even for attractive, masculine, high-achieving males, that act of reaching out to ask a woman to spend date time with him is pretty risky. To make this worse, we males have often-fragile egos. When rejection comes we men are hurt, and it takes some cover-up to disguise the damage. So I ask women to never bluntly say, "No" to a dating request, if for no other reason than to take it easy on our poor male psyche.

If you are learning anything from this book, you know you don't have to bluntly deliver rejection lines. You know 'who you are' (through your Personal Values). Usually, that other person doesn't have a clue what to value or not; even if they did have a 'values clue,' they haven't yet communicated that value set to you. So women, you can simply and honestly say, "Thanks for the offer, but I just don't know you well enough yet." Perhaps this usually true answer will initiate some low-pressure, sharing, non-dating communication time to have those honest discussions (a 'Starbucks connection'?).

Fast forward to this Millennial culture. Men are being pursued by young women (*Unhooked*, Laura Stepp), so the risk level for men has dropped dramatically. And if the woman of interest is not approaching him, a young guy can always ask that woman to "come over and hang out," or to "come on over to the party we're having next weekend." If she shows up, he'll take it from there. With women initiating much of the interaction, young guys are happy to sit back and field the interest. This is sad for women in many ways because they don't get to see how a man can handle the dating request challenge, to see the kind of character which demonstrates his future capacity for meaningful commitment. To the young men and women reading this, it is totally counter-cultural to articulate Core Values. Today's culture elevates lifestyle to top priority. Lifestyle is the driving value and if you recognize this, you may as well be honest about it. The key here is to spend quality time with your 'person of interest' communicating the values you have been working to refine.

Phase 2: Freedom Dating

This concept is, by far, the hardest to wrap your mind around. Today, people move from impulsive relationship to impulsive relationship thinking they are committed, faithful, and trustworthy, while they often are simply deceiving themselves. 'Serial monogamy' is an oxymoron. Relationship after relationship with sexual compromise is promiscuous; don't be fooled. Serial monogamy is promiscuous. People initiate emotional and physically intense relationships that flare up suddenly and dramatically — and then proceed into the breakup 'hurts.' But then it's back to the frustration/loneliness of Singleness, while the search for the next 'perfect partner' begins.

This sort of serial monogamy hurts you in many ways. When you do freedom dating, you must control and protect your sexuality. Without this constraint, you are deluding yourself; you have caved into the hook-up culture. Here's the 'Freedom Dating' concept. First, remember Rule #1: Be very careful about who you date. Once you do make a good values-based decision, you must be ready to enjoy meaningful conversation on that date. See Phase 2 in the shaded oval on the next page?

What is freedom dating? It means you elect to go out with someone because you respect them, you understand their values, goals and aspirations, and you want to know them better — and yes, you are attracted to them — at least somewhat. An evening at dinner with someone who shares those kinds of meaningful personal insights? How bad can that be? During this dating phase, you can begin to *Connect* this person to some of your values-based activities. It's one thing to share the fact that you go to a weekly Bible study home group; it's quite another to invite that person to attend the group. It's one thing to talk

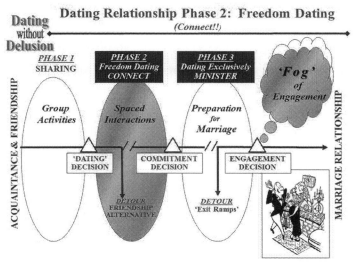

about your work with a charitable/benevolent organization. It's quite another to invite your friend to work at the thrift store with you. It's great to have a personal commitment to prayer; it's on a totally different level to have the opportunity to pray with this person. *Connecting* the person you are now dating with the values-based activities and commitments in your life is part of the dating decision.

What about the insight you will gain from connecting your relationship to your important activities? It's one thing to for a person to hear about your commitment to meaningful activities; it's a whole new and more in-depth revelation to see the person you have dated in the environment that houses your commitments. What is her comfort level? How does he fit into your environment? How does she interact with your co-contributors? Is he comfortable with the people you trust and respect? Do you see the recommended difference between quality *Sharing* in Phase 1 and real in-person *Connecting* in Phase 2? Does that mean the good communication stops? Of course not. Connecting builds upon and continues the great dialogue you began before you were dating. *The difference between a friendship relationship and dating relationship is huge.* The difference between knowing someone and dating someone is 'huge-er' (if there were such a word).

If you are at all like me you hate ambiguity. I like to be clear on my commitments so you can know what to expect from me. I'd like to expect the same from you. Expectations in early dating however are often unspoken and ambiguous; you know it and everyone in the seminars knows it too. So in the last 3 class sessions I often begin this phase by explaining the very intense process of dating exclusively....*before* we even begin to talk about the Freedom/early dating phase. I draw up the scenario of the two Singles enjoying a nice first date dinner at a very nice restaurant. I ask the class to imagine a discussion which goes like this:

- What kind of marriage style do you think would be right for us?
- Let's talk about the emotional trauma in my childhood...
- Let me share the painful lessons I learned from my last serious relationship.
- I think we should develop some conflict resolution techniques!
- Let me share with you some of the ugly details of my last divorce.
- In the past, I have seriously failed to manage money correctly...
- I have some serious debt to deal with...
- Let's work on our combined budget!

Do you see how nonsensical these are? This is the kind of stuff you need to deal with in an *exclusive* dating relationship — the next pre-engagement phase. On this first date you have little commitment, you should have little intimacy, physically, intellectually, and personally. My Single friend, you know what you should be talking about on this dinner date, because you have been through Part One of this book. You talk about, and articulate, and recall the stories behind your Personal Values! So let's continue down the Freedom dating path.

Here's the hard question: what does 'freedom' mean? First and foremost, it means that you protect *your* freedom: freedom to continue to live as you choose, freedom to set your own schedule and — here's the kicker — freedom to meet and possibly date other people. If you thought dating was counter-cultural, how about freedom dating... with non-exclusivity? You will be out of step with the culture in many ways. What's the catch? Freedom dating requires that you have only *very* limited sexual involvement, if any at all. And you preserve the kinds of discussions cited above — childhood trauma and so on — for the next phase.

To have Freedom... First give it away

Singles have taught me about expectations sneaking into dating interactions. Created expectations are always a challenge. Expectations like:

- This has been such a great time, I assume will date again.
- I'll start regularly communicating with you (phone/e-mail/text)
- I'll post a picture of us out on the date
- We'll share a kiss at the door
- I know you would never 'see' (date) anyone else
- Of course you'll include me in your next x,y,z activity

Remember the Relationship Ripper: Expectations created but not communicated breaks down the potential of good relationships. So if you want to do a future activity with this person _please say so_ and be clear about it. Otherwise give freedom to the other person first, and _then_ you will have it for yourself. How do you do this? You're concluding the date — a nervous time — and you simply say:

- Great evening thanks for joining me. No expectations?
- Before we think about another date....please join me at my (service-based) activity.
- Let's take some time to think-and pray-about next steps....O.K.?
- I had a nice time. Thank you. Please....no obligations?
- Before we consider another date I'd like you to meet my good friend (who is your accountability partner).

Do these seem non-committal and a bit evasive? Good! You've been out on one great date, and shared your Values centered life and beliefs. That's a start of a good relationship — but only a start. If you and she experienced a Values-disconnect, you have a reason to avoid any more dating, so say so. Even on the best dates however, it's normal to be unsure, so give freedom to the other person and stake a healthy claim to your own freedom.

Sexual involvement — A river of unspoken communication

Sex is an intimacy which must be preserved. Here's a summary of what many psychologists and medical professionals know. Sexual involvement — and particularly sexual intercourse — creates intense feelings of attachment (well "duh," you say). It's also a 'river of unspoken communication': see the slide below. If you let sex happen, it sabotages your capacity to meet and spend

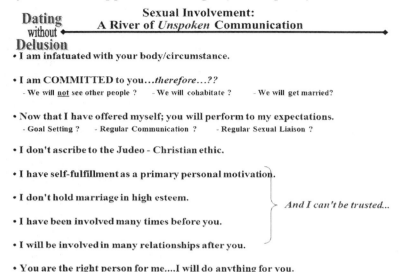

time with other people. Unless you let sex be *the* reason for meeting new people, in which case you're definitely reading the wrong book. If you let sex happen, even in this culture, you will be seen as an unavailable Single person, or just another low-principled individual doing what everyone else is doing.

Here's some help for your decision (see slide above). When you lose the fight to maintain your sexual integrity, you don't know what the other person has *assumed*, based upon your sexual involvement. Is that other person infatuated with your body? Does sex mean that there is now a substantial commitment between you and that other person? What commitment might that be? Again from the slide above: in 'background thinking,' the other person may have all kinds of questions and doubts about your motivation for sexual involvement. If you are a faith person, you are crossing the line when you are driven by physical involvement. What is the motivation for sex? It's often self-focused and selfish. The person pushing for sex may be broadcasting "I do this all the time, and I will continue to pursue other relationships primarily for sex after I have been involved with you." How about the last point down? "I am infatuated with you and I will do anything for you." Get the point? Bottom line is, *you don't know* what they are thinking. In the short term, infatuation is driving you, her, or both of you: not the mutual respect you need to develop a lasting relationship. Here I'm talking about even lower level sexual involvement, not necessarily sexual intercourse. Sexual activity blurs relationships, when you are trying to achieve some relationship transparency.

Looking back at the phase slide. Look inside the oval in Phase 2, where it says, 'Spaced Interactions.' Hopefully this is self-explanatory. You've been out with this person once! This relationship is not ready for a barrage of phone calls, day-to-day interactions, etc. If you are obsessing about this person, please go run a marathon or something else to help dial down your infatuation. Space your interactions! If the person insists, or if you can't stand it, you and she should do a value activity-faith people can fall back on church activities, for example. But watch out when you two show up for the church service: now you'll have to deal with the gossip. Gossip is a difficult reality that very often demeans you and the other person you have dated. Do you see the fragility of a new dating relationship?[63] Usually one person is experiencing more attraction than the other, and that person has to deal with those intense feelings of attraction. Slow down! Space your interactions over time. Perhaps you meet twice in one week. Perhaps you do a second date in a week or so. Here, *none* of my recommendations are prescriptive, meaning, "Do it exactly as I say." Instead they convey, hopefully, that you must deliberately slow down. I've made this mistake and suffered for it; perhaps that's why I'm sensitive.

The Binding Circle

Deeply felt attraction can be the beginning of a very painful sequence. It starts with the emotional slide that is set off by sexual attraction, infatuation phenomena, and sexual. involvement. Looking at the sequence of attraction/ infatuation, we talk about the 'Binding Circle' (below). I have heard it said that without testosterone, men would never enter into the complexities and commitments of marriage. That may be true from a logical standpoint because we all know the 'drive' that testosterone injects into relationships. To top it off, we have the brain stimulus that comes from the phenomena of recognition. Does this emotional swirl happen in a nice little sequential process like you see on the graphic? No, but I want you to understand the power

---

[63] Please 'dog-ear' this page, or put a paper clip in it so you can refer back to this list. We will discuss every point... every mind-set tip... from top to bottom.

of the hormones working on you. It's like, do I even have a chance? Does the stimulus of infatuation and fog of attraction lead sequentially to sexual

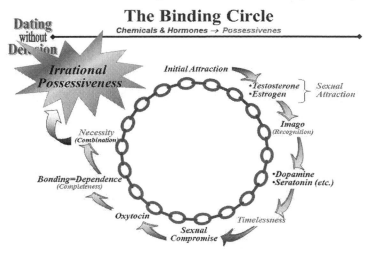

The Binding Circle

Chemicals & Hormones → Possessivenes

Dating without Devotion

Irrational Possessiveness

Initial Attraction

•Testosterone •Estrogen — Sexual Attraction

Imago (Recognition)

Necessity (Combination)

•Dopamine •Seratonin (etc.)

Bonding=Dependence (Completeness)

Oxytocin

Timelessness

Sexual Compromise

compromise and irrational possessiveness? It doesn't have to. Anyone who has been in the throes of these feelings knows it's like an intense emotional soup that you have to wade through. In these hormone-driven mindsets, the feelings swirling around in your head are intense. You do know for sure that those "I have to have her; I can't live without him" feelings are ones that will not last. Restating the essential:

> *Everything good that has ever come into your life or ever will come into your life comes as the result of commitment, either your commitment to someone else or someone else's commitment to you. (Jay)*

Lasting commitments are not feelings-based. They are values-based. Intense infatuation is not commitment; it is guaranteed to fade. If you irrationally commit to someone, your commitment is fragile and guaranteed to be followed by the sad disintegration of the bond that you thought was so incredible. Do your own research on Oxytocin (no, not OxyContin, the pain reliever) and see how powerful it is, particularly for women. This hormone creates intense attachment feelings after intercourse. If you fail to keep away from sex, you are adding all of the possessiveness and feeling of attachment which comes after intercourse. Follow the binding circle clockwise around the chain. You and I probably can remember these phenomena from our past relationship history, and 'Irrational Possessiveness' is powerful. Hopefully you avoided the potentially disastrous conclusion depicted at the end of the chain and in the airplane collision in the graphic below. In spite of the chem-

Impatient Sexuality:
The Logical Consequence

Dating without Delusion

You Marry The Wrong Person!!

Go Directly to the Worst Kind of Relationship

ically driven surge of attraction, I am suggesting you change your way of thinking. For Christians, I love Romans 12, verses 1 and 2. "I urge you therefore brethren, by the mercies of God to present your bodies as a living and holy sacrifice, acceptable to God which is your spiritual service of worship. And do not be conformed to the world, but be transformed by the renewing of your mind, so that you may prove what the will of God is, that which is good and acceptable and perfect" (italics mine).[64]

Win the battle in your mind first

Dating with Freedom (non-exclusively) requires a different mindset and a different way of thinking. Having a dating experience, even a good dating experience, is an important first step... but it is only a first step. We've discussed the problems with sexual involvement; sex has serious implications. Internally you know this, but the culture teaches the try before you buy attitude. Beyond that sexual encounter is a whole list of expectations you and she, or you and he, don't begin to understand. You can be so convinced that this is the right person...and so you make the critical wrong choice; and just like an airplane collision, annihilate one another in a marriage collision — better known as a divorce. So the get ready for the battle. Move slowly, intentionally, and with limited expectations. Ask the Lord to help you do this (if you are

[64] Romans chapter 12 vv 1&2. NASB.

a Christian). Spend time with your close friends, and talk about the vulnerability you are feeling (or maybe you're not). In every situation try to go slow.

Mindset tips for Phase 2

Now let's look at some mindset tips for Freedom Dating: Phase 2 (below). The slide refers to 'new paradigm' thinking. Yes, dating with freedom and patience requires a shift to a new thinking framework… a paradigm… a re-

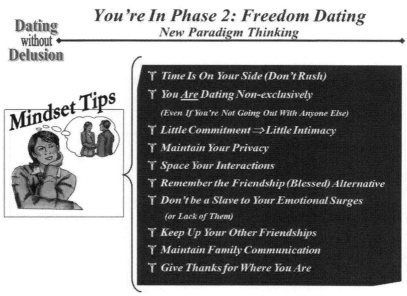

You're In Phase 2: Freedom Dating
Dating without Delusion
New Paradigm Thinking

Mindset Tips

- ⴲ *Time Is On Your Side (Don't Rush)*
- ⴲ *You Are Dating Non-exclusively*
  (Even If You're Not Going Out With Anyone Else)
- ⴲ *Little Commitment ⟹ Little Intimacy*
- ⴲ *Maintain Your Privacy*
- ⴲ *Space Your Interactions*
- ⴲ *Remember the Friendship (Blessed) Alternative*
- ⴲ *Don't be a Slave to Your Emotional Surges*
  (or Lack of Them)
- ⴲ *Keep Up Your Other Friendships*
- ⴲ *Maintain Family Communication*
- ⴲ *Give Thanks for Where You Are*

structured mindset. Again, look at the slide above (with the little weight-lifters). The first point is yet another reminder to go slow:

Time is on your side (don't rush!). That's the opposite of what a person flooded with Infatuation would do. Always, no matter what you feel, *go slow!* Looking at the mindset tips, the first point is critical. Time *is* on your side, so don't rush. People who are caught up in the Imago-based phenomena of recognition readily tell me to butt out: "I *know* this is the right one, Jay!" At this stage, be honest and admit that you really don't know how this relationship will work out. If you know where you are in the relationship, you are equipped to protect yourself. Here's another mindset tip for this phase:

> *"Never make anyone a priority in your life, when you are*
> *just an option in their life." (Unknown)*

Believe me, I have seen so many Singles practically jump out of their skin with excitement over a new dating relationship. Patience is very important. Usually these emotional tsunamis do not last.

You are dating non-exclusively... Even if you are not going out with anyone else. Point two is that you are dating with FREEDOM, both for you and for him. The practical upshot of freedom is *non-exclusivity,* even if you are not going out with anyone else. Why? Because if you were asked out by someone else, you *could* go because you didn't get swept away by your emotions, you didn't compromise sexually, and you maintained your integrity. Knowing this was a first date, you didn't get involved intimately (right?). Great, that was appropriate because you and she had little commitment to one another. Your relationship was unsure and in the 'discovery mode' (pretty exciting though, huh?).

I am often challenged in the seminars because women, in particular, cannot imagine dating more than one person at a time. Attractive women are constantly offered hook-up opportunities. They are being hit-on by men who are engulfed in our hormone driven, infatuation-based, pornography-soaked culture. Honestly, this barrage wears women down.[65] They are tired of it. The first and most important skill for these women is to learn to communicate that they are only interested in building relationships with people who share similar Personal Values. Women, please explain to the thick-headed guys that values are the challenge. I know that attractive men experience the same kind of challenge on a less frequent scale, but the answer is the same: communicate clear Personal Values! Here are some answers to help shift your thinking....combined with the totally fictitious story of Mary Beth.

1) The chance of meeting even one person who is a high-integrity, values-based person is pretty small. And you know it.

2) The chance of meeting two reasonably attractive guys who share compatible values with you is even smaller... almost minuscule. So when women say, "I'm not going to date four or five guys at the same time!" I heartily agree. You won't have four or five values-centric guys in your sphere of influence any one time, either.

---

[65] Women, if you bear the blessing and burden of physical attractiveness, here's an empathetic verse from the book of Proverbs: Proverbs 11 v 22: 'Like a gold ring in a pig's snout is a beautiful woman who has no discretion.' Be polite, be clear, be careful.

3) We all have the fear of the gossip culture labeling you as a loose, low-principled women or man. Get ready; the culture is nasty, with all of the social media fueling it. So your fear is well founded, underscoring the need to avoid the temptation of sexual involvement and to regularly communicate your freedom from needy emotional attachment. Communicate your confident independence....over and over again to everyone you care about.

4) If you accept that first date with a well-meaning values-grounded man, the gossip wheel will still try to grind you down by a thousand and one whispering voices trying to label you as a 'couple' on the expressway to marriage. You are not! You have to clearly refute those greasy little gossip innuendos coming at you, maybe even in the church foyer. And whatever you do, don't tag yourself on Facebook as being 'In a Relationship'... and he better not, either.

5) Suppose Mr. Values-based man enjoys a high-integrity, great-communication date with Mary Beth. Good follow-up communication practice suggests that you touch base with her the next day or at least within a couple of days, to thank her for the enjoyable time. Maybe you want to enjoy another date? Maybe you should Connect with some of the common-ground stuff in Mary Beth's life that you really found interesting. If you know her well enough to date her, then it's time to Connect her with important parts of your life.

6) Here's the tough part: Suppose you received another offer from another person who you know is a high-quality, sincere individual. Yep, you both share some nice, fundamental values. Do you think, "Gee, I'd like to ask her to go out, but I just took Mary Beth to dinner." What do you do? First, see if you can share some time with this second person in safe activities. If you spend more time with this woman, and you still see her Integrity and attractiveness, I say ask her out! Courtesy and restraint will go with you again on that next date, right? Good. Then look for an opportunity to share with Mary Beth that you are going to ask someone else to dinner. If you treated Mary Beth well, perhaps she'll see that your motives are good. Maybe she'll blow up in your face, in which case you've learned lot about Mary Beth. Maybe in the long run, you'll see that Mary Beth is the one who was subtly but undeniably the person of integrity, with all

the inner attractiveness you recognized in the first place. Because of the freedom you offered and lived by, that door will probably be open to you.

7) Look back to pg. 202 to continue the Mindset Tips/suggestions: discussion below.

Little commitment means little intimacy... even if your hormones are screaming at you. Men, in particular, are being bombarded with society's pornography and it is difficult to maintain personal restraint. So men, get this under control, using prayer and every other resource you can dig up, as soon as possible. The degree to which you lose your sexual restraint, that's the degree to which confusion (and possessiveness) will reign in this relationship. Remember the 'River of Unspoken Communication' slide and all of the negative uncertainties broadcast by your choice to start down the sexual road.

Maintain your privacy. What privacy? Your house, your living space, your finances, your deeper ongoing challenges. Everything from your living space to your finances to your diet to your other relationships; these things are not necessarily topics for discussion... yet. Whatever you do, don't fall into the trap of, "Come on over and watch TV with me on the sofa." Early dating does not warrant the sharing of unneeded information or premature disclosure of your living environment

Space your interactions. Do you understand 'space your interactions'? Here it is again. You could be fielding six to eight phone calls/texts a day; don't do it! That's a key mark of Infatuation. Space your interactions by leaning on your other relationships and activities. Remember this equation: Freedom + Confidence = the Fire of Romance. You will be more attractive without neediness and desperation; most of which values-centric people have little of, anyway. *Space your interactions.* Particularly for people whose 'bells and whistles' have been triggered, and they can't think of anything else but the person they just dated. They'll start obsessing in their minds and moving towards the cell phone every 15 minutes. The complexities and immeasurable impacts of Facebook/Twitter/Instagram maneuvering are really bad. Even if you post a picture of you and her on the bike trail, you might be starting up the gossip engine. Particularly if you're addicted to Facebook, you can blow up this relationship by messing with your status and posting the wrong picture. If you are being jerked around by your feelings like this, remind yourself that your obsessing might actually scare away the other person. You don't like to be smothered; neither do they. SPACE YOUR INTERACTIONS.

Remember the 'friendship alternative.' Look back at the Phase 2 timeline chart. It's that 'Detour' arrow pointing to the bottom of the chart. If you achieve this objective of developing the relationship slowly and without physical entanglement, you have the opportunity to 'shift' the relationship into a wonderful friendship (that's why it's called the 'Friendship Alternative'). We'll come back to this very important concept in a moment.

Don't be a slave to your emotional surges (or lack of them). My recommendation to you is to buy *Getting the Love You Want* and realize that if someone does, in fact, share your Core Values, they are great people to be dating, even if your 'bells and whistles' are not screaming at you. See if you can date someone who is solid and values-centered, *even if you don't feel those infatuation responses.* You might be surprised at the great conversations you get to share.

Keep up your other friendships. Particularly with your accountability partner. This is critical, particularly when you are in the bells-and-whistles mode. Your accountability partner knows you and all of your personal quirkiness; they *want* to give you honest feedback. If the situation were reversed, wouldn't you do the same for them?

Maintain family communication. You do have relationship Core Values, right? Better keep making good decisions regarding family events and relationships. Perhaps even some limited interaction between your new relationship and your family is warranted. You know they will give you valuable feedback. You also know that they might put undue pressure on you because you have introduced them to a person who has romantic potential for you. I call that 'friendly fire.' "Look who John brought home; she looks like the one for him!" (and other very stupid comments). Be careful.

Give Thanks for where you are. What does it mean to give thanks for where you are? Let's see... you've met someone who respects your Core Values. They thought that you were interesting and attractive...they asked you out. You spent quality time with them, enjoying something besides airhead conversations. You are intrigued by them, but you don't know where this relationship will go. But since you kept the sexual interaction in control, you have maintained a measure of personal freedom. What's bad? Nothing! This is all good! Give thanks!

Remember the friendship alternative

A concluding story. When we complete this discussion, you will fall into one of two groups. The first group consists of those people who are highly interactive (Influencers or 'high I's', in DISC terminology), who really do want

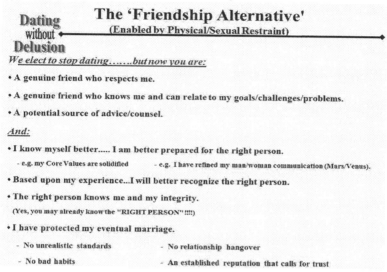

The 'Friendship Alternative'
(Enabled by Physical/Sexual Restraint)

We elect to stop dating.......but now you are:

• A genuine friend who respects me.

• A genuine friend who knows me and can relate to my goals/challenges/problems.

• A potential source of advice/counsel.

And:

• I know myself better..... I am better prepared for the right person.

   - e.g. my Core Values are solidified   - e.g. I have refined my man/woman communication (Mars/Venus).

• Based upon my experience...I will better recognize the right person.

• The right person knows me and my integrity.

   (Yes, you may already know the "RIGHT PERSON"!!!!)

• I have protected my eventual marriage.

   - No unrealistic standards   - No relationship hangover

   - No bad habits   - An established reputation that calls for trust

the interaction and depth of interaction which good dating entails. If you are one of these people, pay careful attention to this section. The second group consists of people who could *never* date different people at the same time, because of past scars and emotional hurts. I understand both. Work through this section with me to see which one you are and how you want to 'set your mind.' A couple of seminars ago, we were discussing the non-exclusive dating concept. One of the guys is a highly social, interactive, gregarious personality who really enjoys interaction with women. He is a Christian (I think), and he enjoys the character and honesty and spiritual depth he sees in Christian women. His personality is such that I easily see his need for good social activity and interaction. He is maintaining his integrity as a Christian man by controlling his sexual urges (I think), even though he has been married. Like all of us, he is trying to mature personally and spiritually. In my from-a-distance opinion, good non-exclusive, non-entangled, quality relationships with Christian women may be a real help for him. I trust the Christian women that I know in our church to give him honest feedback when he needs it.

In that same session is a woman who has just been through a tough divorce. She is emotionally damaged, and really needs some healing time before she dates again. In fact, it is going to take the right man with a lot of empathetic patience to help her to slowly develop trust and depth in a new relationship.

From my vantage point, the man in this story *must* learn to Freedom date non-exclusively. Even in the most benign scenarios, he wants to go beyond casual interactions to the deeper levels that a date entails (I hope he's ready to share his Personal Values). This woman, on the other hand, is going to have a difficult time going out with *any* man even once. For him, Freedom/non-exclusive dating is essential. For her, patience and no dating until she has really gotten to know a good trustworthy Christian guy is a more logical path. For her, non-exclusive dating would be very disorienting.

Two different people. Two different life circumstances. Two different conclusions about dating relationships. Whatever conclusion you arrive at, I trust that it will be based upon the life direction your Personal Core Values have set for you.

Freedom dating: Now what?
Admittedly early dating is by far the toughest phase to manage and navigate, so here's one more pass at tips and tricks to help you. It is divided into three suggestion areas. These three areas are very mistake-prone. The idea is to avoid these common mistakes, which no doubt you will recognize.

Communicate, Communicate, Communicate. The first mistake is to forget what you are communicating to the person you are dating. Reiterating your values and your commitment to your Core Values is obvious. If possessiveness starts to creep into the dialogue, *reclaim your freedom*. A date does not mean you have established any exclusivity with that person. You are a sufficient and competent person; you don't 'need' a relationship. Christians, dialogue your trust in the Lord. Remember Chip Ingram's summary:

> *"The people who are ready for a serious relationship*
> *don't need one."*

That is what confidence, contentment, and sufficiency in the slide on the next page are saying. As hard as these suggestions might be, if you do them, you will be more attractive to anyone and everyone you know — including the person you are dating. These confident and sufficient attitudes are the opposite of needy and dependent. As you behave with confidence you will be creating a persona which is attractive, and your attractiveness will encourage your dating partner to further rush the relationship. 'Tap the brakes!' Always remember to slow down.

Dating without Delusion

You're In Phase 2: Freedom Dating
Now What?

Communicate, Communicate, Communicate,
1. *Communicate Your Core Values*
2. *Communicate Your Commitment to Your Core Values*
3. *Communicate: Re-Claim Your Freedom*
4. *Communicate Freedom: Demonstrate Confidence & Contentment*
5. *Communicate Sufficiency*
6. *Communicate Trust (In the Lord)*

Two-Way Activities
1. *Maintain Yours*
2. *Be Open Minded to New Things (Reasonably)*
3. *Invite Sharing of Your Activities*
4. *Remember Group Activities*
5. *Watch out for 'Dead' Time*

Build a Friendship
1. *Empathize......Listen*
2. *Advise......when asked*
3. *Offer No-strings help (e.g. Moving)*
4. *Pray/Read Together (Careful!!)*
5 *Demonstrate Personal Integrity through Your Values*

Two-way activities. You've all seen people 'drop off the radar' when they start a dating relationship, which is usually the beginning of trouble. Yes, that person is interesting; yes they have a busy and engaged life. But so do you. Make sure that there is some balance in the activities that you share. Remember to *Connect* with one another's values-based activities. Look to see this person in their life involvement; look at who they associate with; experience a small piece of their life patterns. You should also include that person in the 'living' of your life. If you forsake the pursuit and expression of your Core Values for involvement with this person, alarms should go off and the red lights should flash.

A quick story from the Christian world. We call it 'Missionary dating.' An attractive Christian woman gets many offers from guys who think she is great, and she finds one of them interesting and attractive. She gets her spiritual values into the conversation, and he seems receptive. Funny thing is, he attends church with her when it's convenient, and seems a little uncomfortable around her Christian friends. Her friends see less and less of her as she spends more and more time with him in his activities. She rationalizes, "I know that I can bring him closer to God... he is discovering himself as a spiritual person," as she slowly drops out of contact with her close friends. Even her best friend and accountability partner is hearing less and less from her. You see the problem. Many faith-based books before this one have warned against 'Missionary dating'. Again remember Rule #1: Never date anyone who does not understand, appreciate, and respect your Core Values

Build a friendship. A last reminder. Even though you are dealing with the emotion of dating, you are still building a friendship. Remember Phileo from the Love chapter? Sharing life through ideas, circumstances, and situations. Laughing at each other and yourself. Laughing at life. Laughing at circumstances. Sharing of the tragedies and difficulties. Don't forget the relationship basics. See again the last part of the slide: build a friendship. Good dialogue between two people requires meaningful sharing on the part of both people; no monopolizing. It also has real empathy, patience, understanding, and honesty.

A Reminder

Recall the woman in the infatuation driven dating scenario. The one who drops-out of her values-based activities and loses contact with her best friends and family. Can you see that she is denying herself? She is abandoning her Core Values for the sake of her new guy relationship? Can you see that she is slowly immersing herself in his world, at the expense of her values? This is 'self-abnegation' and it is tragic on many levels. She is no longer thinking for herself . This 'self-denial,' is what I call 'values-denial,' and it will become ever-so-subtly less attractive to him. She has lost her values-commitment; some of her best lifelong relationships are eroding; she is now in a deteriorating relationship with someone who is finding her less interesting and, ergo, less attractive. It all comes back to Rule #1. Perhaps a woman who knows, speaks and consistently lives her values will be the one who has depth of character and a deeper 'style, charisma, and charm'?

So here we are, having navigated the vagaries of early dating. Hopefully you will use your values, your best relationships, great communication, and sexual restraint to get through the craziness of this phase. As you choose to date, ask yourself: Did you use the process? Have you built a relationship with someone you respect and 'love'? Does that person know *the real you* through your values? And, of course, vice versa; do you know him through his deeply held values? Remind yourself — great relationships are constantly growing. Has this relationship become more and more transparent and supportive over the weeks and months of early dating? Great! It's time to move on to exclusive dating.

Decision point #2
Phase 3: Should we date exclusively?... with a purpose?

Remember way back when? At the very beginning of this book section, in the dating phases, **'To date or not to date?'**. is the first big decision. Here comes the second big decision: **To commit or not to commit**? Commit to what, you say? Commit to each other; *to get this relationship ready for marriage.* It is not Engagement; Engagement is so hectic and confused that you often can't get any real relationship work done during those months before the

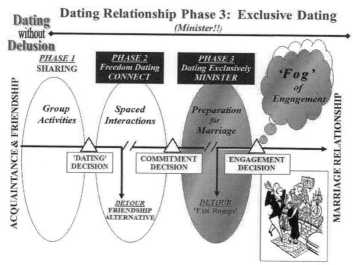

Dating Relationship Phase 3: Exclusive Dating

wedding. That's why I call it the 'Fog' of engagement. You're better off to do your relationship preparation now, or else you might head into marriage with some very serious blind spots. If you have 'Freedom dated' this person non-exclusively, you have had great opportunity to know them: to know their values and to experience their values challenges, their personality problems and strengths, and the situations that make up their lives. So you know them and they know you. Remember this concept?

Every relationship has a best outcome. (Jay)

You both have decided, with level-headed thinking, that the best outcome for this relationship, for *the* relationship that you both 'own,' is a lifelong commitment in marriage. Are you absolutely sure yet? No. But you want to commit to see only one another. Moving into Phase 3, you *both* have decided that the best outcome for this relationship could be a lifetime marriage commitment, and you clearly communicate that decision to each other (sometimes very hard for guys who are allergic to Commitment). Can you be 100 percent sure that this relationship will move to marriage? No... especially if the infatuation hasn't subsided yet. You may find out, as you work on your relationship that you should move back to being an autonomous, confident, and content Single person.

In this next phase, I'm going to give you nine tasks to do, and a timeline to do them by. The tasks are tough, and they get tougher as you go along. You may not get them all completed, but if you do even half of them and add some good relationship analysis, you'll understand why you should — or should not — get engaged. Let's look at the decision hurdle of getting into this exclusive dating phase. Check out the next slide. Men are always in a hurry for physical interaction; but they also are often 'commitment-phobic.' That's simply saying they are sometimes afraid of commitment and dating exclusively should be seen as a big commitment. We've discussed in depth the unspoken communication that happens with physical interaction. You can almost say that the better the sexual restraint/control, the better the communication. Look at our cartoon characters on the next slide (next page). He is hanging onto his freedom but oh, by the way, he really enjoys companionship interaction (we'll say, for example purposes, that they have not caved in and had intercourse). Still, he shows up regularly, enjoys spending time with her, and yes, they have even shared some of their values-based choices. With lack of communication, lots of physical innuendo, and his blasé assumptions about her availability, she starts *assuming* that they have an exclusive relationship. He, on the other hand, really doesn't communicate with her consistently and has some commitment-based reservations about this relationship moving forward (meaning, he is afraid). Enter STRESS. She assumed this, that, and the other: how could *he* even think about seeing other women? He hasn't said anything about exclusivity: how could *she* think that they were moving forward with this kind of commitment in their relationship? You've seen relationships which muddle along for a long time without clear commitment Perhaps the man-woman roles are reversed? Maybe they are in different seats in the graphic? There are perhaps an infinite number of scenarios men and women face as they move towards exclusive dating. It's

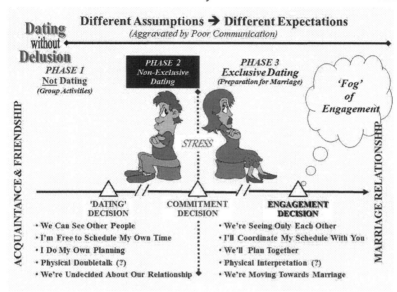

not an easy challenge because it requires great communication between the man and the women. It is a life-changing decision. Hopefully you can make this decision based upon both of your well-understood Personal Values. A key note to men: do you want to be a decisive, values-centric leader who knows how to communicate? Here's your opportunity. Be clear; if you want more time to do values interaction, say so. Women, if a man you respect can't make the decision to move forward, you should respond with appropriate, reserved confidence, and *be ready* to go out with other quality guys (even if they are not on the horizon). All easily said, which is why we spent so much time discussing WHO you are and working on your Personal Values refinement. OK, that's one 'Let's not do it that way' scenario. Here is another scenario which seems to be more prevalent in this post-modern world.

The above scenario described a man (or a woman) who *do* have a good values-base, and couldn't see it clearly enough to move forward. As I listen to the Millennials in the seminar, I hear them saying that's not what they see today. They see the opposite. They see couples (who don't know what values are) rushing past the Freedom dating phase and into an exclusive dating relationship, They don't really know or understand each other yet they want to rush pat the Freedom dating phase in a big hurry. What the Millennials share with me is that often this is a big mistake. Is this infatuation-based impatience? Is it a response to the culture's influence which makes you feel as if you're worthless unless you have 'a relationship'? Many young people see the emptiness of the culture and the lifestyles in it and want to get out — as quickly as possible. It's an understandable impatience. Remember the quote from the Millennial woman in Laura Stepp's book? In her heart she wanted to enjoy the relationship journey?

A milestone discussion

Now, let's talk about the things you should communicate as you start an exclusive relationship. In the next slide, I have these 1940s-looking people who are having some kind of serious discussion. The artist was probably envisioning a

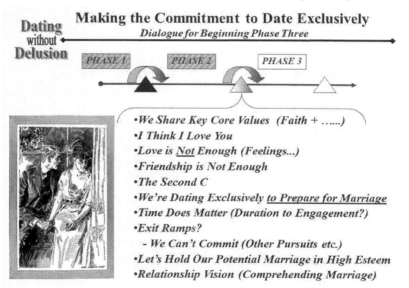

'let's-get-married scenario'. Looks like he is broadcasting and she is demurely receiving. Two-way communication is falling short. Moving to an exclusive relationship is a decision worthy of some serious two-way discussion. It's man-to-woman, woman-to-man: "Let's take this relationship to the point where we *know* whether or not we should get married. From this point on, let's see one another exclusively, committing to see no one else." Let's talk through the slide.

We share key Core Values. At this point, talking about Core Values further is always good, but hopefully you understand your and your partner's Core Values. The second point bears lots of repeating. "I think I love you" is empty if you don't understand what love is — all three aspects. Go back and read the Love Chapter, if necessary. But why would you date exclusively if you don't believe you love the other person on many different levels?

I think I love you. If you both have embraced the full meaning of love, you can discuss why you believe your relationships has the quality to 'Not take into account a wrong suffered,' for example. Once again go back and look at the chapter on Love. Read and re-read 1 Corinthians 13. Do you have that kind of love?

Love is not enough. Well actually Love *is* enough if you bring all three aspects of Love — Agape, Phileo, and Eros — exercised with steady commitment over the long haul. And of course that is what marriage is all about. Today's feelings which are so unreliable, and subject to the big ebb and flow, are the vulnerability. The character to live your commitments is the key. You'll both stand up at that altar and say 'Till death do us part' — will you mean it?

Friendship is not enough. Our friendship is a good one, and we share some wonderful give-and-take interactions, and some fun and uplifting compatibility activities. Phileo-friendship is there and it's great, but we both know changes will happen for both of us. Does your friendship have an enduring quality which will help you weather the tough times and life challenges?

The second C. Great and lasting relationships are based upon Commitment, the second C of the 4C's. You know this other person has demonstrated solid commitment in their life. You have made and kept commitments in many life venues — work, family, faith. Now, both you and he are making a Commitment to each other to do the hard work to get your relationship ready for engagement. The ability to commit is essential for both of you. Do you have it?

Time does matter. You don't want to rush into marriage, but you don't want to drag out this phase, either. Can you get your relationship work done in 10 months, in 12 months? When should you get engaged? Speak this intent to one another. Time does matter; you and she are about to close yourselves off from other dating relationship opportunities. If you can't get to a decision in a specified time, like 12–15 months, then be ready to back away from this relationship and move on. Based on the reading and research I have done, I recommend no more than 18 months (extended situations, such as overseas deployments, etc. are special circumstances). How short could this period be? Look at the nine marriage preparation tasks and decide. Doesn't it seem to you that relationships that drag on and on over the years are lacking something? You have seen it: two people let the relationship drag on; they don't seem to grow, but they still are together. That's lack of Commitment. On the other hand the culture will always try to rush you.

Exit ramps? Are there pivotal situations which might cause you to see that you and he are headed in different directions? She wants to solidify her commitment to overseas missionary projects. He doesn't have a missionary bone in his body. He decides that he doesn't want to have children; she has dreamed all her life about being a great mom. These are really Core Value hopes that diverge. Much of this can be sorted out while you are in the freedom phase of dating. A quick story. Two very high-quality Christian people I knew developed a very solid and exclusive relationship. With a son from a prior marriage, she could never achieve comfort with the idea that her potential future husband felt he would have to (at least on occasion) discipline her son. For many reasons, this became a 'detour'; an 'exit ramp' for this couple. Though they shared key faith values, this situation became a deal breaker and they chose — very wisely — not to marry. These exit ramps are essential; they avoid a likely future divorce.

Let's hold our marriage in high esteem. Restraining our physical drives now, before we are married, has lasting benefits. Restraint demonstrates that he values you. If he can exercise restraint now, you know that you can trust him later. The benefits of sexual restraint are numerous: it's what this slide calls 'holding your marriage in high esteem.' Stop and think; if you can hold your impulses in check with your future mate now while you're dating, how much more do you think that he/she will be able to trust you later in your married years? A lot.

Have a relationship vision. If you agree with these ideas, now is the time to start envisioning what your future marriage could look like, to start dreaming of all the good things that might be yours as a couple in a values-based marriage. The slide calls it sharing your 'relationship vision.' Judith Wallerstein's *The Good Marriage* defines four marriage types, each with its own set of strengths and challenges. Her book deftly describes good marriages because they work. In my view that's a good place to start, as you both define how you are envisioning married life together. As you listen to your potential future spouse describe how she thinks it will be, you will be gathering valuable insight.

What about marriage as the 'great mystery'? From the spiritual vantage point? How will you continue to pray with one another — you are praying with one another, right? In the Book of Ephesians Chapter 5 (v 20–33), there is an expansive and challenging description of marriage. If you are a spiritual person, do you want your marriage to look like that? _Love and Respect_ (Emerson Eggeritchs; see Relationship Library) is an entire book wrapped around the challenge in verse 33: "Let each individual among you also love his wife as himself; and let the wife see to it that she respect her husband."[66] Go get _Love and Respect_ and read it with your future spouse. If you don't like this one, find another book that you both can read and discuss. Open your minds to the challenge in front of you. Let your reading jump-start your communication.

In the seminars, on one or two occasions, I have taught the session on exclusive dating _first_. Remember the crazy discussion at the start of Freedom dating? Let's discuss our budget! In the seminar... just to illustrate how crazy it would be... we discuss exclusive dating _before_ the discussion of the Freedom dating phase. Think back to the early dating time: lots of infatuation and the excitement of meeting someone you are attracted to. The excitement of the relationship potential swirls around in your head — and probably his also. Excitement, a future full of unknown potentials, and guess what? Lots of ignorance. At that stage, you don't know _any_ of the relationship downsides. Infatuation, delusion, and ignorance are the hallmarks of those early days. In the Freedom dating phase, would any of the items on the exclusive dating discussion be appropriate or wise? Absolutely NOT. The man-woman communication described by this chart is appropriate for two people in a mature and maturing relationship. The culture will tell you to rush into this exclusive phase. Today's culture tells you to skip over the Freedom dating phase completely. Wisdom tells you to follow the process, take your time, be appropriately transparent, and get to this decision point when the time is right.

What about divine intervention?

A good friend on church staff leads _Marriage Mentoring_, a really great resource for married couples looking for some guidance. I ask him if there is one thing which marks solid marriages. He says, without a moment's hesitation "They

---

[66] Ephesians 5 reference: all versions.

pray together!" So here's a great prayer opportunity: to ask the Lord for His stamp of approval. Should you expect a sign? Many people say no because it is so easy to deceive yourself. Nevertheless I say you should ask for some confirmation from God. Many people do not receive because they do not ask. So I say *ask,* if you are a prayer person. Let's not think we can manipulate the Lord, however. If He gives you an unpredicted, supernatural sign, great! Remember the story about the flying garter? God is very interested in you becoming you, and the marriage that you are contemplating will enable you — or hamstring you. As Gary Thomas says over and over in *Sacred Search,* it's not about who you marry, but why. The whole concept of finding the perfect soul mate proves itself to be a delusion, over and over again. That's why we always come back to the process. Follow the process, and God will show you whether or not the marriage you are contemplating is right. Whether His affirmation comes flying through the air or through subtle spiritual revelation... the means is not the issue... His direction is.

A final thought on entering this phase. Please look back at the phase slide and see right below exclusive dating is the term 'Minister.' This Bible term really is the simple idea of doing the service-oriented tasks: the chores, the menial tasks of daily life, on behalf of the other person. This exclusive dating phase should demonstrate great understanding, communication, and commitment. If you are on the path to marriage, you should be discovering ways to support the person you love; the person you might marry.

Here's a real-life example from my Phase 3 life with Debra. As a Single mom, she faced all of the challenges of trying to balance a busy life with being a good mother. On one occasion, her Honda Accord needed critical repairs. I was able to take her car to the local Honda expert, whom I knew well. I provided the logistics and the finances to get this job done. Would this kind of support (ministering) be appropriate if Debra and I were in the earlier dating phase of our relationship? I say no. Now that we were seeing each other exclusively, does this make sense? I think so. Are you beginning to see why phases are so important? OK, you and she have decided to continue down the path, and you both are committed to growing together. How can you do it?

Cardinal Rule #2

I have been saying to you for most of this book that every person — every individual — is absolutely unique. And of course each person's Core Values should reflect their uniqueness. In the same way each man/woman relationship is unique — each one has capacities and powerful potentials, and also a unique set of challenges. Makes sense don't you agree? Even in the most romantically intense relationships between seemingly perfectly-matched couples there are issues to be dealt with. Remember JD Greear and his wife? In the first 6 months of their marriage their arguing quickly caught up for all of their 'perfect' courtship time. Being a realistic values-based person, you know if you can understand these challenges early-on, it will give you and

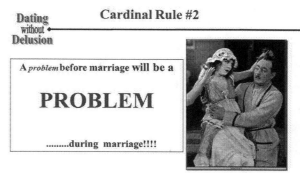

Cardinal Rule #2

A *problem* before marriage will be a

PROBLEM

.........during marriage!!!!

Therefore Do <u>Whatever Is Necessary</u> to Unravel and Defuse the Problem While You Are Still Dating!! (or Detour!!)

your potential future spouse a chance to understand and deal with these issues; as opposed to letting those issues sneak up on you in the early months of your marriage. This concept is captured in the slide above which depicts Cardinal Rule #2. In the slide Rule #2 says:

A problem before marriage will be a PROBLEM during marriage

Remember Rule #1; about dating only people who understand, appreciate, and respect your Core Values? Entering into exclusive dating with mutually respected Core Values is a strong base to work with. Rule #2 simply reflects the reality of human relationships — there will be problems! With this thought in mind, I offer you nine tasks to work on as a couple. Doing these tasks will hopefully uncover the specific challenges you and he will face. It will help you to lose the 'soul-mate' fantasy. Most of all it will help you and he to see the areas where you can exercise Agape-based love — I Corinthians 13 style — on behalf of your partner.

Whatever you do avoid the *delusion* of thinking simply more time will be sufficient to grow your relationship and prepare it for marriage. Avoid this trap! Growing a relationship must be intentional on both your part *and* her part. How can you be intentional? Glad you asked — on to the 9 tasks for exclusive dating!

The Nine tasks in Phase 3: Exclusive dating

The nine tasks are extracted from good psychologists and researchers (primarily Judith Wallenstein's descriptions in *The Good Marriage* and Harville *Hendrix's Getting the Love You Want),* and from other credible sources. They start with backward-looking 'recovery tasks' and move on to forward-looking relationship tuning, 'marriage preparation' tasks. Once again, they are not prescriptive, meaning that there is no longstanding history or custom that is being recommended to you. I am giving you a starting point. I hope you will refine this list to meet your and your future spouse's needs. Rest assured that very few people have ever used these exact nine tasks to hone the quality of their relationship. If you and your future spouse hurdle all nine tasks, please let me know (you might be the first).

So why do I offer them to you? Because stagnant relationships are really deteriorating relationships. Relationships that are not moving forward are really moving backward. If I could, *I would explode the notion just spending more time with one another means your relationship is growing.* More time and patience is good, but relationships grow when people consciously decide to help them grow. I think that many couples move onto marriage as a way to grow their relationship, simply because they don't know what else to do. Suppose you are crippled, not able to use your legs. You meet someone you love and they, in turn, love you. That beloved, because he loves you, will want to learn all there is to know about managing the complexity of your wheelchair. Do you see the parallel?[67] We all have issues and past hurts which require special knowledge and accommodation. The idea is you *can* be intentional and work to determine exactly what you can do to make this relationship more effective, Most of us have scars and situations from the past that merit special consideration and adaptation. Remember in this phase, we are learning the accommodation and adaptation which can protect our relationship.

Should you decide to do even three or four of these tasks with your future spouse, you will have moved your relationship forward. You know yourself — you are learning to know your future spouse. You both have been damaged to one degree or another — remember Jay's anger? To do your best, you have to

[67] In fact, we do have a friendship with a couple that has a good marriage relationship. She doesn't have use of her legs, and he has refined his expertise on managing the chair, even on overseas travel. A great real-life example of caring commitment. His skills minister to her physically. Let's do the same with our relationship 'hot buttons' etc.

be ready to skillfully handle those personal special circumstances.

With that background, here is the slide (below). We will discuss each task (#1–9) and offer a short description of what each task entails. Then you can go to your Relationship Library and do the groundwork to be able to discuss

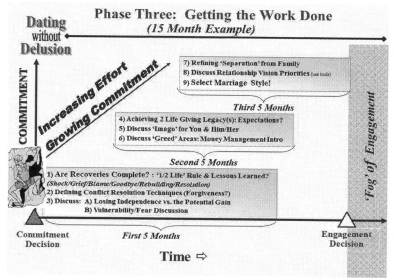

the needed process and benefits with your future spouse. Perhaps one or two of the tools in the Part Three tools section will meet your needs? Most importantly, if there is an area where you know you need help and there is no task described above that addresses your particular need, _please add that task your list_. Then, take the needed task to the pastor/counselor you are going to lean on during the days leading up to your engagement and marriage.

Now, look at the slide. See the rock climber on the left-hand side? He represents the effort and focus you need to step-by-step _move up_ your relationship commitment and expertise. The bottom of the chart shows the timeline for this phase. The idea is that over time, through your combined efforts, you will work to improve your relationship _and_ improve the depth of your commitment to one another — remember the second C (Commitment)?

I've suggested a 15-month period. Why 15 months? Two reasons. Number one is many psychologists/counselors teach that Infatuation (the 'evil little twin') subsides after 14, 16, 18 months. By taking 15 months to do Phase 3, you allow the intense feelings of infatuation to calm down. If you believe that you and he can get a good number of these tasks done in a shorter period of time, go for it! Remember, in the seminar I suggest these tasks, but really only as a starting point for you both to consider. If you both find an additional task that you feel needs to be added to the list, please let me know the insight you've uncovered. Getting *any* of these tasks done will be a help for you both. The more the better. Please note that during each five-month period, I have suggested three topics to discuss with your future spouse. None of this makes any sense unless you have spoken your commitment to be exclusive with this person, and she with you. It's really a life milestone when you commit to see only that person. Celebrate it! With those caveats, let's begin to look at the sometimes-gnarly nine tasks.

Task #1: Are your recoveries complete?

In this world, many people are coming out of live-together situations, divorces, gray (over 50) divorces, sexual addictions, and difficult/possessive relationships. Chances are you or your potential spouse is one of them. How about people who have lost a spouse? In all of these situations, relationship trauma has happened. When you have trauma, you don't use just a Band-Aid. You go through the whole recovery process. If you are one of these people, do this now, even if you are not in a relationship. Faith people want extended prayer. Some of the very best counselors offer therapy to people suffering because of the loss of an important person in their life. They guide people through the five steps (shock and grief, blame, goodbye, rebuilding, resolution) of the healing process. If you have 'lost' a significant person, make sure you have dealt with the trauma.

When I was single, one of my adopted brothers wanted me to go out with a woman he respected. She was a woman with spiritual depth who had several strong commitments in place in her life-career, family of origin, and church/spiritual values. So I said, "Sure," and proceeded to invite and take her out to dinner. She was physically very attractive and our discussion over dinner was interesting, with good communication about our respective lives. Lingering in the background, in the 'parentheses' of our conversation, was an unspoken wound. She had come out of a long relationship with a guy and, however it ended, one thing I knew: it was painful. She was still in the grief phase of recovery. As we sat in the car after dinner, her grieving was tangible. Without significant time and healing, she wasn't ready to go on *any* date, let alone enter into a new long-term relationship (don't worry; that thought never crossed my mind). Apart from prayer and therapy, which she needed

ASAP, an exclusive relationship and even Phase 2/Freedom dating were all going to be problematic. She needed time. She needed recovery.

Many of you have been hurt in the past; have you truly accomplished closure? At this exclusive dating juncture, you probably have already completed this discussion. If not, why don't you begin with the honesty of what you learned in that painful breakup? Hopefully, you will be able to maturely talk about the things you learned and the things you learned about yourself. In an honesty-based conversation, share those with your now-significant other. Is this a one-time discussion? Obviously not — make sure to spend some quality communication time on this challenge.

Task #2: Define conflict resolution techniques

Every relationship has issues and disagreements. No surprise; you will have your share of them. Better figure out how to handle those conflicts. How are you, as a couple, going to handle those inevitable situations? How are you handling them now? After you have an argument, does the other person know that you need some space, you need to go for a walk on the beach, you need a workout, whatever? The worst thing you can do is to follow your most important person to the gym! Or maybe the most important thing you can do is to follow your most important person to the gym because you have enjoyed that activity together in the past.

After you do your calming down, how will you come back together? Here's a Jay principle:

When there is a break in relationship, we both have to accept and take responsibility for our parts in what went wrong. I can always ask forgiveness for my bad behavior in the disagreement. (Jay)

There is sometimes pretty one-sided wrongdoing in a relationship. You've seen manipulators and selfish people trample all over their most significant other. Not pretty, is it? Often a party-minded guy ignores his responsibilities to his more-reserved wife or girlfriend. He does the activity-intense running around without communicating with her what he's doing, where he's going, what time he'll return, etc. etc. So you think well sure, he's being stupid, but what did she do wrong? Perhaps, at the very least, she did not make her expectations clear, and she can ask for forgiveness for that poor communication. Perhaps she should have addressed this situation — and her concern

— before they make the big decision to exclusively date one another.

If you have made it to Phase 3, Exclusive Dating with Intentionality and Integrity, then you know that you better be prepared to deal wisely with the inevitable differences and disagreements that will emerge. People taking a bath in infatuation may *think* they could never have a disagreement... you know better. To help you with your conflict resolution, go back into the tools section of this book and pull out the tool titled, '*Stopping the Downward Spiral of the Four Horsemen.*' Noted psychologist John Gottman, through lots of research, has identified four specific behaviors that lead to marriage destruction. In the tools section, I'll suggest techniques for holding off the damage these behaviors can do to your growing relationship. The behaviors are: Contempt, Criticism, Defensiveness, and Stonewalling.

Task #3: Please set aside time to discuss:

A) Losing my independence vs. the potential gain, and
B) Your vulnerability and fear

Let's look at A first. When you commit to anything, you have to forsake other things to get your commitment rolling. Same thing in relationship commitments. You both have just made a commitment to each other, which oh, by the way, leaves some of your other commitments in a receding state. How does that feel? You have lost some of your independence; how do you handle that? On the other hand, you love each other, which holds life-changing potential for you both. Go on a date and discuss that over a nice glass of wine! That's really a fun discussion. If it isn't fun, you have a serious problem before you even get started.

There is B — *fear*. You have made yourself vulnerable. You will have to be honest about your issues and feelings. The reality is, this relationship might not work out, and you will feel like a failure — even though it might not be a failure at all. If you have done your Core Values work, I believe you will be well on your way to a great relationship. But there is all of that Imago stuff. You — or he — might have baggage that makes daily living just too hard. You might have learned behaviors/expectations which are too hard for her to handle. There is nothing worse than being trapped in a relationship that is not right for you. It's the reason why we have done this step-by-step progressive dating process. The other kind of fear is simply the loss of your independence, loss of your personal freedom — on several levels. I would guess, if you have followed my advice, your depth and quality of relationship should far outweigh this 'fear.' But now that you are committed to dating exclusively, your relationship will consume a lot more of your time. Other activities will have to take a backseat. Parenting could consume your early marriage life. That should be no problem. Go ahead and have some in-depth discussions about these inevitable changes. And then there is the fear of returning to the lonely life of a Single, because that is the alternative to you and she moving forward.

Task #4: Achieving two life-giving legacy(s): your expectations?

Remember all that discussion about Personal Core Values? You know the person sitting across from you because you have struggled and worked at describing your Personal Values and understanding hers. You know what he values, and you can see and hear his life commitments through those Personal Values statements. He will have to spend time realizing these callings. He will have to spend time at work. She will have to spend time with her prayer person and her accountability partner. Her career requires long-distance travel. You are 'called' to serve in the _____ ministry (fill in the blank).

Our spiritual perspective leads us to believe that living out these values is not optional. Our practical perspective leads to the same answer. Our values-based activities *are who we are*. Living out your essential life elements is essential. Not living them out will be ultimately frustrating and unfulfilling; your frustration, or her frustration, could easily be the reason for a future divorce. So I'm asking you to ask very deep and complex questions about your lives and your 'callings.' Maybe task #4 is the most important one of all. There you are, wrestling with who you are separately and trying to envision who you will be when the two of you become one. To achieve any kind of personal legacy, you both must use your gifts and callings over the long haul. As a couple you could have tremendous positive impact. You must achieve together. And if you've made it with me to Phase 3 in your relationship, I believe in you. I believe in your genuine motives, and your real integrity.

One more reminder for faith people. Maybe you're praying, "Is this right for us, Lord?" If you ask for a clear sign from God, He may — or may not — answer. Once again, your job as a Faith person is to *ask*. If you are not a praying person, these tasks will still create meaningful communication and deeper interpersonal understanding. For you, these tasks may be even more critical.

Task #5: Discuss Imago for you and him/her

When we were discussing Imago in Part One, I shared my childhood frustration (one of them) and my childhood response. When I was six, seven, eight years old, I wanted to have a home with warmth and stability; I wanted a wonderful 'home' in the depth of my being. Then the screaming would start accompanied by serious violence. Do you remember my response? It was *escape*. I went to my friend's house. The house that was so well-kept. The one with the basketball hoop. The one with the mom and dad who were so stable. Frustration → Response. I practiced this Frustration → Response sequence over and over again (because my parents were a mess). Reminder! My frustration response was to get on my bike and escape. In a grounded marriage relationship, escaping and disconnecting cannot replace great dialogue and forgiveness. That Frustration/Response sequence was essential for me then — *but as an adult, it is unacceptable*. I can try to make my escape look very 'adult,' but in mature relationships, the escape response is very dysfunctional. Remember how Harville Hendrix talks about the conscious marriage? I'm encouraging you to have a conscious and committed dating relationship.

My wife Debra is a tremendous home-builder. How much do you think I love that? But she used to have an angry tendency to scream (like *her* mom and dad): very bad for me. My relationship task was to explain to Debra that I had this deep Frustration → Response cycle built deep into my mind and being. Because I understand it, I can be aware of it and fend it off. When she understands it, she can be very careful not to pull those triggers.

OK, now I'm asking you, as intentional people committed to one another, to have this discussion before you get engaged... *before* you get married. If necessary, go back to the 'Unpacking Your Suitcase' section in Part One. Pull out the 'Things I wanted, but didn't get' and the 'Frustration → Response' sheets. Go over them with one another. How are you going to be sensitive to your partner? Do you understand his previous life and how it has shaped him?

Task #6: Discuss 'greed' areas: money management intro

Money discussions are positioned at the end of the second chunk of tasks. Why? First, because discussing budgets and financial vulnerabilities is not something to do right out of the exclusivity gate. Everyone knows finances can sink relationships; money pressure can destroy intimacy and marriage relationships. The other 'honesty' is that almost everyone in America has a vulnerability to over-spending, an over-attachment to 'things,'[68] and lifestyles that are potentially unsupportable. I have this problem. If you are one of the rare people who have this under control, please bear with me because even though you have tamed this beast, chances are the other person has not. So doing a budget is key. Being honest with him about how you will unwittingly try to torpedo the budget is the hard part. For both of you, the idea is to help the other person with their financial challenge areas. All of this takes time, honesty, and perhaps help from a financial expert.

Task #7: Refining 'separation' from family

You're now into the months just preceding your engagement. If you've made it this far, you can make it the rest of the way. If you have come this far, perhaps you can come the rest of the distance! You have taken off the rose-colored glasses of infatuation. You have worked on your blind spots and relationship sensitivities. With your well-understood Personal Values, you are positioned for an engagement and marriage that will have resiliency and quality. All great stuff.

Now, let's look at a recommendation from Judith Wallerstein. She — and really every common-sense person — knows your future *priority* relationship will be your spouse. For people of faith, God may be your #1 relationship priority, but among your earth-bound relationships, your partner will be first priority. Not your parents. Not your kids from a previous marriage. She will be in first place. It does *not* mean that your parents, kids, and friends are no longer an important part of your life. It does mean that you will have to create subtle boundaries. It does mean that there will be areas of your life where you and she will make key decisions. These are areas where you will not allow outside, inappropriate intrusion into your new lives. There must be a subtle but clear boundary put around your future marriage so that external influence, even from your parents, must not be intrusive. Yes, you must 'hon-

---

[68] Remember 'Lust of the eyes' from 1 John 2 v 16.

or your father and mother' and yes, you must carefully manage how you will participate in family traditions that were formerly unspoken commitments and expectations. Chances are you now have two or more families to accommodate. Do it with understanding and grace, and decide how you and your future spouse will do it together.

Task #8: Discuss relationship vision priorities
(a simple communication tool)

Task #8 is very simple and surprisingly revealing. Here's the worksheet below. You and your future spouse independently fill in the blanks by scoring your priority for each item in the list. Some items seem so obvious — like 'We trust each other' or 'We are sexually faithful' — I sure hope so! So hopefully you both score those as top priority, and you both score it as a '1'. For each relationship item both of you scores a priority item using the 1 to 5 scale. Very simple. Now, look at your respective scorings. Is there a difference of more than two? What a nice opportunity to discuss why you made an item a

Your Relationship Vision
(Harville Hendrix)

Dating without Delusion

A Communication Tool ...Discuss Them All → Focus on Differences 2 or greater

Your Priority(s) (1 is highest; 5 is lowest)		Your Partner's Priority(s) (1 is highest; 5 is lowest)
( )	We Worship Together?	( )
( )	We Settle Our Difference Peacefully?	( )
( )	We Have Satisfying and Beautiful Sex?	( )
( )	We Are Healthy and Active?	( )
( )	We Communicate Easily and Openly?	( )
( )	We Have Fun Together?	( )
( )	We Are Each other's Best Friends?	( )
( )	We Have Secure and Happy Children?	( )
( )	We Trust Each Other?	( )
( )	We Are Sexually Faithful?	( )
( )	We Both Have Satisfying Careers?	( )
( )	We Share Important Decisions?	( )
( )	We Have Daily Private Time?	( )
( )	We Feel Safe With Each Other?	( )
( )	We Share Our Primary Sport/Activity?	( )
( )	We Have the Same Friends?	( )
( )	We Live Close to Our Parents?	( )
( )	We Have Similar Political Views?	( )
( )	We Have an Orderly House?	( )

higher priority than she did. Why he thinks an item is more (or less) important. How about 'We share the same sport/activity'. Personally, I don't really care if Debra wants to play golf. What about you? If there is a significant priority difference (and there usually will be) it's going to require some understanding and compromise between you. 'We have the same friends?' I for one sure am thankful Debra has a wide spectrum of friends, some of whom I really don't interface with. See the chance for discussion? Make this #8 task a fun one, and it will serve as some nice prep for the pre-marriage counseling testing, which is substantially more complex. This stuff is all about the third C: Communication. Communication is a trademark of great, sustainable, life-long marriages. Have fun. If you have done all seven tasks leading up to this one, there won't be many surprises. This is a simple tool; the more complex personality disposition tools that marriage counseling will take you through will have more depth, and require some expert analysis from the pre-marriage counselor.

Task #9: Select a marriage style!

You're closing in on the end of your 15-month exclusive dating phase. With your Personal Values as a foundation, you have worked through the tasks to discover the strengths and weakness of your future relationship. Hopefully, you have allowed Infatuation to calm down. Without Infatuation, you may have felt the romance was gone. But you know better; you know that most young marriages experience this emotional lag and decide the marriage was a mistake. You, on the other hand, have your well-communicated core values as a foundation. No gray divorce down the road for you! Through those values, you see her as a person who really loves you, even though she understands all of your weaknesses, childhood damage, and vulnerability. You see him as someone who knows and understands who God wants you to be. Congratulations! That is very fine relationship work!

For the last task, let's go into your Relationship Library and pull out *The Good Marriage* one more time. If you remember, Judith studied 50 good marriages and 'typed' them. Remember, when a therapist or counselor reaches conclusions or recommendations, those results may fit you but they probably won't fit you exactly. For marriage types, Judith has defined four basic types that are very insightful. What's more insightful are the strengths and challenges of each marriage type. Way back at the beginning of this book, we talked about equipping you to build better relationships — across the board. Now, at the end of the journey, it's time to equip you for the most important on-earth relationship of your lifetime. This enables you to be aware of the challenges you will face in the marriage type that most suits you both. Your parents probably had a traditional marriage. In this marriage type, the roles are clear: the man is probably the sole breadwinner, and the woman is committed to creating a 'home' that has both stability and warmth. We Boomers watched our parents model this marriage style, and many of the marriages we saw as kids actually lasted. Chances are, particularly as a Millennial, your marriage will probably have much more negotiation of roles, daily chores, and challenges. You better see Judith's description of the Companionate marriage to understand these intricacies.

Decision Point #3:
To get engaged or not?

This is the easy part. I say this because you and he have exercised restraint and patience, and you really do understand one another at a very honest and un-deluded level. You know each other thru your values — and your values are going to sustain you and your relationship (marriage?) over the course of a lifetime. It is a life-changing and life-long commitment, and so it is only normal to question your *decision to get married*. If you want to have some final confirmation and validation, please consider the 10 day technique.

The 10-Day Technique (Jay)

You notice that there is no decision point like 'Should we get married?' I believe that if you have added rigor and patience to the dating process you will have a clear understanding of your relationship and all of its potential and challenges. The commitment and patience you have demonstrated will make the decision to get engaged & married an easy one. Dating by its very nature, wants to degrade into vagary and nebulousness. By using the timeline and process in **Dating without Delusion** you have been intentional and forthright. As a couple you are relationally intelligent. Nevertheless to help with your engagement decision let's do this one last thing. It's called the 10-Day Technique. Remember how you carefully navigated Phase 2 into Phase 3 — Exclusive Dating? During those months in Phase 3 Exclusive dating, you did at least some of the nine tasks, I hope. Now looking at the chart (next page). You both have full-spectrum 'love' for each other, in the face of the realities of each of your shortfalls. It's time to make a decision; if you want to be sure, *the 10-Day Technique will either send you on to engagement and marriage* or *give you a chance to escape a flawed relationship*... hopefully the former.

Here's how to do it. You both sit down and have a good chat about what you have learned, particularly over the months of your exclusive dating. Do you love each other...all three aspects? Of course you do. Remember the 'Dynamic Migration of the three loves? Now, you want to go into engagement with a rock-solid certainty. So what is the technique? The idea is you're going

Dating without Delusion	The 'Ten Day Technique'
	(10 -12 days without seeing or talking to your partner)
How to do it	_What you'll Accomplish_
Make a Statement of Purpose - to Consider Engagement	Test your/your Partner's Commitment & Intent
Not for 'Dating' other People	Consider the Desirability of that Option
Do a Lost Activity	Was that a Worthwhile Sacrifice?
Spend Time with your Friends	See the Value of your Partner's Friendship
Introspect - Think Quietly	Is it Comfortable / Free without him/her?
Sexuality (if you are entangled)	Regain Objectivity: Use the Tools with Clarity
In-Depth Prayer Time	Hear God's Direction

to spend 10 days without seeing or talking to one another. The purpose? It's to carefully consider the rest of your lives together in marriage. It is obviously NOT for dating other people; if that is on your mind, you may have a warning light to consider. These 10 days will seem like an eternity. Remember, in the big picture of 40–50 years of marriage, this is a small commitment — it won't feel like it, though! You may have lost an activity due to your dating relationship; do that activity. How badly do you miss that thing (golf)? Spend time with your key friends, accountability partner, parents. Those friendships are good; hopefully, the friendship you have with your partner is, in many ways, better. Hopefully your best-relationship people will have objective guidance for you. Listen to them carefully. During those 10 days, you are sure to have some down time, some quiet time to think and pray. Does it feel different without her? Of course it does; is it better or worse? If you have been entangled in sexual activity, getting away is doubly important to regain your objectivity. For us faith-based people, this is the time for in-depth prayer. Maybe you both have developed a good prayer routine. As you pray on your own, listen for God's direction. Maybe He has already given you direction and you have been too busy to see it.

As far as I know, Debra and I have been the only ones to use this tool, although I really don't know because people come to a seminar and then go on with their lives. I may never see them again. I *can* tell you very specifically about the 10-day technique Debra and I agreed on. Telling it from my perspective. A confession first. Debra and I (actually I was the weak one) only made it only through nine days. Remember my Imago discussion? On several levels, I was attracted to Debra through my childhood experiences. Remember how I desperately needed a stable home environment? Debra's strength as a 'Harmonizer' and her gift of 'Hospitality' were very attractive to me. I hated conflict, and she was expert at avoiding it. I am a 'high I' — Influence and interaction — and Debra is a gifted person of hospitality: for me, a great fit.[69] Of course, there were the other not-so-wonderful Imago aspects that were working on me internally. Her mother was a screamer and a manipulator (on occasion), and I saw all of those up close in my childhood. So the Imago triggers were working on me. To some extent, those are here for life. The good news is, Debra accepted the Lord in that church service in La Jolla. And over the years, she has spiritually matured into a *very* accomplished prayer person. Most times, I defer to her ability to ask God to intervene in the many and varied circumstances in our lives.

What about the Singles ministry? If you ever meet Debra, go ahead and ask — she has been reasonably comfortable with my ongoing call to work with Singles in the Singles world. Part of the comfort is that many of the people I work with are very spiritually mature Christians, who care very much for the stability of our marriage. 'Trusted Husband' is a Personal Core Value for me — one of the reasons I know the power of Personal Core Values — and it makes a difference. On many occasions, Debra uses her gift of hospitality to host Singles at our house, to make meals for class/seminar people, and to enable the very precise role that God has planned for me. Add up all of these factors, and throw in the humorous direction from on high (the Flying Garter), and you can see why the decision was not so hard to make.

If you and your future spouse use the 10-Day Technique, please share your story with me. *Your* story can no-doubt be a powerful encouragement to others.

---

[69] Debra is a high S in DiSC, Steadiness: very strong on cooperation and working together. For me, a very strong Personality Profile 'fit.'

Can great marriages make great 'disciples'?[70]

In the faith world 'discipleship' is talked about a lot. The simple approach is to think of a disciple as a 'student'. In the Christian realm Jesus is the teacher, and we keep looking to Him for guidance and instruction. The straightforward avenues are prayer, worship, and a steady dependence on the Bible. From these aspects we all can encourage and 'disciple' one another. In marriage two Christians can steadily encourage and disciple one another in these disciplines. When it comes to using your service-based gifts and strengths you may look for a mentor to guide you. Someone to push you to the next level. If I were an evangelist (and I am not) I would look to Greg Laurie or Billy Graham to spur me on, and to share the very unique challenges of that calling. As I write this to encourage you to find a mentoring relationship I am reminding myself to look to the mature Christians in the Single world to push me upward. Will you and your future spouse 'disciple' one another in these very specific gifts and service areas. Maybe. Maybe not. You do know what your future spouse's gifts and callings are... make sure you are ready to provide the emotional and practical support to help your future spouse to be effective in her ministry areas.

Thoughts and advice for 'courting.'

I do not really understand 'courting', and every time I run into someone who is in a courting relationship I ask them to explain what they are doing. Apart from a clear recognition of the authority of their parents, and a measure of patience, they don't seem to have a clear plan. They do know they are courting in order to be intentional — to declare their intention to marry. I recommend you move to exclusive dating with the same clear intention. Courting seems to be a way to break away from all the dysfunctions associated with dating. A very good idea. When you Date without Delusion I recommend you do the same thing

Testing, testing, testing

Please forgive my pushy behavior in the primary parts of this book. Spiritual Gifts! Personality Profiles! Strengthsfinders! I understand that the 'analysis

---

[70] This the 'D' in the Real Life Ministries SCMD sequence.

push' might be a little much. But please reflect back. All of those tests were about *self-discovery*. And there is a lot of work to do. Chances are you're still working hard on that task. Now, we're talking about you and your potential lifetime spouse moving through exclusive dating and into engagement! At this point the institutions and churches will offer a pretty broad spectrum of marriage preparation tests. With the tests that are designed for you at this stage, you will uncover some of the issues that wait for you *as a couple*. What, us? Issues? You bet, and although your exclusive dating may have revealed issues to overcome, there is a whole family of pre-marriage assessments which are worth your time and effort. Remember Cardinal Rule #2? So be really smart and use the counseling/church resources to do these assessment which are uniquely designed for pre-marital couples. Check out the Taylor-Johnson graphic below.

What you see is one of many 'tools' that marriage counselors use to help couples get ready for the challenges they are prone to encounter as a married

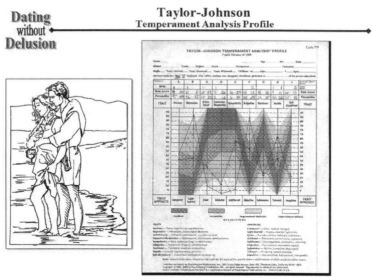

pair. This is a different sort of testing which is comparative — it assesses the strengths and forecasts the problems in your upcoming marriage. There are a number of these tools. Although I like Taylor-Johnson, I am going to recommend something different to you. Usually you will be using the expertise of a marriage or church counselor or pastor. I recommend that you find out what tool your counselor has been trained in, which one *he* understands the best.

With specialized training and experience, she will probably be best-prepared to help you and your future spouse by using the tool she knows best. If it's Taylor-Johnson, fine, but there are a lot of good pre-marital tools to choose from.

A Life Inflection Point

Facing life as a Single is just tougher in many ways. Loneliness. All the bills are yours. Life goes along with many, many ups and downs, and there are always work, family, money, health, and relationship problems to deal with — often it feels like you are on your own. Despite what the culture tells you there will be many more challenge days than days of giddy happiness. There are so many routines which can easily become 'ruts' and ruts are numbing and boring. Many of us need an 'inflection point' where we aim the trajectory of our lives to a higher level. Hopefully **Dating _without_ Delusion** has given you this fresh perspective. Hopefully the self-discovery you've experienced has provided some real enlightenment on the 'who' of who you are. Articulating your Personal Values with some honest self-discovery should provide

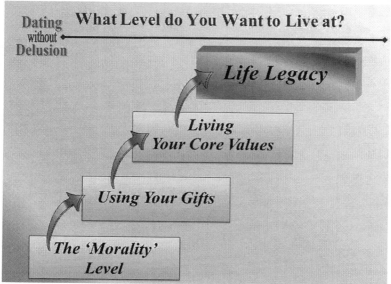

the inflection point. But the choice is yours. As depicted in the graphic above, you have to deliberatively choose to move up to the next level. Trying to live a 'Moral' life without moral standards is a delusion. Being aware of your very personal gifts is a big step up. And of course getting to some very precise Personal Values which you can 'Know, Speak, and Live' on a daily basis can be a life-changer. And here's one final encouragement. Using your values you *can* think differently about life and most of the choices you make. The living of those values with consistency and commitment — long haul commitment — will be what people remember you by. On the chart the top level shows 'Life Legacy'. Isn't that what you want? Don't you think that's what the Lord designed you for? Life is short, and the way we live and serve others with our gifts, talents and strengths will move your life to the higher level. Like the example Charles Schultz gave us with Peanuts, quality, day-by-day living of your values will be the way you leave a legacy people will remember.

So Mr. & Ms. Single I hope you have embraced who you are — never ever thinking that a new relationship will solve your problems — but at the same time being ready to embark on new dating relationships with a renewed sense of purpose and understanding. Or not? Being a confident and content Single person sure beats being in a lousy marriage. Dating with intention and process is not easy, but chances are you've felt the pain of past failures. After your journey through ***Dating without Delusion*** I hope you believe that only great, well-built relationships are worth risking your life purpose, independence, and freedom. For Faith people I pray you receive God's guidance as you navigate today's broken culture. For those of you who are searching for the answers, I pray you find the Maker's supernatural design in yourself as the ultimate testimony to His creative power — and a revelation of His love for you.

Part Three:
Tools for Singles

Tools for Singles

Imagine you're a craftsman, a long-time expert in your field. You have experience and deep knowledge of your trade techniques. When you go to the job, you know what to do and how to do it. All you need is your full com-

The Dating without Delusion
Dating without Delusion
Toolbox

4C's & The Dating Timeline

When life starts happening:
- Do NOT Trust your Feelings
- Face the Facts
- Stay Connected to Your (Christian) Community
- Get help from your Accountability Partner
- Time is on Your Side .... Go SLOW!!!

• **Always: Core Values (& Bible) first**

• **One tool used well is much better than many misused**

• **..... or not used at all (Ignored warning signals)**

plement of tools. Over time, you have narrowed down your tool selections to the ones that you can use most effectively in the shortest time, leading to the best results. The same thing is true for relationships. The only thing is, relationships are much harder than a job. Jobs have straightforward goals and expectations. Before we fill up your toolbox, let's talk about the slide above.

The first thing is to *not* be driven relentlessly by your feelings. That is going to require help from your accountability partner and intelligent friends. The second key is to GO SLOW because *time is on your side.* As I have told this to many Singles, sometimes I have been angrily blasted because "I *know* this is the right person...so we've got a handle on this Jay!"

Look at the bullets below the toolbox. The first point is to focus on your Personal Values and, if you are a Christian, your Bible-based values. The second point is to pick one or two of these tools and use them. One well-used tool is worth a lot. If you pick *just one* tool, I suggest the 4C tool that we discussed in detail in Part Two. A good tool like this will help you see the warning signals. But, you'll have to pay attention to the warning signals, so don't race through the yellow light, although it's very difficult not to. As you read relationship books, including this one, some tools are going to be tailored for you and some aren't. The ones that fit your personality and demeanor are the 'keepers.' Once again please start with the one tool I think is easiest to remember and use the 4Cs (Core Values, Commitment, Communication, Compatibility).

God has a plan

Remember the base of the pyramid back in the 40'000' view? The starting-point logic contends that God has a personal plan for each of us, and it's a very specific plan tailored exactly to fit only *You*. How do I know this? Partly because I'm in the process of discovering His plan for me. The other reasons are:

1) The empirical evidence for intelligent design that demands a verdict.

2) The three real-life examples: (which you have already read) one from our twenty-first century, one from ancient Israel, and one from my family.

3) Let's start with the empirical evidence. Did you hear recently about the enhanced Hubbell satellite telescope data? Here's the Horsehead

nebula, taken by the Hubble. I offer this one simply because it is so beautiful.[71] Very interesting. Scientists now believe there are 170 billion additional galaxies. The smallest galaxies contain ~10 million stars (a star being like our sun). The largest galaxies contain ~a trillion stars. Beyond inconceivable. When we were up at Priest Lake in northern Idaho in the fall, we walked out under a heavy canopy of stars. In northern Idaho, you can imagine there isn't much ambient light from adjacent cities and industry: it's a pretty remote northern location. On this particular night, the sky was clear: no clouds or overcast. Looking up, the stars were dramatically innumerable. In the intense darkness, the distant stars in the Milky Way had that 'hazy' effect. All in all, a pretty remarkable and awe-inspiring evening. J.D. Greear (in *The Gospel*) does a nice job of describing this in terms that are at least remotely conceivable:

"Astronomers tells us that if the distance between the sun and the earth were the thickness of one piece of paper, then the distance between the earth and the closest star would be a stack of paper 70 feet high. The distance across our galaxy would be a stack of paper 310 miles high. And our galaxy is but one of hundreds of thousands of galaxies in the known universe."[72]

The picture right is 30 Doradus.[73] 30 Doradus is an intense star-forming region where millions of baby stars are birthed inside the thick clouds of dust and gas. 30 Doradus is a 'small' satellite galaxy of the Milky Way. The picture captures a little bit of the awe we felt that dark evening at Priest Lake.

If you want a more up close and personal account, read the book by a modern neurosurgeon who experienced a days-long journey into deep heaven while he was lying unconscious in a hospital bed, without a functioning cortex. It's called *Proof of Heaven*. The neurosurgeon writer (Eben Alexan-

[71] View yourself at https://esahubble.org/images/archive/category/galaxies/
[72] *The Gospel*. p. 92
[73] https://www.nasa.gov/multimedia/imagegallery/image_feature_2105.html

der) was attacked by a meningitis-like infection that left his cortex total-ly non-functioning. Ignorant of many theological basics, he was also a re-nowned expert on brain functioning. My guess is that God chose him to have a tour of the heavens precisely because he was spiritually ignorant, and also because he is perfectly equipped to rebut the medical and scientific skep-tics.[74] When, against all odds and most medical professionals' expectations, he came back to health (after an extended hospital stay), he was compelled by the experience to write the book. *Proof of Heaven* provides a first-hand account of someone who has been into the deep heavens. If you're willing, this is a great read.

From the inconceivable size of the universe, *let's now go in the other direction,* towards the micro-complexities of creation. As I'm writing to-day (it's early March), it's snow-ing like crazy. Perhaps trillions of snowflakes are piling up out-side the front door. Below is a close-up picture of a single snowflake.[75] Look at the intri-cate design. Go to the web and you can see similar shots of many other snowflakes. Look at the variety of structure and design of each snowflake. Have you heard (as have I) that *no two snowflakes are alike?* "How can that possibly be?" you ask. Once again, it is difficult to fathom the intricacy of cre-ation. Keep moving down in

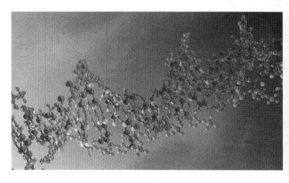

size to the DNA and sub-atomic level; once again, it is difficult to compre-hend, let alone understand. Continually, scientists slowly are beginning to understand the complexity of the brain and how it operates. Now, DNA se-

---

[74] Alexander, Eben. *Proof of Heaven*

[75] Macro shots of natural snowflakes, snow and hoarfrost crystals from photogra-pher Alexey Kljatov.

quencing is becoming a 'tool' that doctors can use to predict our susceptibilities to various forms of cancer and other diseases. Check out the DNA picture above: micro-complexity beyond imagination.

Scientists use tremendously complex accelerator systems to discover particles that are nearly undetectable. 50 years ago, two physicists (Englert and Higgs) predicted the existence of the 'God Particle.' In 2013, scientists used accelerators to create sub-atomic collisions that are detectable (picture right). The Nobel Prize was awarded in 2013 to two scientist whose theory about a sub-atomic particle was validated in accelerator tests in Europe. Going down to the cell level and further to the chromosome level (23 of those), we start to see through DNA sequencing that there is no one exactly like you.

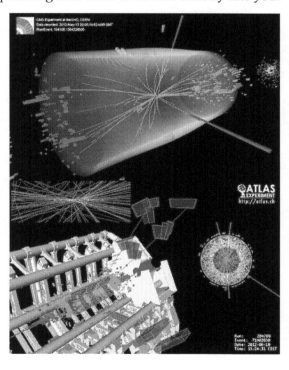

Here's a wonderful little tool to let you see the whole 'spectrum' of creation: it's called 'The Scale of the Universe' and you can access it and click up in size or down to the micro-complexity at https://htwins.net/scale2/.

As a relationship guy, I kind of already knew this. When you 'factorial out' the personality dispositions with the spiritual gifts with the talents and strengths (34 of those), once again you start to see unimaginable complexity and diversity in each of us. This is not a book about apologetics; it's a book about relationships! What I'll argue, with all of this evidence, is that you are unique. And I'll lean on the Bible when it says, "Your eyes have seen my unformed substance; and in your book were written the days that were ordained for me, when as yet there was not one of them." (Psalm 139:16; NASB). How do you discover this? Let's turn to intelligent and scientific self-discovery. When you do the self-discovery work in Part One of this book — remember the three assessments I asked you to use (reminder to the right)? — You are discovering the intricacy of creation existing within your very being.

Monopoly: Where should you invest?

Recently, I volunteered to speak at a Christian Singles gathering, and the theme was tagged with the 'Monopoly' moniker. Of course the idea was to discuss the 'investment' of our time, treasure, and talents. Everyone makes 'investment' decisions every day, and the very good idea was to step back and ask if our investments and choices were paying returns. For us Faith thinkers this is an essential question which has eternal signifi-

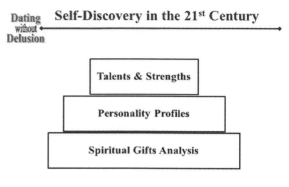

cance. If you have worked your way through Part One of **Dating _without_ De-lusion** then you can see how Personal Values offer the easy answer; *if* you have them. First here's the verse excerpt from Ephesians 4

> So Christ Himself gave the Apostles, Prophets, Evangelists, Pastors, and Teachers to equip His people for works of service so that the body of Christ might be built up until we all reach <u>unity</u> in the faith and in the <u>knowledge</u> of the Son of God become <u>mature</u> , <u>attaining to the whole measure</u> of the fullness of Christ. (Underlines mine)

Here's the discussion slide we used (next page) based upon Ephesians 4 verses 11–3. Staring at the top of the graphic you see the reference to the idea that Jesus is the Creator. He is the creation agent of the Godhead and He has created us.[76] As His creation we are totally unique and precious in His sight, and we are 'equipped'. See how the figure progresses from the top of the circle then clockwise around? As you can see in Ephesians 4 we are equipped for *works of service.* Have you found the ways in which you are equipped to serve? Once again the culture will try to convince you to choose your own path — to focus on yourself, not others. But this verse says very clearly that your 'equipment' is tailored for very precise acts of selfless service. The idea is for you find your pre-ordained works of service by understanding *how* you

---

[76] The validation for this is largely based upon verses like Col 1: vv 19 & 20.

are equipped. Remember the analogy about the 300 pound football player? This is the same idea. When you use your very special personal equipment to serve others, they will be blessed — they will be 'built up'. When you do self-less acts, expecting nothing in return, the people you serve will be amazed, and you will feel free — free of the expectation game and all the other rela-

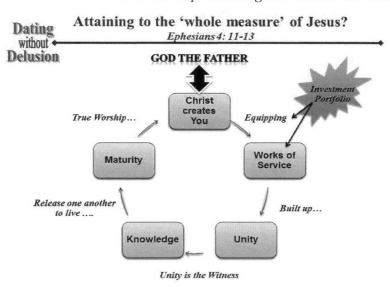

Attaining to the 'whole measure' of Jesus?
Ephesians 4: 11-13

Unity is the Witness

tionship complications. Look back at the list of gifts I gave you — the one with the quote from Charles Schultz. The list is wildly divergent; it's all over the place! Somewhere in there is YOU. When you serve like this a strange thing happens — you start to fit together with the people around you. They know what to expect from you, and they appreciate you for it. This is what the Bible calls 'Unity': each person; each part doing its precisely defined role. A person doing their perfect roles is releasing. You know what to expect from them, and within the bounds of our humanness, you get it! When you see unity working in this perfect way, you will be amazed, and you will under-stand why the Bible says unity is the best message to the world.[77]

So here's the last effect. Seeing a group of people behaving in this way cre-ates an *understanding* in you. I think this understanding is what the Ephesians 4 verses call 'maturity'. When we have wonderfully accurate expectations of one another we reach a level of insight and comprehension — what the Bible

---

[77] Jesus says in John 17:23, "I in them and You in Me that they may be brought to complete unity. Then the world will know that You sent Me and have loved them even as you have loved Me."

is calling 'maturity'. And once again we have stumbled across a word which everyone loves to use, but very few even begin to understand. I want to think I am mature but I only start to understand when my comprehension of who I am starts to guide my decisions and interactions with other people — it begins to drive my behavior. Think about maturity, and what it means for me and for you; it may be thinking time well spent. Now let's keep going around the maturity circle. When you realize and embrace who you are, and start living that way — I for one believe it makes the God who created you smile. Living the way you were designed to live. Seeing others live the same way. Having great relationships with those people is a wonderful thing. So here's the slam dunk.

When you get to see the no kidding design of how God has truly purposed all of this — really all of us working together — you get to experience the divine design. Yes, it doesn't happen often in our post-modern culture, but when you do get to see it, it's a wonderful thing. So this is the last part of the clockwise circle. When you see God's design it should provoke you to a deep awareness; an acknowledgement of how His design is *supposed* to work. Isn't this awareness a rare but indescribable thing? If you haven't seen it it's a hard thing to imagine. Seeing people doing their best and working together you start to understand how God has made things, and how His intended design is better than anything we have tried to create on our own. So we complete the 360 degree journey around the circle in the slide. *Worship.* Another word which is hard to define — even harder to grasp — but it comes about when we see the complexity and the superseding wisdom of God the creator. Faith people call it worship. I don't have an alternative definition — other than the thankful awe you experience when you see the intricacy and the unsearchableness of God's design for life.

So where should you invest? — the whole Monopoly concept? Look back at the graphic. Figure out how God has equipped you — then invest in those skills and giftings. *Figure out how to use your equipment.* The Strengthsfinders people say you have to discover your innate talent and then spend the time and resources to add complementary skill and knowledge. The result is a true personal strength. When you use your strength or a gift on behalf of others, you'll personally experience God's design. Then you'll be able to Worship Him based on the unsearchableness of His design. His design in YOU!

Where to find Truth?

Recently I was reading Oprah, the November 2012 issue. Yes, I know it's a woman's magazine, but it's a good magazine. You can see the hard work of many people in the layout and in the content. Oprah and her staff look to include short to-the-point articles designed to help people live life more effectively (Oprah would probably say "more meaningfully.") In the November 12 issue, in the closing one-pager, 'What I know for Sure.' Oprah talks frankly about the need to be grateful.[78] How she used to write post-it notes to remind herself to be thankful about people, things, and events that made her smile... or moments that were memorable, warm, and funny. She was chastising herself a bit for letting that habit slip, as she was in the turmoil of launching a television network. Looking back, she reflected:

> *"Only when I began feeling gratitude for the opportunity to serve a new audience in a new way did a shift happen. Viewers started saying the most amazing things — things that aligned exactly with my vision of what OWN can be. She closes with: "But I've learned from experience that if you pull the lever of gratitude every day you'll be amazed at the results."*

Thankfulness. My wife Debra has picked her life verse from Paul's letter to the Philippians. Here's the first part of it:

> *"Rejoice! I say again rejoice! Let your gentle spirit be made known to all. Be anxious for nothing, but in prayer and supplication, <u>with thanksgiving</u> let your request be made know to God, and the peace which surpasses understanding will guard your heart and mind."[79] (underline mine)*

What's the point? 'Be thankful' is one essential point. Congruency is the other point. People may dismiss Oprah, or people may dismiss the Bible, but truth has a way of presenting itself in many different ways. Wisdom and truth can be found in many places. You must seek it. If you are a Christian, please don't dismiss a tool that comes from a secular source. If you are not a Christian, please keep an open mind regarding Bible directives and wisdom. They will build you up in an indescribable way. Now, let's look at some other tool alternatives.

---

[78] *O: The Oprah Magazine,* November 2012; p. 194.

[79] Philippians 4: vv-8; NAS Bible.

Your accountability partner

One of the excellent benefits of knowing your values is the greatly increased possibility of meeting a same-sex friend who really appreciates and understands you. Appreciates and understands me? How great is that?!!! If you have a close friend, draw them closer by sharing your Personal Values with them. If it is a genuine friendship, that person will give you honest feedback on your values discoveries and how you articulate them. If that friend doesn't appreciate your values set, you have to find someone who does.

IF you can build this accountability partner relationship, here are 10 (of a possible 100) benefits of having that friendship; see the slide to the below. This whole book could be devoted to the development and benefits of this kind of transparent relationship, but here at least 10 of the big plus items. Before digging into each item, let's focus on the dating-related features and

Dating without Delusion

Who Should You Choose??

(For an Accountability Partner)

Someone Who .... *and Therefore Won't*

Someone Who	and Therefore Won't
• Knows You	- Miss Your Blind Spots / Weaknesses
• Walks in Integrity	- Violate Your Common Principles/Values
• Is Trustworthy	- Break Commitments or Gossip
• Allows You to Be Yourself	- Get Frustrated With Your Basic Self
• Has the Courage to Confront You in Love	- Ignore Your Mistakes
• Is Forgiving	- Dump You Because You Failed or Got Angry
• Is Sensitive to Your Needs	- Be Absent When You Need Them Most
• Is an Encouraging & Listening Person	- Make Matters Worse

benefits. When you find a person that you want to date, your accountability partner, who knows you and your values very well, can give you affirmation, or they might raise the red flag. And they shouldn't be giving you just gut instinct reactions. They should be giving you their insight on how/why this new relationship person can understand, respect, and appreciate your unique set of Personal Values. Do they have to have your exact values? Not a chance! Remember we are all unique, which means we all have different values. But if two people have a decent articulation of their values, it will be relatively easy to see the complementary (or conflicting) nature of an emerging dating relationship. It's the job of this great friend to give you honest feedback, good and bad, about the relationship you are pursuing. It's the job of the guy who shares your love for _____ (?), and who you know will be a lifetime friend sharing your life milestones as you both move forward. When we have gone over this accountability partner idea in the seminar, it's always refreshing to see someone jump up and talk about the close friend they have — like a good brother or sister — someone who has been there for them through thick and thin, through hardship and celebrating. These people know how important a relationship like this is, and they are not confused about the many benefits. Remember, 'life is relationships.'

I have this little saying: "God doesn't build one-way streets." People who have great friendships are clearly aware of the two-way nature of healthy friendships. It really focuses on 'Is sensitive to your needs' and they won't 'Be absent when you need them most' (below). It's the simple idea that we need to be there for one another at different seasons in our lives. At the decision points. During the crises and sickness. The concept is you can give your friend the same kind of caring and feedback when *they* are in the midst of challenges and relationship decisions. Everyone should have a friend like this; I hope you find a person — a true friend — like this. Please add to the simple guidelines in the slide above. This is so important, let's talk about the leading point in the graphic:

Someone Who... and Therefore Won't. The most important thing is that this person loves you 'because of *and* in spite of:' because of who you really are, and in spite of your weaknesses, childhood baggage, past failures, and weird idiosyncrasies. All of which adds up to they know how you are prone to fail, and *they are faithful to call you* on your about-to-be-made blunders, (Line 1). It is great if you share Personal Values, but let's hope your friend has the integrity to stand on his/her own values set (Line 2). Trustworthy (Line 3) goes beyond keeping promises to not gossiping about you and your struggles, particularly behind your back. Do they accept your little quirks? Can they laugh at your stupid little habits and forgetfulness (Line 4)? Do they love you enough to gently confront you when you are making mistakes (Line 5)? And when they do confront you and you get angry, do they have the fortitude and forgiveness to love you in spite of your angry reaction (Line 6)? In an open relationship like this, your friend will be tuned into the challenges and tragedies that roll through your life; will they be there to help you get over those hurdles (Line 7). And lastly, can this person be 'others-focused', not self-absorbed, to be able to listen to you and encourage you as you walk over the hot coals of some life issue (Line 8)?

Closing this discussion, I am deeply thankful for the friends I have who model this kind of steadfastness. I ask myself where I would be without them. A verse from Proverbs jumps out here, *"One who has unreliable friends soon comes to ruin, but there is a friend who sticks closer than a brother."* (Proverbs 18:24; NIV). While I am thankful for the friends who support me, I also realize that many of the people who come to the classes or seminars don't have a good and faithful friend, and this is a big problem. Perhaps the best place to find that key friendship is in the exercise of your service to others. Someone who shares the same built-in drive to serve others the way that you do? In that service setting, there may be a person who can be this kind of friend for you. 'Life is relationships.' God help us to build these kinds of relationships into our lives.

Loneliness: Use it as motivation to fix the problem (Jay)

If you're Single, you know why I put this tool near the front of the tools section. Particularly if you live alone, you know the ache of loneliness that can

Dating without Delusion

Loneliness: Use it as Motivation
(...to Fix the Problem!)

• **Reduce Time Spent Alone**

• **Increase Time Spent Building Your Personal and Corporate Faith**

• **Decrease Time Self-Preoccupation (Look for Service and Giving Opportunities)**

• **Decrease Mindless, Habitual, Unproductive Routine (Damaging Routines)**

• **Spend Time With Your Parents**

• **Increase Tie Building to Others (Accountability Partner)**

• **Consider This a 'Season' for Extra Career/Education Dedication**

• **Develop a Friendship With a '4C' Married Couple**

Life is Relationships....Start Working Now on Making Them Better

grip you every so often. So do your best to develop values-based friendships, which can help tremendously. I hope you have a same-gender accountability partner, or you're working on finding one. This tool is a list of suggestions that you can refer to when loneliness creeps in. The first point is obvious:

Reduce time spent alone. Kind of obvious, but think about it; lonely day after day is when your mind starts to drift and you start down the path to erosion habits (like TV). Most of us will do much better if we have healthy relationships in our weekly routine. Sports are more than exercise. The book club is much more than a couple of novels. If you are a Faith person, make sure you do some faith building (be creative!). And I would be remiss not to promote weekly Faith-based home groups where I have seen Singles grow and support one another in healthy highly connected ways.

Increase time spent building your corporate and personal faith. Build your faith? How do I do that you say? In a recent Singles Fellowship session we talked about increasing your 'Lifestyle of Worship' activities. Here is the menu of suggestions.

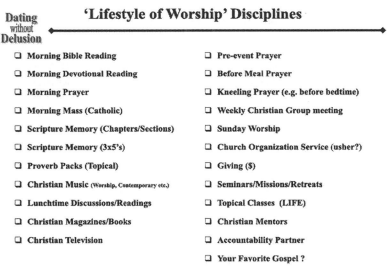

'Lifestyle of Worship' Disciplines

- ☐ Morning Bible Reading
- ☐ Morning Devotional Reading
- ☐ Morning Prayer
- ☐ Morning Mass (Catholic)
- ☐ Scripture Memory (Chapters/Sections)
- ☐ Scripture Memory (3x5's)
- ☐ Proverb Packs (Topical)
- ☐ Christian Music (Worship, Contemporary etc.)
- ☐ Lunchtime Discussions/Readings
- ☐ Christian Magazines/Books
- ☐ Christian Television
- ☐ Pre-event Prayer
- ☐ Before Meal Prayer
- ☐ Kneeling Prayer (e.g. before bedtime)
- ☐ Weekly Christian Group meeting
- ☐ Sunday Worship
- ☐ Church Organization Service (usher?)
- ☐ Giving ($)
- ☐ Seminars/Missions/Retreats
- ☐ Topical Classes (LIFE)
- ☐ Christian Mentors
- ☐ Accountability Partner
- ☐ Your Favorite Gospel ?

This list could be expanded almost indefinitely, but let's talk about one, Christian Radio. 102.1 is KLVJ ('K-love') radio. A simple and effective change is for you to tune into this faith-based station as you do your daily driving. Will this increase you personal faith-focus? It does for me. This list can be expanded indefinitely....but you get the idea. Stay out of the mindless ruts!! Increase your faith foundation.

Get away from self-preoccupation and self-focus. This kind of inward thinking makes the loneliness hurt more. Get out and find some way to serve others.

When you see the misery out there, you'll be thankful for where you are. When you help someone else in a tangible way you'll experience real joy.

Decrease mindless, unproductive routines. Football game after football game, soap opera re-runs, fluffy/sleazy — you name it — fiction. Those routines create ruts (definition of a rut: a grave with the ends kicked out). Let's switch to better alternatives, like spending time with your parents. In a recent seminar, I talked about knowing, speaking, and living the 10 Commandments. The Fifth Commandment is, 'Honor your Father and Mother.' One of the guys had heard this before (he has come to ***Dating without Delusion*** a couple of times). In a tough Northwest windstorm, a tree blew over in his parents' yard: a BIG mess. He took it on himself to get over there and clean it up: the whole thing. Long story short is that his act of service tangibly improved his relationship with his parents and particularly with his dad. How can you close the gap between you and your parents? How can you honor them? What are their needs and wants?

Increase your tie building to others. I'm asking you to be creative with the key people in your life, like your accountability partner. Find out what their 'Love Language' is (Smalley). If it's 'words of encouragement,' make sure to compliment them on their latest effort or project. Take them out to dinner, celebrate their birthday, invite them to a conference or a concert: think creatively. Give them what *they* truly enjoy, not what you would want for yourself. When I was Single, I used to practically invite myself for dinner to homes of good friends who had good marriages to good wives. I knew that these were safe environments and yes, I was a little obnoxious in pushing for an invitation. Thank you if you are one of the couples that helped me. Great meals with quality people in a safe environment; great relationship examples to emulate. Do you have good marriages to lean on?

Consider this as a 'season' for extra career focus and dedication. Very hard, if you're in a job rut. But even if you are stuck in a job that isn't perfect (none are), go to the next level in effort, in service. Help to meet one of your leader/supervisor's tougher goals. Look for an additional assignment; take on a gnarly administrative job that nobody else wants to do. (Be careful here: make sure this matches with your disposition and test-validated strength.) The book of Proverbs is loud and clear when it comes to the benefits that you will receive. Check out the promises in Ephesians 6.

Develop a friendship with a 4C married couple. If you are a Faith person, attend a home group that includes couples who have good marriages. Maybe you come from a broken household. Maybe you come from a solid and committed family. In any case, seeing a 4C married couple operate in their marriage will remind you how marriage is *supposed* to work, including all of the patience, forgiveness, and understanding that are the working parts of a good marriage. To all of the married couples who sustained me through my extended time of Singleness (Bill and Barbara, Mark and Carol, Scott and Sarah, Fred and Shelly, Jim and Toni, all the way back to Navy days Tony and Becky, Butch and Dawn, and many more): thank you.

Loneliness is like an ache, a low-level persistent pain. Any of the suggestions above might help, but you know where the ache really comes from. It's from that natural need to enjoy adult, interesting man-woman interaction. Much of it can be on the Phileo level; see the Love discussion in Part One. In my view, this is very difficult due to all of the culture dysfunction we discussed in Part One. Where can you find relief from this ache? The place that I have seen honest relief is in faith-based Singles home groups: groups of people not only building their faith, but also being appropriately transparent with their struggles, challenges and needs. I have seen men enjoy straightforward conversations with women, and vice versa. In both cases, that internal, undeniable need is met in those interactions. I don't expect co-ed bowling leagues, etc., to provide that kind of safety and comfort. Perhaps the safety aspect of being in a group with articulated faith-based morality enables the kind of healing I am recounting.

The 'hit-on' tool

Over the years, I've heard some pretty bizarre real-life stories from Singles, mostly who are doing their best to live a life of integrity. A situation which comes up often is when you — the Single — are approached by a married individual. Personally, I've heard of this happening more to Single women, being approached by married men. Suffice it to say, you need to be ready regardless of who are. So when a married person 'extends' a friendly conversation into the inappropriate personal domain, use the tool below.

First and most important is the highlighted/boxed principal. If you can 'win the battle in your mind first,' you will be on your way to successfully dealing with this circumstance. Unfortunately, the reverse is also true: if you lose the battle in your mind and start daydreaming about covert liaisons, you're on your way to messing up a family...and your own life. The remaining bullets down the page of the slide *increase* in intensity. They move from conversational techniques (like talking about the person's spouse and oh, by the

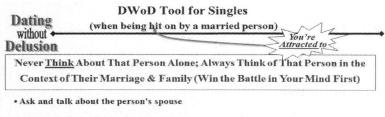

DWoD Tool for Singles

Dating without Delusion (when being hit on by a married person) ————→ You're Attracted to

Never <u>Think</u> About That Person Alone; Always Think of That Person in the Context of Their Marriage & Family (Win the Battle in Your Mind First)

- Ask and talk about the person's spouse
- Ask and talk about the person's children
- Ask what HIS/HER moral standard is?????
- Talk about YOUR moral standard
- Talk about the people you are dating
- Talk about your authorities (who would be offended at this....'suggestion')
- Ask your Father to call (for Women)....dissuading further advances
- Ask your Pastor/Small Group Leader/??? to call

way, the people you are dating) to asking third parties to intervene on your behalf...and really on the behalf of that person's marriage. If all of this is going on at your workplace, you have Human Resources professionals to lean on; the good ones can handle this situation very discreetly. The bottom bullet is, of course, for those people who have a good church/small group connection. As a small group leader, I have had to address these situations and always I had another church leader there for the meeting.

Now, please focus on the little starburst at the upper right of the slide. It addresses he situation when *you* are attracted to a married person. These same techniques will help you direct your behavior and discussions towards healthy boundaries. For Christians, there are a bunch of verses, particularly in Proverbs, that give severe warnings against adultery. For example, check out Proverbs Chapter 7, as the young man follows the adulterous woman "like an ox going to the slaughter, like a deer stepping into a noose, till an arrow pierces his liver, like a bird darting into a snare, *little knowing It will cost him his life*" (verses 22, 23 NIV; italics added). Please recall the devastating effects divorce has on children (from Part One). Adultery is often the root cause of many a divorce scenario.

Having a marriage vision

There are at least two ways to get an understanding of healthy marriage relationships. One is to spend time with committed and successful couples who have established marriages with common values, resiliency, and forgiveness. As well as attraction and compatibility. The other is to look at key resources, such as the one below. Remember Stephen Covey's admonishment to 'begin with the end in mind'? Pick up this book (or find another one that fits your persona) and read it. You may remember the saying, "If you don't know where you're going, you're probably going to get there." You need to have an idea of what a healthy marriage looks like. If you are one of the dwindling number of people who were raised in healthy, no-divorce households, you have absorbed good marriage vision. The more you can reflect on those positive growing-up experiences and be clear about your need for them, the better.

I have enjoyed Judith Wallerstein's book and it's one that I recommend you pick up for your Relationship Library. She studies healthy marriages, and types them. For each of the marriage types, she digs into what makes them work and what specific challenges each marriage style must overcome. For example, traditional marriages have clearer boundaries and expectations than some of the emerging marriage styles. Contemporary marriages are full of negotiation, requiring strong communication skills. The research and in-depth analysis she does will really give you insight on the marriage type that suits you and oh, by the way, the very unique challenges that come with that marriage type. All in all a very good read that will help you *no matter what stage of relationship development you are in.*

As for the Wallenstein resource, she looks objectively at 50 good marriages. Based upon her research, she types marriages into four basic types (Traditional, Companionate, Rescue, and Romantic) and then looks at the way each operates. Beyond an in-depth look at each of the four marriage types, she very succinctly defines 'tasks' that every good marriage must navigate. If you add this book to your Relationship Library you no doubt will find a style that fits your upcoming marriage

So you say, "Jay! Stop taking to me about marriage until we get through the whole conundrum of dating!" I understand why this seems to be premature to you, since you aren't even dating yet, or perhaps you've only been dating a short time. The challenge is to understand marriage so you can use

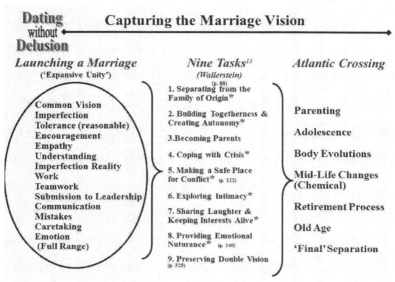

it a mental backdrop for your dating experience. Good marriages have to deal with day-to-day challenges, but they also need staying power and the foundation to go through tough challenges. Using Judith's work, I've constructed the tool above. The analogy is that marriage is like an Atlantic crossing in a steam liner. There are plenty of icebergs and hazards that your ship has to be prepared for to make the crossing. Marriage that aren't fully equipped to make the crossing probably won't make it. A good marriage has flexibility, adaptability, and all of the attributes shown on the left of the slide below. Now we are so used to seeing dysfunction in marriage. Don't be dragged down by those issues; keep envisioning a marriage relationship that works, which is the purpose of this tool. Sure, you have to be a forgiving and supportive spouse (after successful dating). And you want your relationship to keep on improving... a tall order.

The center of the slide extracts from Wallerstein's book the nine tasks that every good marriage must tackle. Remember, these are tasks which good marriages get done. Most marriages *don't* get this stuff done. So what? There will be a hit on the quality of the marriage, that's what. Take Task #1, 'Separating from the Family of Origin.' Good marriage partners put one another on the top of their relationship priority list — earthly, that is. Just for a moment, however, let's assume either one of the spouses can't create healthy distance between the marriage and the in-laws. Those kinds of in-law relationships can create intrusions which tear the marriage apart. Counselors and relationship books deal with this kind of problem, which is potentially huge.

Of the tasks Judith defines, most of them are tasks you can do during dating — I have annotated those tasks with a red asterisk. The nine tasks in exclusive dating lean heavily on these tasks from _The Good Marriage._ If you have reached the exclusive dating phase, this is a great read.

Stopping the downward spiral of the Four Horsemen
(John Gottman/Jay)

If you are driving a car and you get a high-danger traffic alert for the road you're on, chances are that you're going to reroute in a hurry. The same thing should be true for relationships. Unfortunately, nothing like a relationship warning is going to come at us over the radio or through a digital sign. Maybe the warning will come from a trusted mentor or accountability partner, if you have one. There are four very relationship-toxic behaviors that erode a marriage relationship. But this is a dating book, you say! Yes, but the whole point of dating is to build relationships safely, and to protect the potentials and possibilities of finding a relationship that is marriage-worthy.

So if you knew eventually, even in the best-for-you relationship, you were going to face an 'irreconcilable difference' challenge, wouldn't you want to be forewarned and forearmed? Let's look at the Four Horsemen. They come from a respected psychologist, John Gottman. He contends that the contempt between couples emerges in a destructive way that leads to other negative emotional reactions and behaviors, specifically criticism, defensiveness and stonewalling. I have added the graphic depiction that suggests the sequential downward spiral. Do these negative emotions and behaviors always happen in the tight sequence I have shown? Likely not. But if two people are aware of the erosion that can attack their relationship, it would only be common sense to try to prevent the downward spiral. I agree with Gottman that this downward disintegration is at the root of the irreconcilable differences that are often cited as the reason for thousands or millions of divorces each year.

Why are we talking about irreconcilable differences in a dating book? First, because I contend that differences of opinion, different beliefs and attitudes, and different situation assessments are *always* present in *every* relationship, particularly in man-woman relationships. In everyday co-worker, friendship, and family interactions, we can very easily choose to dial down the level of interaction and to spend less time with that person when we have disagreements. Even in dating relationships, it's easy to dodge real issues and spend less time with that person, thereby avoiding the conflict and contempt which are actually present. Not so in marriage relationships: your marriage partner is at your side... daily. Remember, successful dating will allow you to manage the problems in your relationship. It may enable you to marry someone you truly love (all three elements of love). If that happens and you don't have the delusions about conflict-free relationships, how much better prepared will you be for a successful lifetime commitment to a marriage? So let's look at the Four Horsemen spiral and its downward progression. This progression is the one to avoid!

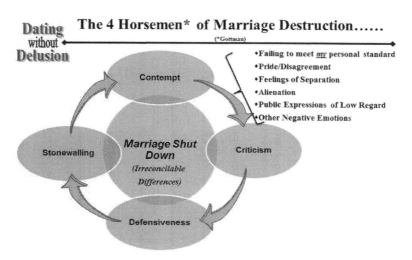

The 4 Horsemen* of Marriage Destruction......
(*Gottman)

Dating without Delusion

- Contempt
- Stonewalling
- **Marriage Shut Down** (*Irreconcilable Differences*)
- Criticism
- Defensiveness

- ◆Failing to meet *my* personal standard
- ◆Pride/Disagreement
- ◆Feelings of Separation
- ◆Alienation
- ◆Public Expressions of Low Regard
- ◆Other Negative Emotions

The Downward Cycle Starts...How Will You Break the Cycle?

What's the definition of an argument? Two people in the same room. This is an obvious exaggeration to highlight the fact that no one is just like you. Those differences make you beloved (hopefully) to many people, but they are also the differences at the root of our differences and arguments. Many people successfully contain their negative emotions — and some don't — to avoid the argument pain, but the differences are still there. So what are the root causes? Please see the Four Horsemen chart annotated above. Check out the list of causes for the contempt that you will inevitably feel. Even the most 'Compatible' couples — even couples with values compatibility — will face this challenge over the course of their marriage. The first issue is when you have learned to live at a higher standard and your spouse does not live up to your expectations. You feel that you are superior in that aspect of living (in your opinion). That, of course, is a prideful opinion that creates a feeling of contempt in you. Even if you don't articulate any of that contempt, it's still in you, doing its nasty little erosion.

My adopted parents had a very solid marriage. They would often have to swallow the critical words when their contemptuous differences of opinion emerged. The essential thing: they learned the stupidity of vocalizing those little feelings of contempt when they showed up during the course of the day. Not vocalizing those feelings of alienation and separation is a wise first step. Particularly important: no demeaning the other person to your friends and family...especially in public. This is a challenge that Debra and I have to face on occasion. Personally, I hate it when she criticizes me to other people in public over some difference that we are experiencing, and I'm sure she feels the same when I violate this principle.

Do you see that the contempt worms its way into a verbal criticism? (We're working our way around the Four Horsemen slide clockwise from the top; follow the arrows). From here, it is natural to be defensive: the third oval in the diagram. I am very prone to this behavior because I am emotionally vulnerable. The strong and silent persona that so many men fall into is the danger; but, of course, women can respond that way, too. All of which brings us to the last step in the spiral, stonewalling. Guys who have hurt feelings use this technique to punish their spouses. A wall of silence hurts women who often love interaction, and it hurts men who need input and encouragement from their wives. Once again, this sequence is much more dynamic and overlapping than I have depicted it, but you get the idea. There are empty feelings of alienation and isolation. There is a feeling of aloneness. This kind of negative emotion is what John Gottman would say is at the root of irreconcilable differences. Step back and think about a couple that *had* such great interaction and now can barely speak to one another... this is a tragedy. The question is — what can you do about it?

If you believe at all in the downward spiral created by the Four Horsemen, the obvious answer is to *stop it* before it gains destructive momentum. The next chart (next page) suggests some thinking and pro-action to deal with the feelings of the contempt which typically start the cycle. Again, this is about learning to do Conflict Resolution and avoidance while you are still dating. Learning this while you are exclusively dating is Task #2 of the 9 Exclusive Dating Tasks. 'Define your conflict resolution techniques'.

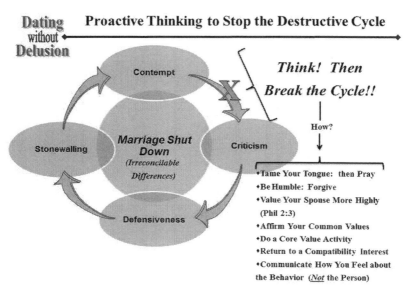

Tame Your Tongue: then Pray. It is so very easy to lash out, to be verbally demeaning, and to angrily snap back. When you recognize this is about to happen, take a moment of silence; breathe; sit down for a moment. If you are a Faith person, this provides you with the opportunity to pray, and pull up the Bible verses that help you the most. Example: 'Even a fool, when he keeps silent, is considered wise. When he closes his mouth, he is counted as prudent. (Proverbs 17 v 28 NASB). During that silent moment, remember how you and your significant other share essential and similar values in life. How important is that person to you? Tremendously. How about 'A gentle answer turns away wrath, but a harsh word stirs up anger.' (Proverbs 15 v 1 NASB). Pick your verses.

Be Humble. Forgive. The key to this is to remember the times *you* have been critical and unloving. Owning your own failures creates a sensitivity, which allows you to forgive the other person. Ask for the Lord's help as you go down this path.

Consider your significant other more important than yourself (Phil 2:3). Think about her value to you. Remember the commitments you are sharing with him. Think about the last time you spoke badly and he forgave you...which leads you to forgiveness and humility. The culture teaches you to elevate yourself. Selfish, self-focus is going accelerate the downward spiral. My recommendation is to pause and remember the key Personal Values that you share, and have spoken to one another. Do you have kids or step-kids? They're at the center of your family/relationship values. Remember the hurt and displacement which arguments with your significant other works on the kids.

Do a Core Value Activity. Prayer is often cited by many Christian counselors as the Single most important thing you and your spouse can do to come back together. I want you to learn this principle while you are dating. I recommend that you ask forgiveness, and pray very soon after the contempt and criticism start. It's very hard to even think about praying together when you are defensively stonewalling each other. Many times, once the downward spiral starts, feelings can get worse. Prayer can deal with the emptiness and criticism you want to blurt out. If you are not a faith person, you have to find help in your other best relationships. Church is another obvious answer. I can truly say that when Debra and I are at odds over an issue, the negative feelings are really slowed down by time spent in a good, spiritual service. Or, if you have commitments to a service/giving activity, go out to support that cause. Seeing people you are trying to help in various impossible predicaments will take your mind off of the contempt for your spouse, and it will make you realize what a good life you really do have.

Return to a Compatibility Interest. Although I always say Compatibility is the fourth of the 4C's, it's still a good thing. If you both love to do something, get together, go out and do it. Do you both like to go to the gym? Great, go hit the gym together! If you love to go on great bike rides in the outdoors, wonderful! Get out there together and let the fresh air blow over your nasty emotions.

Communicate How you Feel about the Behavior — Not the Person. The last contempt-stopper is a suggestion about what you *still* think *you have to say.* As a last resort, if it's absolutely necessary that you tell her; you can't go another minute without letting him understand. (Remember, my #1 stopper is to tame your tongue!) If there is an issue that is eating at you, please don't demean the other person. Help them to understand that when they do or say _____, (fill in the blank) that behavior makes you feel badly. How does it make you feel? Your feelings are real and you own them. Don't communicate another criticism. That's the beginning of a back-and-forth Ping-Pong discussion. No; please help the other person to understand how you feel. Help them to see and feel the hurt you feel. The dialogue might go like this. "I love you, but when you do (whatever the behavior is), it makes me feel unloved, not valued (again please honestly fill in the blanks)." By doing this, you *are* being critical, which is why I offer this as a last resort. Be sure you are criticizing a specific behavior and *not* the other person — a vital difference.

A tool for Single parents: the Parenting 'Target Zone'

Being involved in what churches call Singles ministry has been interesting, frustrating, and rewarding, all in one. Along the way, I have been asked to lead Single parenting classes of various types, **Dating _without_ Delusion** being one of the broader Singles offerings. Like the number of Single adults in America, the number of Single parents continues to grow at a rapid rate. I have been influenced by great teacher/psychologists such as Kevin Lehman, Chip Ingram, Foster Cline and Jim Fay (*Parenting with Love and Logic*). In particular, Kevin Lehman (author of *Single Parenting*) digs into the complexities of parenting as a Single parent, having to balance the child's need for both parents with the fact that the divorce has split the marriage apart. Much has been written about helicopter, hands-off, laissez-faire parenting. Ditto for over-controlling, authoritarian parenting; *we all tend to err* in one direction or the other. Do you see the two extremes on the chart? Another parenting style which drives kids crazy is inconsistency. The best parents in my opinion are parents who know and live their Personal Values. The big problem is parents often get divorced over values differences. So now as the kids bounce from home to home they have to adjust to each of the parent's rules and environment. This one a many reasons why kids experiencing divorce have such a difficult time. What is worth emphasizing here is the 'Power of Influence' shown in the graphic below. For example, showing respect for the other parent (see the top bubble in the graphic) enables a child to have access to both of his/her parents, even in a tough after-divorce situation. Respecting God's design (again, top bubble) recognizes the need for us to allow the child to become who they have been designed to be. How different is that from 'You can be whoever you want to be' or 'You do it because that's what we've always done'?

Let's take a closer look at the bottom bubble (look at the 'Positive Influence'). If you're not a Christian, you want to know where your morality comes from; that leads to the virtues of honesty, integrity, and trustworthiness. Giv-

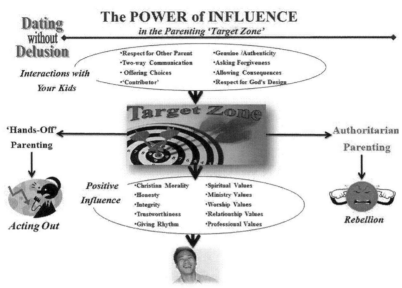

The POWER of INFLUENCE
in the Parenting 'Target Zone'

ing of your time and money sends a strong message to your kids about the need for us all to be 'others-centric.' The values list sits in the right half of that bubble. The Power of influence, I contend, is tremendously powerful when your values are clearly in view for your kids to see. If you know, speak, and live your values, your choices and actions have foundation. When your kids ask you, "Why?' you will have an answer. Kids may not like the direction they get from their parents, or from their Single parent, but they can depend on the clear values rationale the parents use to make decisions.

Here's an example. Let's do the real-life example of going to church again. Using the Personal Value 'To Know, Speak, and Live the 10 Commandments.' Sometimes I twist in a little sarcasm by talking about the 10 'Suggestions.' As a reminder, the Fourth Commandment goes like this: "Remember the Sabbath to keep it Holy. For six days you shall labor and do all of your work, but he seventh day is a Sabbath unto the Lord your God" (Exodus 20). As it turns out, this personal value fits very nicely with 'Spirit-abiding man of Christ' (remember my #1 Value?). So here comes the weekend and the question comes up, "Do we need to go to church this weekend?" Going to church does not keep a day set apart to focus on God, but it sure is a good start. Both Debra and I feel a tangible and discreet difference — kind of like an emotional hole or gap — if we don't go to church. As parents, when the question came up, "Why do you go to church?" the answer was, and is, easy. My values are grounded in Christ, this is what He says to do, and we do it. There are many, many examples where my values were the small voice in the back of my head telling me I had to make the values-based choice. Of course I say that was God; you may say that I am deluded. If it was the Lord, I think He used my values to provide a small but critical reminder to make values-consistent choices.

The going-to-church example is one of many situations where values allow a straightforward explanation for your kids-they allow you to clearly explain your actions and choices. You've heard the buzz-phrase 'lead by example,' and that's a part of this story. With values, 'lead by example' becomes 'live by example' with a values-based rationale. Will your children agree with you? Maybe not, but they will not be aggravated by hypocrisy or authoritarianism: the things that drive teenagers crazy. As you look to the psychologist professionals to develop your parenting, see if the 'Power of Influence' can't play a strong role in your life and the life of your kids.

Your Relationship Library

There are so many self-help relationship books out there, it's daunting to find one that 'fits' you. **Dating _without_ Delusion**, as a little side benefit, synthesizes time-proven resources for you. I've tried to select and adapt some of the best relationship principles from some of the best relationship books, Bible-inclusive. This condensation will offer you some really key learnings, and it may inspire you to get one or two of these books to read and interpret for yourself. These books, in my opinion, have 'stood the test of time.' They also bring practical insights that I have applied over and over again in many different **Dating _without_ Delusion** classes and seminars. People know truth and understand practical living when they see it. As a person of Faith, I have always attempted to see the author's perspective and assess the alignment with Bible relationship principles. In retrospect, this has been a very simple and straightforward process because the congruence between these quality books and the Bible is very compelling. It's a congruence that needs little defense. The issues we are going to confront, however, are at big odds with our broken culture.

You will find that many of these published works are 1990's vintage, which is a reflection of how long I have been encouraging Singles. It also reflects the fact that the principles embedded in these volumes still hold true. For example, in developing the 4C's,[80] we discussed the third C, which is Communication. In this section, I offered adapted graphics from John Gray's *Men Are from Mars, Women Are from Venus*. Specifically, understanding that 'Women are like Waves' is an important reality in my marriage, which has short-stopped my bad thinking and even worse reaction (on my part) to Debra's occasional emotional housecleaning episodes. John Gray believes, and so do I, that many marriages face this same phenomenon. Is this understanding a benefit to me as a Christian husband who is called to 'love his wife as Christ loved the church'? Absolutely. But why wait until marriage to start the learning? Delusional dating expects women always be rational and men to always be emotionally available. Delusional dating leads to marriages with damming and unrealistic expectations. So I believe, with Judith Wallerstein, John Gray and many others, that relationship training is essential early on. If better relationships are the only result, so be it. If better marriages are encouraged and enabled by better dating, my goal will be achieved.

A very few of you will get the whole book-set and start your own research. Many more of you will get one of the books that captures your individual need and imagination. I hope in this book you Faith-oriented people have found unambiguous Bible support and direction.

So here is a start to your Relationship Library. I list the books alphabetically by author and offer a paragraph synopsis supporting why I included this book as a starting point for your selection process. A complete bibliography is offered at the back of this book.

***Now Discover Your Strengths*. Marcus Buckingham, Donald Clifton.** The Bible is full of references to our gifts and callings. From my perspective, most churches make a passing nod to spiritual gifts tests, personality profiles and strengths analyses. Let's believe the Bible and the scientific evidence in order

---

[80] The 4C's are Core Values, Commitment, Communication, and Compatibility.

to embrace the complexity of human composition. Yes, we *are* fearfully and wonderfully made, and understanding yourself is a *big* discovery task. *Self-discovery* is the demanding task, and this is one of the best tools to help you.

Now a part of the Gallup organization, Strengthsfinders experts tell me that they are closing in on *30 million* people who have taken the assessment. The Strengthsfinders assessment is a positive psychology assessment that identifies an individual's innate talents. Talents, combined with knowledge and skill, become strengths. These assessments have proven to be effective in both business and church settings. As the tool is refined and applied to many organizations and businesses, the Gallup Organization continues to collect data and sharpen their analyses. Are you still skeptical? In 2005 and 2007, Gallup looked at over 65,000 employees who received strengths feedback and concluded that *turnover rates were 14.9 percent lower*[81] than with those employees who received nothing. Looking at over 500 work units, managers who received strengths feedback showed 12.5 percent greater productivity relative to those units where the manager received nothing. Hard statistics like these reinforce the fact that we indeed are unique individuals. Understanding how we are wired makes a difference. It makes a difference in the business world, and I argue that strengths self-awareness combined with values self-awareness can make a tremendous difference in the world of relationships. Someday, it would be wonderful to see how values/strengths self-awareness can reinforce the stability and longevity of marriage. A future goal.

I use an older version of Strengthsfinders (Strengthsfinders 2.0 is the current publication) because it has a nice section on 'How to manage a person with the (fill in the blank) strength' that has served me well. My talent/strength of 'Individualization' is a built-in propensity to appreciate and enjoy the special complexity of each person as a one-of-a-kind individual. My Individualization strength is the one operating to encourage *you* to become the unique person indicated by *your* strengths, uniquely designed by God to execute His unique plan for you. All of my strengths are woven into my values, and this is the approach I recommend for you. Personal awareness can transform *all* of your relationships and, very importantly, inform your day-to-day living through the entire dating process.

---

[81] Buckingham, Marcus. Clifton, Donald. *Now Discover your Strengths.* Copyright 2005, 2007. The Gallup Organization, Princeton, NJ.

Are You the One for Me?* Barbara DeAngelis.** A Los Angeles Ph.D. psychologist, Barbara is definitely secular in her approach, but also intensely practical. I have adapted some of her summary checklists into the Part 3 tools section of ***Dating without Delusion. Look to see not only the practicality of her thinking, but also the natural congruence with spiritual principles. Happily, I find plenty of alignment between her very well developed lists and scripture. For example she warns against relationships with people suffering addictions. What is an addiction but a pervasive idol? That's the Second Commandment. What about anger? Paul in Colossians and James both warns against anger and its consequences.[82] Remember the admonitions about finding truth.

***Love & Respect.* Emerson Eggerichs.** Dr. Eggerichs has been leading Love and Respect Marriage Conferences for many years, and this book has well over million copies in print. The summarized message of this book? It provides a fresh understanding of the significant differences between men and women. In our gender blurred society this is tremendously significant, and within the context of marriage it is intensely practical. For marriages it provides practical coaching for men, and practical coaching for women. "This book is about how the wife can fulfill her need to be loved by giving her husband what he needs — respect"...and here's one woman's testimony:

> *"Let me say after the close on Saturday we spent the best afternoon and evening with each other we have had in years. It was like we were in our twenties again and so in love, Emerson. I can honestly tell you, I never realized how important, how life giving, respect was to my husband."*

We have used *Love and Respect* in the Singles sessions, and I can say that the people who learn about the gender sensitive tools and perspectives were unanimously appreciative of the great learning they were achieving, even if they were not in a dating relationship. In general it is much better to learn the Love and Respect tools while they are still single, and perhaps not yet in any kind of dating relationship. If your future relationship grows into *engagement*, the church may very well offer this training. Please take the training again... it will be be doubly effective in light of your impending marriage.

***Men Are from Mars, Women Are from Venus.* John Gray.** Man-woman communication is a mystery to most people, and it is often confounding. If you

---

[82] James 1 v 19, 20: But everyone must be quick to hear, slow to speak and slow to anger, for the anger of man does not achieve the righteousness of God.

don't get this book (which was very popular because it is very good), find an inter-gender communication book that fits you, then read it! This resource will *not* help you to articulate your Personal Values, which are the most critical element of your communication. It will help you to get a grip on the very substantial challenges of inter-gender communication. Needless to say, poor communication in dating is a BIG problem. Poor communication in marriage sets the stage for a divorce. Remember the third 'C'.

***Getting the Love You Want*. Harville Hendrix.** Our childhood experiences often create pre-influenced reactions that will be frustrating and incomprehensible to the people you are dating... and these frustrations will be just as incomprehensible to our future spouses. Harville works in his book to expose the 'Imago' (Greek for image) embedded in our psyche. These are the outcomes of the childhood frustrations we all experience. The frustrations, in turn, create feelings and emotions that strongly influence our behaviors and our attractions, as we move into adulthood. Harville wants marriages to be open and healthy. I want *dating* to be open and healthy. This book will help you understand and manage the source of the infatuations that you may feel so deeply. Keen Imago awareness on your part is an important element of the practical solution. Deeper self-awareness helps you to relate spiritually and intellectually while managing your emotions in the midst of developing relationships. My goal is to encourage you Singles to develop and use this awareness *before* you date. Certainly *while* you are dating it would also be very, very helpful. Do otherwise and you might find yourself in crisis marriage counseling and therapy. All of this work is to avoid many of the repetitive relationship disasters that may wait for you around the bend, in the next dating relationship.

***Unhooked: How Young Women Pursue Sex, Delay Love and Lose at Both*. Laura Sessions Stepp.** Feminism in the 70's had a strong influence on the parents of the current young adult population. 'Don't be exploited by men' and 'success at all costs' has been strongly broadcast to today's young women. These mantras deeply influenced the culture and the behavior of today's college-age women: a large segment of the Millennial generation. In this work, Laura helps you to understand this culture and its devastating impact on young women. It's a tough read. It's objective, valuable, and written by a skilled and empathetic researcher. A must-read to understand today's cultural 'baseline.'

The Gospel. J.D. Greear. I was passing the 200-page mark in writing this book when our church's senior pastor launched a new sermon/home group study called *The Gospel*. The pastor had just been on a sabbatical, and took some of his away time to read this practical discussion of the difficulty that churches face in encouraging their people to live spiritually relevant lives without getting trapped in the 'Working for God' mentality.

If you are a church person, you know this dilemma plagues us all. If you are not a church person, this little book is a clear presentation of Christian basics without a lot of the buzz phrasing. The lesson I recall from Sunday school and the

one J.D. reminds me of is the simple locomotive analogy. Without an engine, which is the gospel, your train is going nowhere. The 'works,' — the results of our faith behavior, are the practical outcome of honest service to people who are in crisis. From a personal perspective, I am a prime offender... meaning that I get caught in the 'Working for God' ambiguity all of the time. And you already know enough about me to know that I hate ambiguity.

So as the new sermon series started, I was busy teaching a new Singles **Dating _without_ Delusion** class, I was writing this book, and I was taking on a new consulting challenge. Like you, I was busy! I have been a Christian for over 30 years; I have two piles of books stacked up on my desk; and my office is deteriorating into a clutter. I thought to myself, "At this point in my life, I pretty well understand the gospel, and I don't need another book." God had another plan, however. My wife zipped over to the church bookstore and the next thing I knew, I had the book in front of me. Next, our small-group leader effusively stamped this book as 'really good.' Still I couldn't understand WHY! Then, as I picked it up one morning, I began to see J.D. Greear's 'fresh' perspective on the Bible and how it tells us to live.

The fresh perspective from *The Gospel* has provided some key insights that put some 'steam in my locomotive,' which I will share with you as you go through **Dating _without_ Delusion**. As depicted in the little insert (right), the idea is to make sure that my Faith is the catalyst that creates 'works of service,' and *not* the other way around. This book reminded me, and I'll remind you: *Make sure you have the right cars hooked up to your locomotive.* Make sure that your true self is at work when you engage in giving and serving activity. *The Gospel* very specifically was a catalyst for Devil's Ping-Pong, which you will find in the section on 'Your Fight against the Culture.' Other key points and references are also included throughout.

I summarize the message from this book with a verse and a thought. The seventeenth verse from James 1 is, "*Every* good and perfect gift is from above, coming down from the Father of heavenly lights who does not change like shifting shadows." And the thought? See *every* good thing and *every* good relationship as a blessing. Always remember, God is the Source. That's big-picture thinking. J.D. summarizes by saying, "You cannot confuse the effects of the gospel with the gospel itself."[83] The Lord used *The Gospel*, a very timely book, to tell me: "Write the book; depend on Me to do it."

Sacred Search. Gary Thomas. This book is written specifically to Singles, based upon Matthew chapter 6 verse 33 that says, "Seek first the kingdom of God and all these things will be added unto you." Gary is acutely aware of the havoc that divorce is wreaking on our country, and he says that many times and in many ways, people who marry in the throes of infatuation are doomed to live ineffective lives. Anyone struggling to deal with the dysfunction and dissatisfaction of a poor marriage can be diverted from higher goals and more effective living. Of course, many of these poorly designed marriages end in divorce, which embroils even the most well-meaning person(s) in the legal and emotional hassles that go along with divorce proceedings. Hear (again) what Gary says regarding poor relationships choices: *"You have no idea how much kingdom time* (Gary's term for God-directed activity) *is wasted on ill-matched people trying to make their marriages a little less insufferable."*[84] The 'life has lost its purpose' phenomenon is the earmark of bad relationships. Conversely, integrating your Personal Values into your relationship building is the best way to avoid this quicksand that is so ingrained into our culture today. Gary speaks in a very different voice than I do, and so I often quote him along the way in order that you might hear some of the most critical relationship concepts from a different vantage point.

The Unexpected Legacy of Divorce. Judith Wallerstein. This talented and em-

[83] *The Gospel.* p. 228
[84] Gary Thomas. *The Sacred Search* (David C. Cook, 2013). p. 250.

pathetic researcher from Cal Berkley is no longer with us (she passed away in 2012). She and her staff did landmark studies, meaning that they interviewed people and families and then continued to interview and assess those same people *over 25 years*. This book is a landmark study, and it takes you on the 25-year journey with kids as they live through the divorce of their parents and then try to come to terms with the resulting deep personal effects as they proceed into adulthood. She destroys some of the myths regarding divorce, and suggests that the impact of a divorce on the kids is much more significant and longer-lasting than we ever imagined. This is a must-read for Singles, to help overcome a divorce (if it happened in your own family) and to understand that many of the Singles you meet (and might want to date) are probably facing similar divorce-related challenges.

***The Good Marriage.* Judith Wallerstein**. What does a 'good marriage' look like? How does it operate? What are some of the key characteristics of a good marriage and how can we learn from them? Judith looks at good marriages (again, over a 25 year landmark period) and studies the reasons that they function so well. She established four marriage types, and helps us understand the key 'operational' principals for each of the types. The four types are:

- *The Traditional Marriage*
- *The Romantic Marriage*
- *The Companionate Marriage*
- *The Rescue Marriage*

As you read *The Good Marriage* you will gain fresh marriage insight, but I want to momentarily highlight the Rescue Marriage as one 'type' having growing significance in our culture. The Rescue Marriage allows the husband and wife to find deep internal 'repair' from traumatic childhood experiences. Listen to Judith:

> *I was therefore surprised and elated to discover through this study a group of long-term happy marriages in which one or both partners had suffered terribly cruel childhoods including early abandonment sexual and physical abuse, severe mental illness in one or both parents and other serious traumas. Remarkably, the tragedies these people experienced as children did not spell doom for their marriages. Eventually a fifth of the couples in this study fell into this category...The*

discovery of these lasting successful rescue marriages is one of the major findings of this work, one that should bring hope to countless people.[85] *(Underlines mine)*

So many people I encounter in the seminar have come out of a traumatic childhood, and all the therapists and psychologists know this spells trouble for those people when they try to create their own marriages. When the Wallerstein study offers a glimmer of hope for future marriages in spite of the trauma I think it is a 'landmark' in itself. Of course this brings us full circle back to your Personal Values. People with 'values-based compatibility' are the ones who can weather the downturns, the disagreements, the crises, and inevitable upheavals of life. Marriages like this get past the 'Imago' imprint of a tough childhood and look forward to lives which share the capacity to give to others. Just listening to a recent Christian song about being 'Broken Together' (Casting Crowns) reminds us of our inevitable personal frailties and blind spots. Every healthy marriage is grounded upon the partners' ability to accommodate, understand, and encourage their most significant-other — their spouse. And always there will be opportunities to forgive and to ask forgiveness. 'Broken Together'... sets the right expectations.

Beyond the marriage types I particularly like Judith's nine tasks. She suggests every good marriage must navigate these tasks. These are a primary input to the nine tasks I recommend for couples who are dating exclusively. The tasks (see Part Two) are crisp guidelines for couples trying their best to prepare their relationship for the lifelong commitment of marriage.

Occasionally I will pick up *The Good Marriage*, and sit for a quiet read. On every occasion I have been enlightened and reminded. Reminded of 'the Great Mystery'...for this reason a man will leave his father and mother, and be united to his wife, and the two will become one flesh. This is a profound mystery...."[86] Is Judith Wallerstein a valuable addition to your relationship Library? I think you know the answer.

---

[85] Wallerstein, *The Good Marriage*. Pg. 91.

[86] Ephesians 5 vv 31 & 32. NIV.

Appendices

Appendix A: Singles Ministry Practicalities

The challenge faced by many churches comes down to inexperience. Many churches are pastored by people who were raised in whole and functional households. Growing up, they attended churches where the majority of attendees were married and raising their own unbroken families. That will no longer be the case in the United States. The pastors of tomorrow may be supported by the whole and functional families they grew up in, but the

Singles Ministries Practicalities
(Jay's Italics)

5 Reasons for Singles Ministry[1]

1. A church that ignores single adults fails to underwrite tomorrow's leadership.

2. A church that ignores single adults fails to appreciate the pattern demonstrated by the early church in Acts 6.

3. A church that ignores single adults fails to follow Jesus example.

4. A church that ignores single adults is a slave to the past rather than a previewer of the future.

5. A church that minsters to single adults will help them mature, make spiritual commitments and establish kingdom priorities that will lead them into better marriages. *(maybe)*

Singles Ministry Leadership Principles[2]

1. We want to raise the consciousness of the whole church of Jesus Christ to understand that singleness is natural and healthy.

2. We want to bring the entire congregation to a deeper understanding of marriage divorce and remarriage.

3. We are totally committed to the integration of single adults into the whole life of the church.

4. Single adult leaders need to understand that the predominant goal of the people in their ministry groups is to find and develop healthy relationships with males and females usually with the hope that they will eventually marry. *(or not)*

1. Franck, Dennis. *Reaching Singles Adults: An Essential Guide for Ministry.* Baker Books, 2007. p52-54.
2. Flanagan, Bill. "Priorities for Singles Ministry", in *Single Adult Ministry.* ed. Jerry Jones (Colorado Springs; Singles Ministry Resources, NavPress, 1991), p44-45.

demographics tell of future congregations which will have many, many more Single adults. The 'Practicalities of Singles Ministry' tool shown above will is a needed resource as churches and church leaders face the challenges associated with the makeup of their new congregations. Authors with Singles ministry deep experience, such as Dennis Frank (quoted above left), are essential to guide us through this transition.

Appendix B: "The Demise of PR-03"

In the Navy, I was stationed on Guam in an A-3 squadron (a long-since re-tired twin engine electronic warfare plane). As a bombardier/navigator (BN for short), I was tasked to ride with this crew to get from Guam to the Philip-pines. There I was to meet a pilot (who was already on the base) to ferry an-other plane back to Guam. The plane call sign and side number was Papa-Ro-meo 03. So this story has been affectionately dubbed, 'The Demise of PR-03.'

The crew loaded in, and a plane captain and I loaded into the back for the ride over. Things went well (it seemed) for most of the flight. The pilot and two other BNs were doing routine training exercises as the plane headed west with hardly a bit of turbulence. All in all, it was a beautiful sunny day as we flew from east to west with the objective of arriving on time at the naval base at Cubi Point in the Philippines. Roughly three hours into the flight, it was normal to pick up the Tacan (a range and direction finding beacon) from Cubi, and with that assistance fly to the approach pattern at the base. When the crew turned on the Tacan, however, instead of the needle locking onto a bearing and range, it just did a slow spin. We looked at one another with that 'what the heck is going on here?' puzzlement.

"Let's fire up the radar and get a fix from Luzon (one of the large islands in the Philippines chain)," said Joe the pilot. Normally, radar was not a necessity on this kind of ferry flight. The plane captain powered up the radar...smoke in the cockpit, so he turned it off. With the radar shut down and the Tacan nee-dle spinning, we didn't have any idea as to where we were (GPS was not even a dream in an engineer's brain in 1973). If you draw a line from Guam north over Iwo Jima to Japan, then from Japan through Okinawa to the Philippines, you have a massive expanse of water with nothing in it. It's like the Pacific version of the Devil's Triangle (by Bermuda), only bigger.

As the plane was steady on our heading of 271°, we could look out from the cockpit (from ~38,000 feet) and see a vast expanse of seemingly serene ocean, with nothing in it. No land mass of any kind. No worries; there was a safety navigational service called the Bullseye Net. The simple idea being that if we did long-count broadcasts with our radio, the various bases in the Philippines and Okinawa could direction-find our broadcast. With three or four bearing lines, the Marine base at Okinawa or the Air Force base at Clark (or somebody?) would be able to triangulate our position. With a triangulat-ed position, it then should have been a straightforward matter to compute a heading to the closest landing facility (which we guessed was no longer Cubi Point).

"PR-03...Long Count, Long Count, 10, 9, 8, 7... " The broadcasts went on long enough to allow the land-based equipment to get a bearing on our signal. "PR-03, we have a fix standby for vectors." All seems to be progressing well. "PR-03, we hold you xxx miles *west* of Cubi." (Sorry, I don't remember what the reported mileage was.) Suffice it to say, we didn't have the range to have flown into the middle of the South China Sea. And to reach that position, we would have to have flown over the Philippine Islands (remember it was CAVU: Clear and Visibility Unlimited). We all were worried; at this point, I was scared. We didn't know where we were, and the Air Force didn't have any idea where we were, either. If they sent someone to rescue us, would they send the Search and Rescue effort out into the South China Sea?

While this whole long-count direction-finding thing was transpiring, the gas needles were falling. I could see Joe mentally computing how long we had before a bailout was our last course of action, and the math was not good. Joe started to talk about the bailout procedures; fortunately he was a Navy professional and maintained his steady demeanor as we went through the emergency checklists. After another 45 minutes, Joe decided that we were going to bail. And it was 'bail' because the A-3 didn't have ejection seats. The entry hatch was in the bottom of the fuselage. In a bailout, the hatch is blown down to a locked position in the airstream, and it becomes a slide. "Slide for life' was the joke around the squadron.

We descended to ~10,000', and Joe slowed the plane to around 250 knots (as I remember). We blew open the hatch to the bailout position (which is like a small explosion in the cockpit) and, as we planned, I went first. I tightened my torso harness as tight as I could get it; I had all the flight gear strapped down hard; helmet, oxygen mask, nomex gloves all on and in place. When that hatch went down, the air blast was severe... and I was severely scared. It was at this moment when I remembered God. My cry-out prayer was short: "God, I need your help. Please save me." I remember a short calm, and then I step into the open fuselage. You can imagine the impact of hitting a 250-knot airstream. As I hit the airstream feet first, the high speed airstream hit my boots first and launched me into a back flip. Without much hesitation, I pulled the parachute D ring and the chute started to deploy.

On the Navy chutes (and most others), there are canvas risers that are hooked into the aviator's torso harness. The risers go up and provide the connection to the finer thickness shroud lines that are attached to the edges of the actual parachute. As I did the huge roll through the air, one of the canvas risers slid under my neck. When the air hit the open chute, the jerk was violent and that riser under my neck was jerked hard, almost like a punch underneath my lower chin. As I would find out later, the riser took a lot of skin off of my neck, and that's what knocked me unconscious. I took the ride from 10,000' to around 1,200' totally unconscious.

The first thing I remember was being slumped over in the airborne chute and coming back to consciousness, staring down at the sea below me. The Navy goes to extreme lengths to train, train, and train. Looking back, I understand why. From that waking moment, my training kicked in and I started to shed flight gear at a rapid rate. When you hit the water in flight gear, you're ready to sink like a rock, so you want to have as little of it as possible. And, most importantly, the Integrated Life Preserver needs to be inflated. From ~1,200 feet to the water, you can imagine that all this transpired in just a few seconds.

From 38,000', the sea looks very calm and tranquil. On the sea surface, the 15-20 knots of wind and the 'calm' sea state are a whole different deal. The immediate problem is that the nylon chute propelled by the wind can drag its hapless victim to a quick drowning. There is also a whole set of Navy folklore (meaning I'm not sure if this is true or not) about naval aviators (trying to avoid this chute-dragging phenomena) releasing their chutes early in the descent...a hundred feel early. Like jumping off a cliff. After I shed my excess gear and inflated my integrated preserver, the training once again kicked in. Focus on the horizon, get your fingers in the quick release fittings, and then wait for your feet to hit the water. When my boots splashed, I pulled the release fittings and — no exaggeration — that chute was downwind 50-75 yards in two seconds, never to be seen again.

You can imagine those few seconds were dramatic and frightening, but I didn't have time to think...just react. I was in the water (tropical water), my neck was bleeding, and I was going into shock. The other bad news was that the 'calm' sea state was a constant barrage of 3-5' foot waves. I get the personal raft out of the seat pan (you are actually sitting on the deflated raft when you are in the crew seats). I pulled the CO_2 bottle and it inflated properly, with no issues. I crawled into the little raft and started the bobbing up-

and-down ride that you get in a one-man raft in the open ocean.

From the raft, I look out over the horizon: not one of the other guys was in sight. No ships, no airplanes, no land...just water. Shock was taking over: I started to defecate in the raft, I started to throw up. When we were going through Navy training, they showed us a survival film. There was the bailed-out aviator in a little raft. A seagull landed on the edge of the raft...the aviator grabbed the bird, wrung his neck, and proceeded to eat him raw. This was not an encouraging memory for me. In the back of my mind, I was envisioning the Search and Rescue (SAR) effort drilling around in the South China Sea, looking for the guys from PR-03. The thought of raw seagull made me feel sicker.

Going in and out of consciousness, I think we were in the water for about two hours when a P-3 aircraft (a four-engine land-based turboprop) came over the horizon. It looked as if he was at about 300–400'. From that flight profile, I got the impression that he was looking for us (wishful thinking?). He was about two miles west of me, and I broke out two flares and fired them in his direction. He turned towards me and my raft, waggled his wings, and turned away. What a great moment! Call off the South China Sea SAR effort.

But knowing that this aircraft was from some distant land base, it was going to be a long time before we could get picked up. I wasn't sure if there was a 'we.' Still no one else from PR-03 was in sight. I tried not to envision a full night on the open sea, but it was in the back of my mind. For some reason, I never once thought about sharks, even though I was trolling for them with my bleeding neck. The waves had mostly filled the raft with water, and I tried to settle down for the wait.

I honestly don't remember how long I bobbed around, but the unmistakable sound of an SH-3 helicopter snapped me out of a daze (the SH-3 was the Navy's standard helo on aircraft carriers and other surface combatants). It was also one of the key SAR assets for the Navy, meaning that it was made for open sea rescues. How was that helo able to reach us in the open ocean? I'd find out later.

The helo came to a low hover about 30–40 yards from my raft and lowered his rescue horse collar. I bailed out of the raft and made a weak swim over to the horse collar. All of this was under the intense down-blast from the helo rotor blades. I hooked myself into the horse collar and they started to winch me up. I got up to the open door of the helo and there was the smiling face of a Japanese Defense Force sailor. The other four guys from PR-03 were already in the helo, and I was amazed and dumbfounded at what just happened... and that everyone made it.

The helo went back to its ship, the JDS (Japanese Maritime Self Defense Force) Haruna (DDH-141[87]), a destroyer with helicopter-carrying capability. As God would have it, Haruna was 40–50 miles away from our bailout location. When the P-3 located us, it was a good feat of international coordination to get the Haruna to launch its SH-3 to pick up the PR-03 crew.

When we landed on the ship, the Haruna Japanese sailors stood me up in the shower and did some medical work on my neck. Then they took me to a stateroom and put me in a bunk with the most perfectly ironed sheets I have ever slept on; I proceeded to sleep for 14 hours.

There is a little post-log to this story. When I got back to Guam (via Japan), I went to church simply to thank God for delivering me from that circumstance. I had stopped going to church, but when I was a boy, we used to go to Catholic Church. So I found the nearest Catholic Church and headed over for a 'Thank You' visit. I remember vividly sitting in the pews and watching the incense and robes marching down the center aisle. Lots of ritual and procedure. I watched that and remembered the emptiness of religion. My parting thought was, "Thank you, God, for getting me home alive." But I also thought, "....this religious pomp and circumstance is not me, and it's not going to honor You." My whole being had been delivered, and I knew it. I had encountered God. Just about a year later in the Newport, R.I. Bible Study, I accepted Christ.

Appendix C: 'Alternative' Dating without Delusion Titles

So one night, three couples from our home group gathered for an evening dinner. 'The Book' (this one) was in process, and we started to talk about the book title. The argument was the title — *Dating without Delusion* — was too limiting. I argued, "Well, there are ~90 million Singles in the U.S." so I wasn't too concerned about limiting the audience. Nevertheless, that started the banter: what *should* the title be? Here are some of the tongue-in-cheek alternatives that were creatively offered, all for your entertainment:

---

[87] DDH-141, the Haruna was commissioned on 22 March 1973 (six months before this incident). It was a 502-foot destroyer, and the lead ship of its class. It was decommissioned on 18 March 2009 after more than 35 years of naval service.

Dating with Delusion

Dating with Delusions

Relating with Confusion

Baiting with Confusion

Dating with Confusion

Dating with Illusions

Baiting with Illusions

And my favorite: **Mating with Illusions** As you can imagine, we were laughing out loud at some of these alternatives: *great* entertainment. There is a limitless pool of hilarious combinations. Just think of ...*sions* words like 'Intrusion' or 'Diffusion,' and ...*ing* words like 'Infatuating.' Then let your creative mind (with a devious edge) take you to some funny and entertaining places: probably why I like Gary Larson cartoons.

Appendix D: Why Dating Matters

Recently I googled some dating sites, looking for a modern paradigm for dating. Over a dozen answers provided zero insight...and no two of them agreed. Really, there were few personal guidelines to be had, and fewer suggestions on how a person in today's culture should 'date'. So what? When I was a young boomer, I tried to 'date' with the same kind of disguised confusion. Why should today's generation have better insight? One big difference...most of my friends had a mother and father at home, and although I didn't have any good relationship role modeling in my home life, my friends mostly did. Fast forward to our culture today where Fatherless statistics speak:

- 63% of youth suicides are from fatherless homes (US Dept. Of Health/ Census) – 5 times the average.

- 90% of all homeless and runaway children are from fatherless homes – 32 times the average.

- 85% of all children who show behavior disorders come from fatherless homes – 20 times the average. (Center for Disease Control)

- 80% of rapists with anger problems come from fatherless homes –14 times the average. (Justice & Behavior, Vol 14, p. 403-26)

Do you remember the adage 'Figures lie and liars figure"? ...numbers always make me a little cautious. Nevertheless, I am reassured by those research agency names behind the percentages. For example, 'Justice and Behavior' sounds pretty authoritative. The grim realities of fatherlessness are dramatic. Who can guess what the negative impact on society might be? Shootings? Drug abuse? Out-of-control anger? So now what? We often look to government to fix society-wide problems like this, but that's like asking government to fix the divorce rate. I just read that ~80% of newly married couples are headed for divorce in the their first 4 to 5 years of marriage (there are those stats again!). Doesn't fatherlessness come from failed relationship building?...whether or not the couple creating the kids is married. Fragile and transient relationship building is at the root of the problem. The divorce rate is just part of the aftermath of poor relationship building. Poor relationship building creates fatherlessness and all of the other behavioral dysfunctions. Now what?

Today, young married couples are carrying the heavy load of a culture which accepts divorce and fatherlessness as a matter of course. These problems run so deep; is there any way to get ahead of the issue? Education on relationship building can be part of the answer. The solution may lie in helping young soon-to-be adults understand themselves (baggage and all) so they can communicate who they are to their might-be-spouses. Can we help kids exposed to dysfunctional growing-up circumstances understand how it has impacted them? Can we create education which helps young people understand the stuff they carried from their childhood? Next, can we help young people forge beliefs to be articulated into Personal Values: Values which they own? Lasting relationships are built when I understand who I am and when I can communicate my beliefs and difficult sensitivities to the people around me. And of course lasting relationships have a kind of transparency which above-all is honest. Marriages built on this kind of honest communication may have a better chance. Honest relationship building during the dating phase of relationship is a part of the solution to the fatherless conundrum.

Anyone else have a suggestion?

About the Author

Throughout his life Jay has exercised his gifts of teaching and coaching both in the personal and professional domain. After a 10 year experience as a Naval Flight Officer (including Vietnam service), Jay transitioned to Raytheon where he worked on Aircraft Carrier Combat Systems and major ship acquisitions. Jay subsequently consulted with Fortune 500 companies at the Executive Leadership level providing forward-thinking inspiration, guidance, and clarity to the organization's interrelationships and overall corporate effectiveness. His expertise and focus is maximizing corporate potential (a Gallup Strength) at the personal and organizational level. *Dating without Delusion* is the culmination of decades of church service, educational study and life experience.

After his first marriage failed in the late '80s, Jay found himself leading a Christian Singles group in La Jolla, California. As a person of faith he expected to see some significant differences between the secular and Christian Singles worlds, however the same kind of emotional upheaval and crisis seemed to be the norm. Jay's calling to 'Encourage Singles to become the people that God has made them to be' now serves as one of his Personal Core Values. Believing that there should be significant Bible-based relationship wisdom, Jay dug in to apply faith based relationship principles to dating. In parallel Jay looked into some quality secular relationship sources (and there are some good ones) to uncover relationship wisdom. You will be encouraged and challenged by the congruency of Spiritual principles with some of the nation's best psychologists and researchers Additionally the Values discovery process contained herein is strongly supported by modern assessment tools. The on-line tools (such as Strengthsfinders) are invaluable as you embark on your journey of self-discovery.

The early Singles venues included weekend seminars both locally and at getaway locations. At Real Life Ministries in Post Falls Idaho Jay taught 6 week Singles sessions, normally three time per year. He also enjoys speaking at conferences and retreats where he hears from Singles spanning the age spectrum, from Millennials to people well into their sixties. Many of those stories are contained in these pages. The real life stories provide a vivid backdrop for the dating process which Jay will offer you. For Singles, Jay suggests building relationships on the foundation of your Personal Core Values. If you are married the Personal Values development process may be great intrinsic learning for you. The fresh view of the culture may help you unravel the culture craziness in which we live.

Jay holds a BS in Physics from Bates College and a MS in Executive Leadership (MSEL) from the University of San Diego (USD). Jay and his wife of 33 years (Debra) reside in San Diego and have two grown sons.

Made in the USA
Columbia, SC
12 August 2024

39891696R00159